TWO SIDES

The Best of Personal Opinion, 1964-1984

Best Wishes!

John H. Redekop

SOME COMMENTS FOR REVIEWERS

"The widest possible readership of these choice essays from twenty years of first class Christian journalism is recommended not only because of their highly readable style, but also because of their most relevant substance concerning Christian thought and life in today's world."

Frank H. Epp
Professor and Past President of Conrad Grebel College, University of Waterloo, and author of numerous books.

"Professor John Redekop writes with clarity and conviction about the meaning of the Good News for our turbulent times. . . . Redekop is an outstanding representative of the evangelical-anabaptist tradition and his forthright commentary on a wide range of controversial issues will challenge and therefore benefit Christians of all traditions."

Harry Antonides
Director of Research, Christian Labour Association of Canada

"The author tackles a very broad spectrum of Christian issues with decisive vigor that makes for interesting and informative reading. Christian life and practices are probed; controversial issues are not evaded—and let the chips fall where they may! The deep commitments of the writer to the Lordship of Christ and to the unquestioned authority of Scripture, to evangelism and mission, and to active Christian discipleship in the world, shines through with a steady light."

Victor Adrian
General Secretary, Mennonite Brethren Missions/Services

"For some twenty years Dr. John Redekop has regularly written the 'Opinion' column in the Mennonite Brethren Herald. As can be readily seen from the table of contents of TWO SIDES, he addresses a wide range of topics—all of them of interest to Christian readers. Although Redekop does not particularly relish controversial subjects, he does not shy away from them either. . . . He writes in a clear, popular style that appeals to many age groups."

David Ewert
President, Mennonite Brethen Bible College

"John H. Redekop, in his 'Personal Opinion' column in the Mennonite Brethren Herald, has over the years consistently maintained a sharp eye on many vital topics. His careful and penetrating analyses have helped us to look deeper than first-glance realities. I'm impressed with the broad range of Redekop's opinions. He chooses topics common to all of us but reveals uncommon insights. His is not only opinion, but wise instruction. You can take it or leave it. Most of the time you take it.

"Here's the best, taken from hundreds of Redekop's short, but important contributions to the Christian/Anabaptist understanding of things, arranged under 15 interesting headings. Reading one is like eating a roasted peanut. It leads to another!

"The bonus of this book is the work of Lorlie Barkman. His ink illustrations add punch to Redekop's prose. TWO SIDES, the Best of Personal Opinion, 1964-1984, is a treat!"

Roy Just
President, Columbia Bible Institute

TWO SIDES

The Best of Personal Opinion, 1964-1984

by

John H. Redekop

Illustrated by

Lorlie Barkman

Kindred Press

159 Henderson Hwy., Winnipeg, MB Canada R2L 1L4

TWO SIDES. The Best of Personal Opinion, 1964-1984

Published by Kindred Press, 159 Henderson Highway,
Winnipeg, Manitoba, R2L 1L4
First Printing, 1984

These "Personal Opinion" columns first appeared in *The Mennonite Brethren Herald* between 1964 and 1984.

Cover Design and layout by Gerald Loewen, Winnipeg, Manitoba
Printed in Canada by The Christian Press, Winnipeg

International Standard Book Number 0-919797-13-X

To Doris
Companion, Counsellor, Supporter
and
Favorite ''Critic''

CONTENTS

PREFACE

It has been a delight to have been associated with the MENNONITE BRETHREN HERALD for more than twenty years. Submitting columns weekly, from January, 1964 until July, 1968 and biweekly thereafter, except for a "sabbatical leave" during part of 1980 and 1981, has been both challenging and rewarding. The several thousand responses which I received added a particularly interesting dimension. Almost all of the responses were affirmative and gracious, some were negative and gracious, a few, unusually unsigned, added a touch of color. I was particularly moved by the letters from individuals who had somehow been personally helped by some particular column. Thank you.

I would like to express my gratitude to the editors who have worked with me during these decades. For many years Harold Jantz has been a patient, supportive, alert, congenial and constructively critical colleague. It was reassuring to know that every column had to cross his desk before going to the typesetter. For shorter periods Peter Klassen and Gordon Nickel also were editors with whom it was a pleasure to work. To Peter, I am particularly indebted for getting the column launched. Our discussions and the subsequent agreement in late 1963 clearly involved some risks, at least on his part.

For many hours of tiresome reading and evaluating I am deeply indebted to the members of the column evaluation committee: Lorlie Barkman, Gilbert Brandt, Harold Jantz, Viola Eckert, and John Eckert. Their rankings and candid comments played a vital role in reducing the almost 600 columns to the 172 which are appearing in this volume. Understandably they were not always in agreement; indeed, sometimes they were in sharp disagreement! But, then, they were invited to serve because of their diverse perspectives. Their contribution was significant but they are not responsible for the final decisions; for better or worse that responsibility rests with me.

My great indebtedness to Lorlie Barkman for his many apt illustrations is obvious. In more than a few instances his pictures say more than my words.

Finally I want to thank Gilbert Brandt and his associates at Kindred Press for encouragement, assistance, and for doing the many tasks involved in getting this book published.

With the exception of minor editorial changes and corrections, and a few abbreviations the columns are reproduced as they appeared originally.

All of us who have worked to get this book completed shall consider the undertaking to be worthwhile if it generates reflection, discussion, gratitude, some discontent, and perhaps even some appropriate action.

John H. Redekop
Waterloo, Ontario
April 5, 1984

THROUGH 20 YEARS OF PERSONAL OPINION

INTRODUCTION

Years ago, so the story goes, John H. Redekop had the reputation in British Columbia's Fraser Valley of being something of a rabble-rouser and rebel within church circles. Possessed of a quick, critical mind and as quick a tongue, he easily struck fear into the hearts of comfortable church leaders. He seemed to be on the way out of the church comunity.

Recently, a Seminary teacher confided the results of an informal poll he was conducting. Wherever he came, he made a point of asking members in local Mennonite Brethren churches about trustworthy leaders. The one name which always came up as trusted was John H. Redekop's.

There are a number of reasons for the transformation of the erstwhile rebel, some of which he explained in an emotional testimony after he was elected moderator of the Canadian Mennonite Brethren Conference in the summer of 1983. He recalled a critical turningpoint he had come to years before with a decision he made then not to give up on the church. His commitment to the fellowship of believers has never been in doubt since.

Nowhere has that likely been clearer than in the column he has written for the *Mennonite Brethren Herald* for twenty years, the *Opinion* column. If it has conveyed any message, it has been his fierce love for the church and his commitment to a vital faith in Christ.

This column has, in itself, probably contributed as much as any factor to the trusted place which John has won in the hearts of many of his fellow church members. His face and opinions have become as well-known to them as any Mennonite's now on the Canadian scene.

The columns in this collection represent a careful culling of many of the best he has written over the entire twenty-year period. They have not been re-worked for publication now. Rather, within subject areas, they have been arranged in the order in which they appeared. And they describe not only his thoughts on a wide variety of topics, they also present a vivid picture of a changing church and world during a two-decade period.

Several aspects stand out about the columns. The ideas are always clear. He writes simply, easily and forcefully. His opinions aren't fudged, even when the opinions are not likely to be popular.

His interests are wide. The mere fact that he has been able to write for twenty years and keep most of his readers interested enough to turn to him — often before they turn to anyone else — is testimony enough of his wide interests.

He is by nature a persuader. His columns have been opinions, all right, but they usually argue their point in a way that says, "Try to see it from my point of view." I suspect that over the years John has persuaded many to his opinions.

There is another level, however, on which his columns have been very significant and which probably accounts for the high regard in which he is held by so many of his readers. It can perhaps be stated in several ways.

One way might be to say that he has always taken his Christianity simply and sincerely. His columns have always spoken for an unsophisticated, yet vital and life-related Christianity.

He has consistently spoken for the

church, not for an individualistic Christianity. He has strongly identified with the themes which might be said to characterize "evangelical Anabaptism" while arguing against the ethnicisms which have so often closed Mennonite doors to new believers. He has been able to criticize Mennonite churches and their institutions without ever seriously raising a question about his love for church. Redekop is a premier churchman.

He has always been in touch with the pleasant as well as unpleasant realities of his world. Few writers — certainly in the Canadian church press — have had as many political leaders respond to his columns over the years as has John H. Redekop. These very public readers as well as the ordinary person in Mennonite Brethren pews from Beacon Hill to Signal Hill have recognized familiar problems and issues in his columns. He was writing about real situations.

The characteristic of his writings which above all others has elevated them and given them such persuasive power and effect is their steady determination to push us to live integrated, whole Christian lives. Redekop, one feels, is consumed with desire to integrate faith and life. We cannot say one thing as individuals, or as Mennonite churches, and live another. We must try to bring word and deed together. Down with petty rationalizations and obfuscations! Our aim must be to think carefully and consistently so that more and more of our life demonstrates what is at its core.

A word needs to be said about the illustrator for this book. Lorlie Barkman is a longtime reader of John H. Redekop's *Opinion* column. Interestingly, the two share a common history: both come from the same area in southern Saskatchenwan. This is the first time, however, that they've collaborated in a work. Barkman is a pastor turned illustrator and television producer. He spent a number of years in the pastorate in Moose Jaw, Sask., and then came to Winnipeg to work in children's television with Mennonite Brethren Communications. Alongside his pastoral and film interests, he has always done some cartooning. His illustrations for this book are in that style. He draws with a comic touch, never sarcastic, and there's clearly a pastoral note there. The drawings complement Redekop's columns very nicely.

This collection of columns will give admirers of Redekop a chance to refresh themselves again at a rich spread of his thoughts. They will discover that even though many were written years ago, they are surprisingly current and instructive.

The book will appeal to those who have read Redekop over the years and who want to go back to reflect again upon issues he has raised. It will appeal to younger readers who want to gain crisp, challenging perspectives on issues with which the church has dealt over twenty or more years. And for those who are new to Redekop, it will be a fine introduction to the thoughts of a churchman who has an intense desire to bring his faith into the marketplace.

As they have done so often in the past, the columns are bound to provoke to thought, and hopefully, to action. For those who believe in what the Christian faith stands for, that would be this book's best reward.

Harold Jantz, Editor
Mennonite Brethren Herald

PART I

Assumptions

ON CONSTRUCTIVE CRITICISM

From time to time one reads or hears statements to the effect that Christians should not be critical; that to be critical is to be unspiritual. I would like to challenge that view. I believe that it is not only acceptable but indeed necessary that we practice constructive criticism.

What is meant by constructive criticism? Some people seem to think that a constructive critic is one who only praises — one who never says anything negative. But is such a person really a constructive critic? Is he drawing attention to weaknesses or shortcomings as he sees them? Is he giving suggestions for improvement? Constructive criticism, I suggest, is characterized by the following:

- it avoids any "character-assasination"; it imputes no evil or questionable motives.
- it does not overlook strong points or desirable aspects; it is aware of the good, while drawing attention to that which requires improvement.
- it avoids all use of strong language which is calculated to hurt someone's feelings.
- it implies, or states explicitly, that any critic may be in error. Constructive criticism is "offered"; it is "offered" in all sincerity, but not as the final word on the subject. It is one person's honest opinion.
- it puts the main emphasis not on the weakness or shortcoming as such, but on the presentation of reasonable suggestions for improvement.
- it never ridicules or scorns; it seeks to help and to understand.

Constructive criticism ought not to be confused with opposition; the former seeks to help while the latter seeks to hinder. Constructive criticism is based on the assumption that good men can disagree agreeably, and that, in the spirit of Apollos, they are willing to learn from one another. It is in the spirit of "proving all things" and of "loving the brethren" that we need to be constructively critical of one another and of our practices and principles.

(The Editor's note for this column stated, "with this issue a new column is being introduced in the Herald. Articles will be classed as 'personal opinion' and may range over a wide area of topics pertinent to the Christian life.")

THE PROBLEM OF THE PIONEER

The democratic concept of the majority being "right" has had a great impact on the basic attitudes of the Christian church. In our own brotherhood this view is expressed frequently; it is assumed that there is safety and "rightness" in numbers.

A few years ago a delegate to a Canadian Mennonite Brethren convention dared to differ openly and strongly with the expressed views of the majority. For this he was publicly denounced as being "unspiritual", an indictment which was neither modified nor retracted. Several delegates stressed that the error of the man's position was proven by the fact that apparently no one agreed with him.

I am amazed by this type of reasoning. Majoritarianism may be the best method of deciding political and social issues but it is fraught with danger when used unthinkingly in the church. The fact of the matter is that new insights generally do not come to large groups or whole congregations at the same time. Even in the Kingdom of God, by and large, individual pioneers of ideas perceive the notion first and then must try to convince the rest.

There may have been some instances where a new view came to many people at the same time but those have been the exceptions in the history of the Christian church. It was not a majority view which authorized the Protestant Reformation, the Anabaptist revitalization, the formation of the MB church, the launching of foreign missions, the organization of Sunday schools, the establishment of Home Mission churches, the initiation of a radio ministry, or the building of Christian camps. Individual "radicals", frequently denounced as being unspiritual, bore the brunt of criticism for each one of these. Only later, when the evidence and logic could no longer be denied, and when it was fully safe to do so, did the majorities change their view.

It seems to me that a truly spiritual brotherhood should pay more attention to the sincere and thoughtful criticisms of individual persons. The views of these people may be just as important for the entire group as the automatic nodding of a hall full of "yes-men." I am not suggesting that the majority of the brethren are automatic "yes-man" but I am saying that in any large organization the danger of apathetic acquiescence is very real.

Many a good idea has been nipped in the bud by the heavy hand of an uninformed and uncritical majority. Dissenters are not always right, but it is in the best interests of the non-dissenters to give them a fair hearing.

NEEDED—MORE DISCONTENT

John Stuart Mill once said, "Nothing is more certain than that improvement in human affairs is wholly the work of the uncontented characters." Improvement in church affairs is also the result of uncontented characters. Right now we need more.

As I observe the demurely sombre throngs of well-adjusted and prosperous members of the middle class in our evangelical churches today I am struck first and foremost by the general air of contentment. People seem to have come to terms with themselves and with the world; they have found their place and they are at peace.

Most of us, I suggest, are actually very easy to please in the whole realm of the building of the Kingdom. We give little and ask little. We think of Kingdom-building not so much in terms of personal involvement as in terms of what the church is doing. The emphasis is on "they" rather than on "we."

Where are the people who are concerned enough about the rate of our spiritual progress to make it their first interest? Where are the multitudes who eagerly shout "Here am I!" when the preacher calls for Christian soldiers? All too often our richly panelled halls of worship are filled with a resounding silence.

We sorely need a wave, better still a storm, of discontent concerning our own lack of concern. The mediocrity, normalcy, adjustment, and peaceful coexistence which characterizes much of the institutionalized church should fill us with alarm. In politics these terms may describe the desired goal, but in Christian warfare they indicate decline and defeat.

The Bible tells us that in godliness with contentment there is great gain. We have emphasized the latter at the expense of the former and have then come out with high marks. And therein lies a great and deadly delusion.

A DOUBLE STANDARD OF FREEDOM

Judging from all the fuss raised by Adolf von Thadden's recent visit to Canada, one would think that Adolf Hitler was asking to become executive director of the Canadian Council of Christians and Jews.

There are several very interesting aspects to this sordid affair. For one thing, it is far from certain that the German National Democratic Party, of which von Thadden is deputy leader, is a neo-Nazi phenomenon. The fact that it is led by ex-Nazis is hardly distinctive, for Chancellor Kurt Kiesinger and many other political leaders in both West and East Germany were also one-time followers of Hitler. As for the policies von Thadden preaches, it appears they are based largely on a near-fanatical nationalism. But that, too, is not unique. Similar views are widely held in other countries, including the United States and maybe even Canada. Even the shades of egotistical and potentially dangerous racism which one can detect "between the lines" are not at all unusual; American and Canadian immigration laws have for decades rested on the assumption that some races are good and desirable.

But the real rub of the matter is that in trying to deny von Thadden the chance to speak, some self-declared apostles of freedom, toleration, and justice have denied their own cause. They have undermined the very principles which they are claiming to defend. Why should von Thadden be denied the opportunity to exercise the right of free speech while an invited guest in Canada? All he asked for was the opportunity to exercise the right to free speech while an invited guest in Canada. Furthermore, von Thadden is a significant German political leader and it is in our own political and legal self-interest to let him have his say: and if his views are wrong and potentially dangerous, is it not desirable that this fact be publicized far and wide, so that his rise to power might be thwarted?

I believe in freedom of expression, in the mass media, for moderates, rightists, leftists, radicals, reactionaries, and wide-eyed idealists. Those of us who disagree with the views expressed need not listen, read or watch the exposition in question. I tend to subscribe to the view that the limitations of all forms of freedom of expression ought always to be nothing more (at times perhaps less) than the laws of the land. It will be a sad day indeed when restraints on freedom of expression are set by the non-reflective, emotion-charged majority reaction of the moment.

Finally, it seems to me that those who clamor loudest to have von Thadden suppressed have often been the first to argue that Communists should be allowed to speak. Why is it that some groups and individuals loudly proclaim the virtues of academic freedom, free speech, and toleration when leftists ask for the floor, but when a von Thadden or Rhodesia's Ian Smith wants to explain an alternate extremist view, these same groups ridicule or laugh them out of court? One cannot have it both ways. Either one tolerates expressions of extremism or not.

Personally, I would sooner err on the side of too much freedom than too little, if for no other reason than that a majority of my fellow-citizens might well consider me a non-conforming religious extremist who makes them feel uncomfortable, and whose freedom should perhaps be restricted.

THE SEARCHERS

Some people, it seems to me, have strange concepts of what it means to be a Christian and what it means to be the Christian church.

Again and again I come across the notion, increasingly even in our own denomination, that the essential quality of a dynamic church is to be a searching community. Somehow, according to this view, a collective commitment to a search for truth, however that may be defined, constitutes the hallmark of a healthy church.

"Dialogue" is the code word. The perspective is actually dialectic. You interact with one another intensely and frequently and out of this interaction everyone involved will gain new insights. Logically, then, since insights flow from interaction, one should make an effort to interact with as many individuals and perspectives as possible. This is, in fact, exactly what happens in many situations.

Rap sessions, exchanges, dialogue and debate are set up all over the place as seekers do their searching. Endless inquiry becomes the benchmark of normality and persistent questioning the sign of Christian maturity. It is all very interesting. But ought such endeavors to be central?

Don't misunderstand me. I'm the last one who wishes to debunk dialogue and interaction as part of effective living and active Christian discipleship; it's vitally needed. We all have a lot to learn. But that should not be our source of ultimate truth. For fundamental answers to crucial questions we look elsewhere. Specifically, we turn to God's Word, requesting the Holy Spirit to guide us as together we try to discern its meaning.

Seeking truth is one of the most laudable pursuits. And seeking truth, as a step in becoming a Christian, is the most praiseworthy pursuit I can imagine. But if we never settle any question we'll get precisely nowhere. Being open to all options is appropriate before a salvation commitment, but not after, at least not if basics are involved.

After all, it is not asking questions but accepting answers, certain kinds of answers, that makes one a Christian. For a Christian, as for a Christian church, some central issues have been settled and the time for dialogue and openness on those key matters is finished. That's hard for some of us to accept. We like to transfer an orientation of relativism and lack of finality from academic, economic and political life to the Christian realm but such transfer is both unwarranted and deceptive.

Christians, I suggest, whatever else we may be, are people who have considered the options and have made a choice. As in marriage—other options are now closed. Christians are people who have made a total commitment, who know in whom we have believed and say so.

PART II

The Christian Message And Mission

DECEMBER 9, 1966

ABERFAN AND CIVIC RESPONSIBILITY

How quickly man forgets mass tragedy. It is only a month or so since a hill of rock and slag killed 146 Welshmen in Aberfan and already some of us must think twice to remember the event.

In the midst of the tragedy it was reassuring to hear of the wide-ranging assistance given by governments and private groups. I was happy to note that the Canadian government made a sizeable gift to the bereaved and battered town. Many individuals showed great kindness in their reaction to the shocking tragedy.

Even so, my mind dwells not on the bereaved, or on those who came to aid, but on a hero who never was. I am thinking of the average wage-earner in Aberfan who lived in the coal-dust covered house just around the corner on Pilgrim Street on the right side of town. Since his name in Welsh is typically long and almost unpronounceable, we'll simply translate it as "Personal Righteousness Is What Matters" and call him PRIWM for short.

It was about two years ago that Mr. Priwm first heard rumors about the possibility of future disaster. One smoggy Saturday while he was pulling weeds in his back yard he learned from his neighbor that the huge mound of slag and rock which the mining company had piled up near the town had been declared dangerous. However, the mine owners had insisted that this statement was false. The town council, anxious not to do anything which might cause the mine to close down, had discussed the matter but had decided to take no action.

Some months passed. In December, 1965, elections were held for a new town council. A number of people urged Mr. Priwm to become a candidate, some even suggested that he should urge an investigation of the slag-pile menace and make that a part of his platform.

Mr. Priwm thought it over for a few days and then decided against it. He was just too busy. As Sunday School Superintendent and Deacon in the local Baptist (or was it Anabaptist) Church he had much to do. And besides, he felt that Christians ought not to get mixed up in politics. At worst politics was dirty, at best politics involved compromise, and compromise was always un-Christian.

Thus the situation continued as it was, and it was as it had been. Mr. Priwm grew busier, the slag pile grew bigger, and the 146 lives grew shorter.

Then came that terrible, heart-rending day of doom. The deadly black wall of death was still advancing when Mr. Priwm frantically set relief operations in motion. Nobody, but nobody, was more efficient, more dedicated, or more selfless than Mr. Priwm. All through the night he worked. Once, during a tea-break, he happened to remember his earlier thoughts, about running for a council position in order to clear up the mess. But he had no time to reflect on the past—there was more work to be done. The Christian principles of love and selflessness spurred him to continued action.

All of which leads me to ask: What is better, to build a railing at the edge of a narrow mountain road or to build a combination hospital-morgue at the bottom? Which is more Christ-like?

MERE KNOWLEDGE OR TRUE FAITH? / OR ASSENT VERSUS COMMITMENT

Knowledge says, "There is a God;"
  Faith prays, "My Father in heaven. . ."
Knowledge says, "Nature points to God;"
  Faith replies, "I have experienced him."
Knowledge says, "God is eternal;"
  Faith announces, "Through him I have eternal life."
Knowledge says, "God is love;"
  Faith declares, "God loves me."
Knowledge says, "God so loved the world;"
  Faith continues, "that he gave his only begotten Son."
Knowledge says, "No man is perfect;"
  Faith admits, "I have sinned before God and man."
Knowledge says, "Christ died on the cross;"
  Faith responds, "Christ died on the cross for me."
Knowledge says, "God will draw nigh unto man;"
  Faith agrees, "If man will draw nigh unto God."
Knowledge says, "Christ showed us the way;"
  Faith explains, "Christ is the Way."
Knowledge says, "Men should follow Christ;"
  Faith answers, "Where he leads me I will follow."
Knowledge says, "The Spirit strengthens believers;"
  Faith recounts, "I became the Spirit's temple."
Knowledge says, "Christ promises eternal life;"
  Faith cautions, "to all who keep his commandments."
Knowledge says, "Christ will return;"
  Faith adds, "Christ will come again for me."

Knowledge agrees;
  Faith obeys.
Knowledge defends;
  Faith contends.
Knowledge investigates;
  Faith propagates.

Knowledge times the race;
  Faith runs the race.
Knowledge measures fish;
  Faith fishes for men.

Knowledge withdraws and lives alone;
  Faith has the same house number as action.
Knowledge believes and trembles;
  Faith believes and rejoices.

JANUARY 5, 1968

REVIEWING THE LEDGER

This is a time of year when many of us get involved in taking stock, balancing budgets, reviewing programs, and generally evaluating the past. In keeping with this spirit more than a few of us individually and collectively review the work of our church.

As one studies the annual church expenditures one point becomes crystal clear, at least in most churches: the rapid rise in the total expenditures has generally not been accompanied by a proportionate increase in "giving to missions" in the traditional sense. More and more money seems to be required for overhead, for so-called operation and maintance. Many people are deeply disturbed by this trend; one discouraged critic observed, "So much for the church and so little for missions!"

There is, of course, a proper and justifiable concern over shortages for missions. No doubt a church can put too much into buildings and instruments, fixtures and facilities (pastors' salaries, of course, rarely reflect extravagance!) but perhaps there is another aspect to the matter. Why should we call it "missions" if money is spent on the development of church facilities in India, but "overhead" if it is spent for the same purposes in North America? The crucial point is, of course, how we view the role of the local church.

Frankly, I would rather belong to a local church which apparently overspent in the area of facilities, staff, etc. and which utilized these assets in true missionary activity than to one which skimped along on very little, yet which thought of missions only as a vicarious pursuit, as something which a church hires specialists to do in far-away places with strange-sounding names.

Missionary activity, in the final analysis is more a matter of being, in its fullest sense, than of doing. The account of Mary and Martha, among other things, illustrates the point. Money spent locally to facilitate Christian outreach, nurture, hospitality, reconciliation, charity, and peace is not a means to some other end, but an end in itself. It should be removed from the column of "Overhead" to the column labelled "Expenditures for Kingdom-Building."

Viewed in this light, local expenses, be they great or small, challenge us to greater involvement, greater concern, and an increased sense of accountability.

A SILENT MAJORITY

During the last few months I have repeatedly heard it said that in our time Christian evangelism may have come to mean quiet Christian living. The argument seems to be that exemplary living is a sufficient fulfillment of the Great Commission. Why allow oneself to develop guilt feelings by "not witnessing"? Why allow oneself to become frustrated and depressed in view of the fact that much evangelical activity produces only failure? Rather, the point is made, live peaceably and appropriately and let God work his will.

The problems which give rise to such a view of Christian responsibility are everywhere evident, however, the view—if I understand it correctly—is unbiblical.

In the first place one should not equate a part with the whole. Being, doing, and saying are all involved in Christian obedience. Each strengthens the other and lends credence to it.

In the second place the biblical imperative seems to be clear—"Go ye." Jesus repeatedly confronted the various types of people in his day and I think he expects us to do the same.

Thirdly, it is highly probable that many people who might observe that certain individuals have a different, more tranquil, mode of living would nevertheless never find out what constitutes the difference. After all, most people do not take the initiative in finding out why other people live as they do. The result would be that the Christian church might function as a detached contemporary monasticism. Ultimately, it seems to me, such an existence is perhaps a way of escaping obligations; a form of self-centeredness. The end would likely be a withered vine.

Having said the above I must add that often I also feel as if islands of relative contentedness is about all we can offer this strife-ridden world. I don't enjoy being rebuffed, misunderstood, or sneered at. Inactivism is a frequent temptation. But in my mind I know it isn't right. "He who is ashamed of me on earth, of him will I also be ashamed. . . ."

When Jesus told his followers that they were to be his witnesses he mentioned Jerusalem but also referred to the uttermost parts of the earth. Have our orders changed?

CHRISTIAN PACKAGING

Surely, there must be fool-proof ways of making friends and influencing people when by our words and actions we tell them that it is incredibly important that Jesus Christ came into this world to seek and to save those who are lost and to give them eternal life.

Perhaps we must find new ways of packaging our product, i.e., the Gospel of Jesus Christ as Savior and Lord. Here are some possibilities:

(1) Somehow discover what people want to hear and then tell them that. Surely no one could be offended by hearing what his itching ears want to hear!

(2) Emphasize theory and deemphasize practice. Maybe more people will nod in agreement if they are clear about not having to change their personal way of life.

(3) Combine Christianity with some other life perspective. Christian-Buddhism, Christian-Hinduism, Christian-Krishna, Christian-materialism, Christian-nationalism, and even Christian-atheism might be acceptable options. People tend to accept new ideas more readily if these can be fused with some that are already known.

(4) Jazz up the approach. Use the language of the streets to get people's ideas off the streets. Maybe the loud jargon will help them move ahead—it might even mesmerize them.

(5) Use big names. Maybe Miss Universe—no insult to Martians or others intended—could lend her weight to the cause by autographing some sound Christian literature. Miss Universe might at least have earthly appeal. We might also consider asking U.S. Defense Secretary Melvin Laird (again) to provide us with guidelines on how to use radio and television more effectively. Many of us obviously were much impressed by his first suggestions.

(6) Hire experts. A good public relations firm might be what we've been lacking all along. If we could put up, say, $500,000 one of the more prestigious firms might be willing to guarantee us at least a 50% favorable public opinion poll response to the question, "Are you in favor of Jesus Christ?"

(7) Use "big-name" Christians. We need not go to the extreme and use Roy Roger's horse "Trigger" during an evangelistic campaign, as once was done, but there are, no doubt, other things that could be undertaken. It might be possible to bring in some of the "Christian" dictators of Asia, Africa, or Latin America to add a dash of colour.

(8) Disguise the contents. Maybe we should simply moralize and avoid any exact descriptions of what we claim to believe. If we live almost exactly like other people do, work where they work, spend like they spend, watch what they watch, go where they go, laugh when they laugh, thus trying to identify with them, we just might be able to add a few Christian words without turning people off.

Of course, some Christians won't like these suggestions. They will insist that Christianity is foolishness as far as many people are concerned. They will argue that we must not be surprised when people see Christ's claims as an offense. Some will even go as far as to suggest that we should diligently obey Christ's commandments and let the Holy Spirit take it from there.

PACKAGING

The March 19th column on "Christian Packaging" has evoked considerable response. I have been informed that we ought to follow Rev. Kennedy's personal evangelism approach if we want to see results; I have been sent the basic literature put out by Campus Crusade; I have been invited to attend a conference at Arrowhead Springs in California; I have been told that the organized church is still basic; I have been told that the organized church has lost its relevancy; etc., etc.

I guess what surprised me most was that quite a few people took seriously all of the eight "new ways" which were suggested. It was my intent simply to point out that, from my perspective, the way to get people to become Christians does not require gimmicks and also that we must keep in mind the element of personal moral choice and the role of the Holy Spirit.

Obviously there is still a great need for "big-name" speakers, relevant approaches, etc., but surely it is equally clear that we ought not to disguise or distort Christ's claims in order to make them more acceptable. In his various writings Dietrich Bonhoeffer has convincingly shown that "cheap grace" is both frustrating and inadequate. We do well to keep his admonition in mind.

I have difficulty accepting the notion that someone, somewhere has discovered some subtle or novel way to "bring them in" real quick and easy! The Gospel is not merely another commodity to be packaged and peddled; it is to be accepted, lived, and proclaimed.

The point which several respondents made, namely, that despite all that has been preached, etc., many of us still do not in fact communicate the Gospel strikes me as being irrefutably true. The blame for this sorry state of affairs (which prevails in most evangelical churches) can doubtlessly be apportioned in various ways. The more important and immediate problem, however, is, "Where do we go from here?"

For whatever they may be worth, here are some personal observations and suggestions:

— Many Christians (I use the term loosely here) are ineffective at witnessing because they have experienced virtually nothing about which to witness.

— Many Christians do not believe that non-Christians will be eternally lost.

— Many Christians have not learned to witness, mainly because they have perceived non-witnessing to be an acceptable norm.

— Some Christians overemphasize individualism and others overemphasize group impact and both forget that God works in many ways.

— We must not rob people of moral choice or fast-talk them into a superficial "commitment." Of course, quick decisions are not ruled out.

— We are obligated to pursue better methods of communication. Where God has given someone a special gift in this area we should be thankful and learn from him if he does what we should be doing.

— Finally, I strongly recommend that very soon our denomination structure a convention which will train people how to witness; the attendance might be amazingly large, at least it ought to be. The theme might be "Propagate or Stagnate."

MAY 16, 1972

FORGOTTEN WORDS

My secret spies and loyal statisticians recently informed me that within one week of hearing a typical sermon 80% of the average congregation forgets more than 70% of what was said. Two weeks later this same 80% of the "listeners" apparently has forgotten more than 90%. Much more is remembered in almost all other communication situations. Such figures are truly alarming and as one who periodically delivers a sermon—and listens to about 75 during a year—I have decided to analyze this forboding situation.

Doubtlessly most of the problem lies with the day-dreaming or mentally lazy listeners. Nevertheless, for the simple reason that on more than a few occasions I have observed these same "lazy listeners" transformed into attentive listeners who months afterwards could still relate the thrust of the message, I shall direct my comments to those of us who preach.

Consequently I shall catalogue a list of possible weaknesses in sermonizing (the order is not significant).

(1) Volume. Some preachers seem to have as one of their operative principles the idea, perhaps penciled in the margin of their notes. "Weak point; shout here!" That only works about three times and even then it

serves mainly to interrupt, temporarily, the relaxed dreamers who have learned how to doze with their eyes open.

(2) Pause. Many speakers, it seems to me, do not know how to use the pause effectively. Perhaps they don't know what to say before a pause in order to make the pause effective or they operate on the erroneous notion that unless they are speaking nothing is happening. (Pause)

(3) Repetition. This is a double point. In general I discern a tendency for people who state the obvious to repeat it too much and for people who present more complicated ideas to repeat too little. An important idea stated clearly in several different ways is not quickly forgotten.

(4) Tone. Rarely have I heard a monotone sermon—although I do recall a few—but not infrequently, and particularly in radio coverage, I have been subjected to twenty or thirty minutes of tiring whining. Personally, I find that the medium gets in the way of the message whenever the latter is delivered in the tones of a weeping operatic tenor.

(5) Rafters. Several preachers of my acquaintance very easily and quickly establish good eye contact with the rafters. No matter how hard I try, I can't rise to the level of their projected pronouncements. If you want us to listen, please look at us.

(6) Communication. The old adage still holds true. There is no communication unless that which is said, is also heard. I have reluctantly come to the conclusion that some of us are unable to ascertain when we are being understood. We must work at it. Merely having said (or read) some words is no guarantee whatsoever that any communication has occurred. (Second Pause).

(7) Questions. Don't hesitate to leave the congregation with some clearly understood questions. If we know that all answers are always given we tend to ignore even the thought-provoking questions.

(8) Feeling. All too often the extent of sincere emotion generated during a sermon is about 1/50 of that generated during a standard sports event. Why?

(9) Stimulation. Finally, preachers ought not to hesitate to raise provocative but relevant points. Not for the sake of controversy but for conflict resolution. Too much of what we hear is too predictable and too safe. A well-prepared sermon should be short on cliches and long on provocation.

OCTOBER 8, 1971

MEASURING SUCCESS

Much ado is made these days about methods which produce successful evangelism. Some Christians seem to be very critical of the "Four Spiritual Laws" while others praise the booklet highly. My personal view, after again reviewing the Laws carefully, is that they state biblical truths, although clearly not the entire Gospel. The adequacy of these 'laws', I suggest, is determined mainly by the user. If they are used tactlessly or superficially they may well prove to be of little value but the same criticism can be made of any form of evangelism similarly utilized.

Be that as it may, my main concern this week is that the various invitations and pressures brought to bear on us to use certain methods to achieve more "success" may, I repeat—may, distort a biblical view of evangelical success.

Clearly, Jesus taught his followers to preach and make disciples, but the emphasis was always on what the believers should do. Jesus, I submit, at least by inference defined success in terms of obedience; we are prone to define it in terms of results. The problem arises from the fact that our society generally defines success in terms of results. The successful business or salesman is not necessarily the most honorably motivated one but the one who makes the most money. Likewise, generally, in the other professions and vocations. The successful teacher is the one who gets promoted. Results are taken as the measurement of worth.

But in the Kingdom of God that's not the central theme. Our society defines success as getting ahead; in God's Kingdom success means following him who is ahead. Our society focuses on externals; Jesus constantly emphasized the importance of "internals." Our society sees a successful person as one who gives orders; Jesus taught that Christian success involves obeying orders. Our society admires him who has acquired much; Jesus emphasized the importance of giving.

I am not suggesting that results are unimportant in the Christian life but I am saying that faithfulness is more important. Let us not permit worldly definitions of success to distort what Jesus taught.

In Mark 6:7-11 we read how Jesus sent out the twelve to spread the Good News. You will recall how he instructed them to shake the dust from their feet when they left a place where the Gospel was rejected. Were the disciples successful in God's sight when nobody believed what they said and when shaking the dust from their sandals they moved on?

FORGIVING, FORGETTING

At local church meetings, at provincial conference sessions, and probably at this year's Canadian and North American assemblies, Mennonite Brethren Christians will again be debating the question of limiting a Christian's church involvement because of his evil deeds before he became a Christian. The issue is an important one and deserves attention—and a Christian answer.

Should we make any distinctions? Or should we simply overlook the past? Would we really be ready to put a former rapist in charge of teaching the young people's Sunday school class? Would we be willing to let a chartered accountant become the church treasurer even though in his pre-Christian days he was convicted of fraud and embezzlement? Would we allow a former strip teaser to be soloist in the choir? No doubt some readers would object; "after all," so some might think, "that would be almost as bad as placing a former persecutor of Christians in charge of the church's missions program!"

But that is exactly what the early church, directed by the Holy Spirit, did in the case of Paul. One of the most zealous Christian killers of all time became relief coordinator, executive field secretary, chief church planter, new fields missions pioneer, and head evangelist all at the same time. And God blessed him and his efforts immensely.

Then there was Zachaeus—an estabishment rip-off-artist of the first order. Should we grant such a person full standing in the saintly fellowship? Apparently Jesus did.

But there must surely be a limit! What if a Christian falls into grievious sin, after his conversion; should we allow him to resume his position as church leader following his repentance? Would we want an ex-liar and an ex-deceiver to lead us? Peter was an ex-liar and an ex-deceiver yet Jesus selected him above all others to lead the church.

Even so, should one not keep former adulterers and others guilty of sex sins so vehemently denounced in the New Testament, in a class apart, away from full fellowship privileges? Jesus' comments to the woman at the well hardly justify such a stance.

"But," you may ask, "does not the evil people do have lasting consequences?" Often it does, as in the case of cirrhosis of the liver, broken marriages, "illegitimate" children, ruined careers, etc., but have we any biblical evidence supporting the view that Christians have a mandate to make sure that these evil effects of pre-Christian sinfulness be somehow cultivated and attention drawn to them?

Accordingly, have we any Christian right to say that a person who was divorced before he became a Christian cannot be a pastor, preacher, or missionary? The answer depends on whether we take our cue from God's Word.

SCHOOL SUPPORTERS

Recently news reports have impressed upon me the fact that at present between 1600 and 2000 students are attending our Bible Institutes, Colleges, and the Seminary in Canada and the United States. In addition, about the same number are enrolled in our high schools. In view of this great opportunity and responsibility that has come to our brotherhood I have prepared a set of suggestions which, perchance, may apply to the odd reader.

- If you hear about some non-Christian students who are misbehaving, be thankful that our schools still emphasize a strong evangelical thrust which attracts unbelievers.
- If you hear that students grow beards, go barefoot, or wear outlandish styles, be grateful that our schools respect individualism. (Maybe the barefoot student can't afford shoes!)
- If you see that the students are wearing peace pendants or even peace beards, thank God for their interest in pacifism.
- If rumor should reach you that wild orgies are taking place right under the teachers' noses, feel sorry for the frustrated person who started the rumor.
- If you have the impression that the students are growing away from the constituency, volunteer to host a few when the school visits your area.
- If you have suggestions about how the school should be changed,send them along to the principal or president; he will be happy to know of your interest and will consider your suggestions carefully.
- If you can't stand the principal or president, ask God to give you a more Christian disposition.
- If you are a critical alumnus of one of our schools, don't forget to express your gratitude to the school that helped you to become so perceptive and enlightened.
- If you hear of a weak teacher, be thankful for all the others who bring up the average.
- If you hear that the teachers are overpaid and underworked, switch the two prefixes in the adjectives and believe it.
- If you are disturbed about the fact that the school you attended has added many social activities, try to be philosophical about the fact that you can't live your youth over again.
- If you hear that fellows and girls are falling in love in our schools, thank God for the fact that they are finding Christian partners in a Christian environment.
- If you read that a certain school requires a subsidy of over $100,000, pause in utter amazement at how efficiently our schools are run; do a comparison with a similar government school.
- If you are asked to give some money, express your gratitude for this personal attention by giving generously.
- If you have no children, be grateful for the fact that in a Christian brotherhood you are as much a part of the operation as if you had a child in every grade.
- If you note that our schools have different emphases, be happy that our educational endeavors reflect the breadth of our resources and perspectives.
- If you are concerned about the fact that the school you once attended has since added substantial sports

activities, try to be grateful for this healthy expansion of the curriculum.

• If you feel that the teachers are not strict enough, send in your specific suggestions; if you feel that they are too strict, be grateful that they are trying to achieve what some parents neglected to do.

• If you cannot see the point of Christian education, ask God to help you improve your vision.

NOVEMBER 26, 1976

PRINCE OF PEACE AND PACIFISM

I am writing this column on November 11; you will probably read it well before December 25. The two dates, I suggest, have more in common than we may have thought, especially if we view November 11 not mainly as military Armistice Day but as a day when we focus on peace.

Somewhere along the line many of us have managed to draw a thick black line **between the Prince of Peace and the** Way of Peace, blithely ignoring the fact that the latter is simply obedience to the former—nothing more and nothing less. At least that's my impression.

For me, the sorry state of pacifist affairs struck home with full force some days ago while attending a peace conference. As I looked over the assembled Christians and listened to what was said, my mind was filled with questions and observations, some of which might properly be directed as follows:

To certain Christian pacifists:

* Please take note that a Christian pacifist need not be a political lefist. Christian theology does not correlate that simply with political ideology.

* Even while he criticizes militarism in all its threatening forms, from Kremlinism to Pentagonism, the Christian pacifist must not hate the inhabitants of those citadels of military destruction. Christlikeness is not measured by the amount of hatred shown towards militarists.

* Why is it that some of us apparently believe that in order to convince others that we are really committed to peace, we must look as if we have just been disturbing the peace?

* Credibility requires consistency. When, as members of the transnational church we quite properly criticize militarism, why are some of us so reluctant to criticize militarism in communist countries?

* Being a Christian pacifist is more a matter of what a person is for, than what a person is against. Pacifism is basically positive.

* Being a pacifist, even a dedicated peace activist, does not in itself make one a Christian. A Christian peace witness is the fruit, not the root, of being a Christian.

To certain church leaders:

* Why is it that Christian pacifism is today in such bad shape, even in many so-called historic peace churches? Why, in some of our churches, is pacifism considered to be suspect and viewed almost as a kind of heresy?

* Do you personally really believe that Christian pacifism is simply peace in action?

* Why do so many of us hold back when it comes to supporting Christian pacifism? Could it be that popularity has become more important than Biblicism?

* Since you, as a minister, have accepted your church's statement of faith it is fair to ask: when have you last preached a sermon on Christian pacifism?

To myself (and yourself):

* Do I really accept the notion that Christian pacifism is a lifestyle affecting all of my relationships, not merely a response to a military draft notice?

* If I had to rate myself on a scale, from a low of one to a high of ten, **concerning my expression of a Christian** pacifist lifestyle in day to day living, how would I rate myself?

PACIFISM
1 2 3 4 5 6 7 8 9 10

EVANGELICAL SALT

Recently I heard a Mennonite Brethren preacher say that in his opinion it was time we paid more attention to evangelicalism and, at least for a while, less to Anabaptism.

I have difficulty with such advice, not because it stresses evangelicalism—I support that—but because it assumes that Anabaptism is not evangelical. Ever since I was taught about my spiritual heritage I have thought that the main strength of Anabaptism lay in its biblical emphasis on both evangelism and discipleship, on becoming a Christian and then living as Christ taught us to live.

But now I am told that too much Anabaptism is not good for me. Something is wrong somewhere!

Let us suggest what I think has gone wrong. I think that some of us have allowed ourselves to be duped, theologically. In recent years, and even now, some people who call themselves Anabaptist and make much noise about it have played down being born again, to use Jesus' words. They have minimized it down to almost nothing.

What a pity and what a distortion! They seem to be advocating a kind of unevangelical Anabaptism, but unevangelical Anabaptism is a contradiction in terms. An Anabaptist is an evangelical person and we dare not forget it. Nor should we let anyone else forget it. Least of all those who by their cultic distortion are robbing our creed of its biblical integrity.

I agree with Myron Augsburger who recently stated the following:

"A few educated persons in the Mennonite church have said, 'We may not be called to do evangelism as Mennonites, we may just be called to be the salt of the earth.' That position is not found in 16th century Anabaptist faith. That is a pseudo, or liberal, interpretation of our heritage that has come from humanistic influence."

Dr. Augsburger adds, "If you are not evangelistic in spirit and purpose, you are not Anabaptist. Theologically, from the Anabaptist standpoint, the only way the church has to perpetuate itself is by converting people."

Amen! That's what Anabaptism means.

Our pressing need at this time is not to abandon the wholeness of Anabaptist doctrine for an "evangelicalism" which often overlooks Jesus' call to faithful discipleship, but to insist that the biblical components of Anabaptism be preached and practiced in their fulness. Better yet, let us not only correct the doctrine of others but let us lead and teach by our own example.

THE MISSIONS CYCLE

Let me stress two points at the outset: first, although I have read about foreign missionary activity with interest ever since my parents first introduced me to some fascinating biographies, I am not an expert on missions; second, the following comments are intended as supportive affirmations of our current missions thrust while also serving as warnings against certain pressures and recommendations one hears from time to time.

Fully realizing that missions programs are dynamic and often in a state of uneven flux, we may, nonetheless, benefit from a review of the various phases or stages which some missions societies have experienced, or at least so it seems to me.

Phase One — The "Pre-Missionary Phase." Christians have experienced personal salvation but have not yet "caught the vision."

Phase Two — The "Pioneer Phase." Here we think of pioneer missionaries trekking through unmarked regions, often paying the ultimate price. Their motivation is to bring soul-salvation to as many individuals, tribes, and peoples as possible.

Phase Three — The "First Settlement" Phase. In this stage we encounter the first permanent physical structures and social organization. The stress on soul-salvation often emanates from a compound mentality derived from an actual compound setting. An emphasis on literacy and on better health conditions tends to be associated with this phase. Also, a growing infusion of Western culture is not uncommon.

Phase Four — The "Total Gospel" Phase. In a sense this phase grows naturally out of the previous one. Its distinctive features are two-fold; an encompassing Christian concern for a person's soul, mind and body, and an inclusive Christian involvement focusing on both prevention and alleviation of misery.

Phase Five — The "Status Quo" Phase. At this stage Christian innovation has largely ceased; the operation of a large program requires much energy and support.

Phase Six — The "Social Gospel" Phase. Nothing changes formally or officially but a very basic, though often subtle, change in emphasis has taken place. Rhetoric still includes salvation but the actual thrust has shifted to the solution of pressing physical problems. Motivation tends still to be thoroughly Christian.

Phase Seven — The "Concern and Dialogue" Phase. In this phase the mission personnel combine mission service with a new dialogical interaction. The results may be spiritually beneficial or they may dilute the Christian message depending on the Christian maturity of those dialoguing.

Phase Eight — The "Missions as Dialogue" Phase. Here the thrust has changed unmistakably. True, the foreign Christian still ministers to important needs but concerning soul salvation the message has become very blurred. It is no longer just a matter of being receptive to the insights or Christian experience of the "natives" or nationals but of seeing considerable merit in non-Christian religions.

Phase Nine — The "Missions as Sharing" Phase. In this phase missions has taken on the trappings of anthropology and mutual learning becomes central. Missionaries come with questions rather than with answers. Social service may persist, provided it doesn't disturb ''native'' natural lifestyles too much but any concern for soul salvation has largely evaporated. Increasingly in this phase, the interest of foreigners is to find out how others live and to seek to understand them. In some situations the ''natives'' become the missionaries and the foreigners the converts as the Westerners become enamored with the virtues of what they find.

Phase Ten — The ''Post-Missionary Phase.'' Eventually, though programs and structures many persist, for all intents and purposes Christian missions has petered out. In terms of motives and message the Great Commission has been transformed into an unrecognizable humanistic open-mindedness. Not surprisingly, such a ''missions'' program is really of no significant consequence to anyone and thus interest, support, and participation all wither.

Such a cycle is, however, not inevitable, indeed, it is preventable.

MISSIONS CYCLE, II

A number of people have commented about my column "The Missions Cycle"; several raised some important questions which require clarification.

Clearly, the various phases which I described are not all mutually exclusive. Depending on the specific situation, missions personnel may find themselves in a pioneering stage which involves a total gospel thrust while being in dialogue with those whom they have come to help. Of course there will be, as one letter writer put it, "mutual learning;" that is not the issue. What disturbs me is to observe such "mutual learning" focus on who Jesus is! If we are not sure of who Jesus is or why he came to the world, then we have no gospel to proclaim, only ideas to share.

The same letter writer adds, "My concern then, is that readers will tend to compartmentalize your ideas into a lockstep codification, and upon hearing of a mission endeavor that involves some of the phraseology mentioned in one of the categories (e.g. 'mission in dialogue'), will paint all such activities with the negative brush. . . ."

The writer's point is well taken. We must be careful not to oversimplify phenomena that are really very complex! And we must always be willing to listen and learn. But I stand by my earlier assertion: we should be ready to dialogue about secondary questions but if we want to dialogue about the fundamental purpose of missions and whether Jesus really lived, then we are approaching the area of "vain disputations" and might as well forget about missions.

A person who does not have firm commitments about the essentials of Christianity can't be a true missionary. Philosophers and academics may search for truth; Christians, while seeking to increase their knowledge, proclaim the truth that they have personally experienced.

Consider the case of the Apostle Paul. The account in Acts 17 tells us that "he was reasoning in the synagogue with the Jews," "conversing" with Epicurean and Stoic philosophers, and discussing religious questions with Athenians at Mars Hill. But always Paul's message was unequivocal and clear. He did not grant any credibility to an "unknown god" but simply announced that "What therefore you worship in ignorance, this I proclaim to you."

Similarly in Ephesus. He "reasoned daily in the school of Tyrannus" but allowed absolutely no place for false religion. He might, I suppose, have been greatly impressed by the strong religious traditions in that city, by the sincerity of the worshippers, by the needs which their religion seemed to fill, by the extensive scholarship associated with that creed, and by the beautiful silver shrines made by Demetrius and the other talented craftsmen.

Instead, Paul apparently had nothing to do with all that falsity. He gave it no credence or standing but preached the true gospel. That is what we should do.

Yes, all missionaries, indeed all Christians, should always be ready to listen and eager to learn—not to accommodate false religions but to become more mature Christians and more tactful and effective proclaimers of the truth.

IS GUILT A MYTH?

Is guilt a myth? The great psychologist Sigmund Freud said so and for decades many, if not most, psychologists have agreed with him. The standard argument seems to be that man has no innate evil about which he should feel guilty, that most "evil" deeds about which Christianity makes him feel guilty are not evil at all, and that parents and church leaders have no right to make young people feel guilty. (The obvious irony in this Freudian argument, of course, is that having shoved the guilt concept out the front door, these Freudians then sneak it in via the back door and try to make Christian parents feel guilty for making their children feel guilty!)

I was reminded of Freud's emphasis when, not long ago, I heard a Mennonite Brethren preacher of considerable reputation lament the fact that in preaching about the love of God, certain MB ministers tended to produce feelings of guilt in their hearers. This presence of guilt seemed to bother the preacher more than a little. When I approached him about the matter he calmly asserted that people should be loved into the Kingdom rather than be made to feel guilty. He seemed to be so assured and spoke so persuasively that I decided to think about the matter a while.

I want to continue my thinking and my study of the question but on one point I am already clear—guilt and love are not mutually exclusive. My Bible studies have convinced me that even as men of God preached the Gospel of Love, God's spirit was already making the hearers feel guilty ("they were pricked in their hearts," etc.)

The more I think about it, the more convinced I am that I must disagree with our esteemed preacher—in our day we need more, rather than less, emphasis placed on guilt. We need it for several reasons.

First, the Bible states that none of us is guiltless; we are all guilty and, unless we accept salvation, we must individually give an ultimate account of ourselves.

Second, if we do not teach the doctrine of guilt, both in general and with reference to specific acts, how can we logically expect people to repent and seek forgiveness? Why should people repent if there is no evil about which to repent?

Third, if we eliminate an emphasis on personal guilt we quickly arrive at a place where the structures of society—all the people out there—rather than we as individuals, are guilty. When that happens any call to

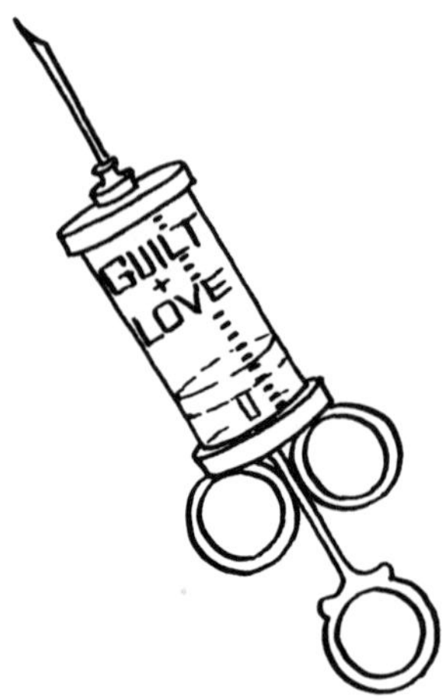

personal conversion makes little sense. Society, not the individual, presumably needs to change. (Here, again, we find that the notion of guilt is not eliminated, it is merely placed somewhere else. The Freudians fail again.)

What we need, I suggest, is a balanced emphasis. Evoking a sense of guilt for its own sake will get us nowhere and, I might add, should make us feel guilty about doing so. Conversely, if we shy away from anything to do with guilt, we will probably also see little repentance, little sense of personal responsibility, and little change in priorities. In short, we will have superficial Christianity and of this we already have far too much!

CARRYING THE WORD

Increasing numbers of evangelical Christians are entering politics. In Canada and the United States the phenomenon is widespread. We think, of course, of President Carter but there are many others at various levels. In Canada there are at least twenty in Parliament and a goodly number at provincial and local levels.

Significantly, growing numbers of Mennonite Brethren are standing for office and being elected. On the basis of an incomplete survey, I find that we now have two MB Members of Parliament and about 50 to 60 MB's holding elective office at lower levels. The numbers seem to be increasing.

For a denomination which at one time had qualms about voting, we've come a long way—the direction depends on your point of view. In Canada we now have enough MB politicians, from MPs to school trustees and council members to Lord Mayors, so that they could call their own mini-convention.

I find this kind of political participation intriguing, partly because of the opportunities and problems I have observed and partly because of the responses of others.

For example, recently I enquired of an American brother how he saw President Carter as a Christian, specifically, whether he felt that the President was presiding as we should expect a Christian to preside in that high office. My American friend was quiet for a while and then said, "Well, he carries his Bible." He spoke seriously.

Unfortunately, that is how we sometimes assess Christian behavior. We focus on externals and on symbols because they are easily seen.

Of course, Mr. Carter should be given high marks for openly and boldly proclaiming that he is a Christian, but surely that is not the real issue. The much more significant question, whether asked of the President, an MP, a mayor, a council member, a school trustee, etc. is whether his decisions and actions embody Christian values and virtues.

It is great to carry the Word; it is much greater to be guided by what that Word teaches! It is great to know that Jesus denounced racism; it is much greater to work for the elimination of racism in our day! It is great to be familiar with Jesus' powerful denunciation of injustice, greed and exploitation; it is surely much more important to utilize opportunities to help the exploited and downtrodden groups in our own society!

To me it doesn't make a great deal of difference whether or not evangelical believers in politics wear their Christianity on their sleeve. They should let it be known who they are, of course, but the fundamental question is whether their Christianity infuses what they do.

Fortunately some evangelical Christians—including MB's—who are active in politics reflect a Christian perspective but some, it seems to me, do not. They may be carrying their Bibles all right but that seems to be the only indication of their priorities. Of course, the same evaluation applies to evangelicals involved in professional associations, pressure groups, labor unions and other similar bodies.

As far as I am concerned, "carrying the Word" in a physical sense is only secondary. If we want to be Christians in politics, in education, in business, in agriculture, in law, in union leadership, in medicine, or in the civil service, then let us truly be Christian politicians, Christian teachers, Christian businessmen, Christian farmers, Christian lawyers, Christian shop stewards, Christian nurses and physicians and Christian supervisors and secretaries. That will be the real test of our faith.

OCTOBER 26, 1979

THE ESSENCE OF THE GOSPEL

The recent surge of activity involving aid to the "boat people," disaster relief and assorted other "good works" has caused me to re-evaluate the fundamental character and significance of such deeds of love and mercy.

More than ever before I am convinced that such ventures are vitally important, not least of all for the giver. But importance is not synonymous with essence. I, for one, am sometimes inclined to make the mistake of equating the two. In order to help me maintain a biblical perspective, as I understand it, I tell myself the following.

To educate people, to bring literacy to those who cannot read, is a great service, but it is not the gospel. Literacy helps people to understand the gospel but it is not a part of it.

To teach people how to grow more food, or to grow food more efficiently, helps them to keep body and soul together but in itself it is not the balm the soul needs. Teaching people how to raise better cattle, goats, or hogs; how to grow better wheat, rice, or corn; how to raise their own fish or fowl; all are vitally important, but these are not the gospel of Jesus Christ.

To teach people sanitation and proper personal care is important, after all, there is some truth to the old adage that "cleanliness is next to godliness", but personal hygiene is not part of the gospel.

To help the sick, the injured, the maimed, and the blind is vitally important. After all, did not Jesus himself spend much time doing precisely that! Indeed he did. But even so that is not in itself the essence of God's gospel.

To assist destitute refugees, (fortunately, North American Mennonites have led the way by sponsoring thousands of Indochinese "boat people"), whether fleeing an oppressive dictatorship, or made homeless by a belching volcano, or drowning at sea, or wasting away in a crowded camp, is one of the most vital ministries in our day, but of itself it is not the gospel.

To give emergency relief when a river floods or a tornado strikes is one of the most commendable forms of service to fellowman but it is not part and parcel of God's message of forgiveness and redemption.

To work at conflict resolution, be it in labor-management situations, racial confrontations, or in arenas of military madness surely constitutes some of the most useful service anyone can perform but that is not the heart of God's gospel. All of the above, and much more that you and I could add, are good deeds, they are acts of kindness, compassion, of mercy and love. If done by Christians they are Christian acts of kindness, compassion, of mercy and love. But they still are only an *application* of love, a partial expression of Christ-likeness; they are not the gospel.

The gospel is God's invitation to people to accept his forgiveness of sin, to accept justification, to become transformed and to accept the eternal life made possible by Jesus' incarnation, death, resurrection and ascension and by the indwelling presence of the Holy Spirit. To proclaim that good news is to proclaim the essence of the gospel.

All forms of service, no matter how desperate the need or how laudable the motive, are secondary. I do not mean to say that service is less important in the sense of being optional; I am saying, rather, that it is secondary in the sense that it can never replace God's message of reconciliation for lost non-Christians.

Let us continue to do "good deeds," for that is a vital part of our mission. But such doing of good deeds is the *result* of the gospel message at work in our lives, it is not in itself the gospel message. When we become Christians, we accept the gospel; when we do good deeds, others experience the consequences of our conversion. The two are not the same. And even the most sacrificial service imaginable does not in and of itself constitute the gospel. Of course, it may be proof of our spiritual authenticity and it may well be a means of bringing the lost closer to God.

This column is not a plea for less emphasis on good works, only on attempt to clarify what they are. The world sorely needs both the "good news" and the "good deeds;" let us continue to proclaim the one and not allow the other to remain undone.

DECEMBER 3, 1982

CONVERSION

Various responses continue to come in about a statement which appeared in this column some four months ago. Concerning "Mennonite Brethren in the 80s," I raised several considerations and problems, including the following: "Will we retain the conviction and explicit assertions that without a personal salvation experience fallen man is eternally lost?"

Some readers apparently overlooked the word "retain" which clearly implies that at present our brotherhood holds to that conviction. Certainly there was no intention to suggest that any pastors, faculty members in our schools, or conference leaders at various levels are moving away from that position. Evenso, I suggest, we have good reason to reflect on the situation. But before I expand on that suggestion, let me explain my view on spiritual conversion.

Clearly, becoming a child of God does not always involve a single, emotion-laden or "Damascus Road" experience. In some cases, as Delbert Wiens explained a decade ago in his classic essay, "New Wine in Old Wineskins," becoming a Christian involves a series of cumulative decisions and experiences. But the bottom line must be a transformation, a spiritual renewal.

My reasons for including the apparently disquieting little paragraph in the August 6 column are at least sixfold:

(1) There seems to be less emphasis placed on "conversion" preaching in our pulpits nowadays than there used to be. Some preachers, perhaps only a few, seem to be uncomfortable declaring the explicit biblical invitations and warnings of eternal damnation unless rebirth occurs, as Jesus forthrightly told Nicodemus. Then, too, for several years we have had no conference evangelist.

(2) Our records tell us that in recent years the number of congregational evangelistic meetings and campaigns has sharply declined. Of course, I realize that Christian camps, schools, etc. are taking up some of the slack and that a more personal approach may be more effective but one cannot assume that all is well.

(3) In our ranks there seems to be less emphasis on categorization; a situation also now common concerning church membership. We have become hesitant to distinguish between the "ins" and the "outs." Such a broader view has its advantages, but also its disadvantages. For some people grey has become a third category.

(4) In some instances there seems to be a subtle shifting of assumptions. From certain parents one gets the impression that their son or daughter is a Christian because the child was raised in a Christian environment and has never rejected the Christian ethic. In a few rare instances the parental stance is something akin to this, "Our boy is a Christian because he has never rejected the faith!"

(5) During the last few years I have encountered a few MB members who, as I perceived it, treated the matter of conversion, especially child conversion, with condescension and humor. One acquaintance was amazed that a certain pastor actually had an altar call.

(6) Finally, we can see all around us numerous denominations which once made much of conversion but now don't.

If the above constitute some evidence for concern, or at least alertness, let me move on to suggest several reasons why such tendencies might increase:

(1) Many of us have become turned-off, if not nauseated, by contemporary misuse of the term "born again." The ads tell us that a car with a new paint job has been "born again" and if we wish to be "born again" we should take advantage of that low-priced one-week sun vacation. Almost any renewal or reconditioning qualifies for the description.

(2) Some of our more sophisticated thinkers are understandably reacting negatively to a shallow, lowest common-denominator (sometimes fundamentalist) preaching which maximizes the conversion experience and minimizes life-transforming commitment and discipleship.

(3) We are having increasing interaction with denominations and groups for whom conversion is no big deal, for whom such a distinction is not basic. Interest is sufficient.

(4) Greater tolerance in many ethical issues has increasingly blurred the distinction between Christians and non-Christians and the need to identify clearly with one categry or the other.

(5) The impact of worldliness, of the pervasive sub-Christian culture, seems to be increasing. We have become more assimilated than we would like to admit. As we become more comfortable in and with the world, the question of conversion drops lower and lower on our agenda.

Well, that's how it looks to me. Fortunately, all things considered, we still have a solid basis for gratitude and optimism.

MARX SAID; JESUS SAID

The writings of Karl Marx and Fredrich Engels stand in stark contrast to the teachings of Jesus of Nazareth. Here are some poignant examples.

(1) *Marx* said, "The criticism of religion is the premise of all criticism." *Jesus* said, "Search the Scriptures . . . it is these that bear witness of me" (John 5:39). "Blessed are you when men revile you, and persecute you, and say all kinds of evil against you falsely, on account of me" (Matt. 5:11).

(2) *Marx* said, "The abolition of religion as the illusory happiness of the people is required for their real happiness." *Jesus* said, "For I gave you an example that you should do as I did to you. . . . If you know these things, happy are you if you do them" (John 13:15, 17).

(3) *Marx* said, "Christianity, like every great revolutionary movement, was made by the masses. It arose in Palestine, in a manner utterly unknown to us, at a time when new sects, new religions, new prophets arose by the hundred. It is, in fact, merely an average phenomenon." *Jesus* said, "For God did not send the Son into the world to judge the world; but that the world should be saved through him. . . . Jesus said to him, 'I am the way, and the truth and the life; no one comes to the Father, but through me'" (John 3:17; 14:6).

(4) *Marx* said, "Thousands of years may have passed before the conditions arose in which . . . this shapeless protein (could) produce the first cell. . . . But this first cell also provided the foundation for the . . . development of the whole organic world. . . . And from the first animals developed mammals and . . . finally . . . man." *Jesus* said, "Have you not read, that he who created them from the beginning made them male and female" (Matt. 19:4).

(5) *Marx* said, "The more man puts into God, the less he retains in himself." *Jesus* said, "He who believes in me, as the Scripture said, 'From his innermost being shall flow rivers of living water'" (John 7:38).

(6) *Marx* said, "This much is sure; the only service that can be rendered to God today is to declare atheism a compulsory article of faith. . . . " *Jesus* said, "Begone Satan! For it is written, 'You shall worship the Lord your God, and serve him only'" (Matt. 4:10).

(7) *Marx* said, "Religion is the opium of the people." *Jesus* said, "You are mistaken, not understanding the Scriptures, or the power of God" (Matt. 22:29).

(8) *Marx* said, "The task of history is . . . to establish the truth of this world. . . ." *Jesus* said, "I am the way, and the truth. . . . Thy word is truth" (John 14:6, 17:17).

(9) *Marx* said, "The Jewish so-called Holy Scripture is nothing more than a record of the old-Arabian religious and tribal conditions. . . . " *Jesus* said, "You search the Scriptures . . . it is these that bear witness of me" (John 5:39).

(10) *Marx* said, "All history is a history of class wars." *Jesus* said, "A new commandment I give to you, that you love one another, even as I have loved you" (John 13:34).

(11) *Marx* said, "Man . . . looked for a superman in the fantastic reality of heaven and found nothing there but the reflection of himself." *Jesus* said, "God is spirit; and those who worship him must worship in spirit and truth"

(John 4:24).

(12) *Marx* said, "Only when the real, individual man . . . has become a social being in his everyday life, in his particular work . . . only then will human emancipation have been accomplished." *Jesus* said, "If therefore the Son shall make you free, you shall be free indeed" (John 8:36).

(13) *Marx* said, "In his changing their mode of production, in changing their way of earning their living, they (men) change all their social relationships." *Jesus* said, "By this all men will know that you are my disciples, if you have love for one another" (John 13:35).

(14) *Marx* said, "Nothing is (real and) eternal except eternally changing, eternally moving matter and the laws according to which it moves and changes." *Jesus* said, "Heaven and earth will pass away, but my words shall not pass away" (Matt. 24:35).

(15) *Marx* said, "The social principles of Christianity preach cowardice, self-contempt, abasement, submission, dejection. . . . " *Jesus* said, "These things I have spoken to you, that my joy may be in you, and that your joy may be made full" (John 15:11).

PART III

The Church

APRIL 1, 1966

ALL WERE GLAD

Perhaps you've heard about Rev. Brown and how he made many people glad.

Rev. Brown and his charming wife arrived in Commonplace, Saskaltoba. in early June. They were a little nervous about the whole thing because this was their first pastorate; they had left the seminary only a week ago.

Their fears and misgivings soon disappeared for everyone was so very friendly. Everybody seemed so glad that they had come. At last, after several years of lifelessness, the old frame church was to come to life again.

The Village Council was glad because the reopening of the church would hopefully quelch the vicious rumor that Commonplace consisted of atheists. Every proper town should have its own church and now Commonplace would no longer be a glaring exception.

The dozen or so merchants were glad because having a functioning church in town was good business. Not only would they now have the opportunity to attend church regularly and thus prove their piety and high morals, but they would also get to know more people. And people became customers, and customers became profit. Eight of the village merchants were in church service the first Sunday morning and they all pressed the new pastor's hand warmly. They were so glad he had come.

The gladness of the merchants was at least equalled by all four of the town teachers. A church does something for a town, especially the children and young people. Now the boy scouts would have a meeting place, the young people would have wholesome surroundings for their Saturday hootenannies, and the younger children, at least some of them, would be off the streets on Sunday morning. It was a good thing that the Browns had come.

Many of the fathers were particularly glad for the revival of the church. Many promised themselves that they would send their children every Sunday. They anticipated with pleasure the quiet Sunday forenoons snoozing in bed. And while they snoozed, the children over in the church would be learning important things. The arrival of the Browns had certainly changed things for the better.

A number of wives also were filled with gladness. Perhaps Rev. Brown would be able to convince their husbands that it was the menfolk who were causing all the quarrels. Several phoned the first week to make appointments so that the new pastor would know the facts of the case.

The young people were glad that their parents would have a place to go (and gripe), and the parents were glad that the young people would finally get straightened out. Old Mrs. Fair was glad that finally somebody would relieve her of the weekly rounds of visiting the sick. Her sigh of relief was echoed by the village constable who felt that his task would become considerably easier.

The whole village was glad. It's amazing what a church can do for even a small town, especially for others.

WELCOME
PASTOR
BROWN

JUNE 24, 1966

WOMEN — SECOND CLASS CHRISTIANS

Historically, Christianity has been one of the major factors contributing to the emancipation of women. In those areas of the world where non-Christian religions are strong, women are often still treated as inferior beings.

In view of the above it is all the more puzzling that many evangelical denominations, our own included, often treat women members so shabbily. If I were a woman I would feel insulted. It seems to me that it is high time that we change some of our time dishonored customs.

One of the practices which disturbs me greatly is our habit of herding the women into some rear corner at our conference business sessions. Why do we do this? I am fully aware of the biblical injunction about being silent (more or less) when it comes to preaching, but I know of no verse which commands us to "come away from the women and be ye separate." Why should not the wives sit with their husbands and be voting delegates?

Recently I was asked to speak at some conference business sessions of another denomination and was immediately struck by the full equality extended to the women members. True, they spoke very little, asking only a question or two, but they had full voting and floor privileges. The whole arrangement seemed very natural. I saw no usher fumbling nervously trying to decide whether to pass out ballots to the rear left hand corner. Perhaps if we treated our women as full fledged church members more of them, especially the younger ones, would be interested in attending and participating in the sessions in question. As it is, the casual visitor to our business meetings might well conclude that our whole denomination is one great big men's fellowship.

Furthermore, why are Ladies' Aids (Missionary Circles, etc.) usually, or at least often, given such a brush off. Personally I know of no MB church where this aspect of church work is given official status. The youth leader, the secretary of the endowment fund, the extension secretary, and even the representative to the burial society are asked to report to the annual church meeting, but the women are ignored. Why? The situation is all the more disturbing in view of the fact that often the women's groups are the most missionary-minded organization within the church. Why do so many of the male leaders tend to be embarrassed when the ladies work is discussed and why do we feel so threatened when the women show any signs of independent thinking and action?

I see no reason why women's work should not be fully recognized as a regular branch of the church and given full representation in the church council, regular or "extended." Is this work any less significant than, let us say, youth work? I suggest that it is at least as important. Usually the youth leader is a member of the council, why should not the women's leader be also?

One could cite other aspects of the problem but let these illustrations suffice.

Christ has taught us that in his sight all people are essentially equal, and that from the Christian perspective physical or social differences are of no consequence. We have made much ado about overcoming racial, educational, and economic barriers; it is high time that we put into practice the notion that Christian equality extends to women as well.

SEPTEMBER 16, 1966

FATHERS OF OUR FAITH

The last decade or so has witnessed a phenomenal change in the social, cultural, and even political orientation of the Mennonite Brethren church in Canada. We have become more heterogeneous, more cosmopolitan, and more sophisticated. Even our church practices have undergone major changes. A new interest in home missions, greater social involvement, an expanded peace interest and witness are all part of this many-sided transformation.

Not too surprisingly, these complex changes have been accompanied by a widespread replacement of our older leaders by younger, inexperienced brethren. Often this change is accompanied by a more or less subdued but nevertheless distinct feeling of relief. The fading away of the revered leaders of yesteryear is often met with cold indifference or worse.

I suggest that those of us who are younger need to remind ourselves whose sons and daughters we are, both physically and spiritually. Before we become too enamored and pleased with our own efforts and innovations, let us admit that we are where we are, and who we are, mainly because of our background and training. Basically, we are not "showing up" our parents but rather complimenting them when we follow their admonition to build, expand, and revitalize. The fact, or so it seems to me, that our denomination seems to be making significant progress in a number of areas is largely attributable to the quality of leadership in earlier years.

Putting flowers on graves is largely pointless. We need to present bouquets and thank our elders while they are still with us. I know that in expressing these sentiments of appreciation I speak for many younger members of our churches.

We thank you, our elders, for what you have done and for what you have been and still are. You have laid the foundations; we want to build on them. The foundation may not always be given due credit, it does not always show, but its role is crucial. Without a solid foundation the structure will crumble. Our foundation, to the extent it is of human origin, has been well built by you. Let us also say that in certain areas we are not building as well as you have.

We sing frequently about the faith of our fathers, and that is as it should be, but let us not forget the human element, the fathers of our faith.

JULY 8, 1966

GLOSSOLALIA AND DISUNITY

From reports by others and from my own observations I have concluded that in at least several regions of our Canadian brotherhood there is sharp disagreement on the matter of speaking in tongues. Feelings seem to be deep and fervent. In some instances relatives have suddenly become cool to one another, friendships have been broken, and feelings of distrust have mushroomed. And in at least two instances some of the brethren have sought to remove others from positions of leadership.

I find the whole matter very distressing. Surely we should be able to discuss our differences in this area in Christian love and mutual confidence. Permit me to think out loud on the subject and to point out several aspects of the controversy to each of the groups in question.

(1) To the Anti-Tongues Movement People.

The Bible does not forbid Christians to speak in tongues. Glossalalia, whatever else it may be, is clearly cited as a gift of the Spirit. (To say that they sound like drunks is hardly original; the same comment was made in Apostolic days.)

Why, I might ask, is there this sudden interest in what people do in their own homes? Furthermore, what a person does in his own home devotions is his own business and not yours or mine. Some of the sharpest critics never have complained one word about fellow believers who have no devotion time whatsoever, but let someone practice glossalalia in his own private room and fires of gossip are set everywhere.

We must always remember to evaluate Christians by their spiritual fruit, as Christ exhorted us to do. Those Christians who practice speaking in tongues should be evaluated on the basis of their joy, their power to witness, their victory over sin, their worship and praise of God, their love for God and man, and their overall spiritual warmth.

Finally, we must remember that historically we have tended to underemphasize the role of the Spirit as well as some of the spiritual gifts. It ought not really to surprize us that a strong reaction in the other direction should set in. Personally, I would rather be guilty of overemphasizing than of underemphasizing.

(2) To the Pro-Tongues Movement People.

Part of the controversy is caused by the fact that people who speak in tongues generally do not explain adequately what they are doing or why they are doing it. You need to explain that the purpose of glossolalia is not to help "foreigners" to hear the Gospel in their own tongues, but rather to commune with God in a purer form — to escape from the limitations and connotations of one's own language.

Another cause of friction is the assertion made by some that it is God's will that all Christians should speak in tongues. To make that claim is to assert more than the Bible does.

Related to the above is the self-righteous claim that Christians who speak in tongues are better than others. Such a view is unscriptural.

(3) All of us need to practice much tolerance, forbearance, and love. We need more open-mindnesses and willingness to re-study Scripture, and less propensity to judge and denounce. A special emphasis on the Holy Spirit

can serve either to strengthen the brotherhood or weaken, even split it. What will it be for us?

RECOMMENDATION 4 (4)

At the Corn, Oklahoma, Mennonite Brethren Convention last November a considerable amount of time was spent discussing the problem of divorce. (Recommendation 4) A part of the recommendation submitted by the Board of Reference and Counsel was adopted, a part was referred back to the committee for further study. The section which particularly perturbs me is section (4), which was added by the delegates as the result of an impromptu vote.

Section (3) involved the question of accepting for membership believers who had been divorced, but had later come "to the point of true repentance." The matter was "referred back." I happened to disagree with the majority on this point because I believe that if we really believe that God has forgiven and forgotten we ought surely to forgive and forget. (I am reminded of the debtor who was forgiven much but refused to forgive others, Matthew 18:23-35.)

But what really bothers me is the theology of our impromptu addition (which was also referred back to committee). After acknowledging that, "If we confess our sins, he is faithful and just to forgive our sins, and to *cleanse* us from all unrighteousness," we nevertheless wrote, "Such members (divorced but repentant and forgiven) shall not be eligible for any office that requires ordination." In effect we are thereby saying that what God has cleansed we still consider to be soiled. For years I believed that after God forgave me, I was, in his sight as one who had not even committed the sin! Was I in error?

If there is any validity in 4 (4) I've got a real problem on my hands. The Apostle Paul was a persecutor and murderer of the first rank yet he exhorts us to love all men, even enemies, and to do good to those who abuse us. Who is he to talk? What an example he was! He was a murderer and by his own admission a wicked character of the first order. I can see where he might have served as head usher for the Jerusalem congregation, or maybe even registrar-statistician, but to have him head up the entire missionary venture, to become a leading brother, and claim to be receiving direct communication from God . . .! Well! After all, he was a mass murderer —a historical fact that cannot be denied! Can anyone supply me with some new version of the Bible in which this mass murderer is kept strictly in a secondary role; one in which he does only those things which the unordained normally do?

HYPOCRISY OR PIETY?

Several years ago the Mennonite Brethren Conference authorized local congregations to accept as regular members Christians who had not been baptized by immersion. It was generally agreed that the substantive prerequisite for members was a committed Christian life, not an outward symbolic form.

Unfortunately, however, the step in the right direction was only a half-step, maybe three-quarters. As I understand it, our present policy still prohibits non-immersed members, of whom we have many, from being ordained to the ministry. Why?

At various places Scripture states that church leaders should be chosen from those members who exemplify Christian maturity in its various aspects. Nowhere are any other kind of prohibitions cited.

The MB Church has traditionally prided itself, in a proper fashion, on the fact that we are a brotherhood, not a hierarchy of pompous bishops, collared clerics, and lowly laymen. Now, suddenly, we start establishing special categories, and, what is even more surprising and unfortunate, we set up an admittedly non-essential, and for many of us non-Biblical, criterion as a basis of differentiation!

Where in the Bible can we find the slighest shred of evidence to support the view that the church should have two levels of membership? Where do we read that a baptism which is admittedly adequate to symbolize a believer's joining the Body of Christ is nevertheless inadequate to permit him to proclaim the Good News about Christ? Where can we find any Biblical justification for a practice which adds to the Biblical prerequisites for the ministry?

It is my view that whenever we make it more difficult to enter our church than to enter heaven, that whenever we make it harder for people to be preachers than Jesus made it for people to be his disciples, and that whenever we legislate in areas where the Bible is at best unclear, to that extent we err!

Personally, I believe that baptism by immersion is the best method, although the significance of the step is, of course, not dependent on the mode. I think we should maintain the practice of using immersion. We should also clearly state that all our ministers are expected to abide by denominational guidelines, not because these are infallible but for the sake of uniformity and because of general preference.

If the above policy were adopted each non-immersed aspirant to the ministry would decide the matter for himself; there would be no wholesale barring by the brotherhood. There is every indication that the ministrial candidates who had not themselves been immersed would gladly abide by church custom.

Jesus frequently criticized the Pharisees for adding to what God had said. I think that on occasion we have done the same thing. If we are totally honest we may have to admit to ourselves that despite our frequent zeal and honourable motives, something of what we heretofore have taken to be piety is, in fact, denominational pride and hypocrisy!

APRIL 17, 1970

A "CHRISTIAN" GHETTO

A "Christian" ghetto is a strange phenomenon. In the first place it is not at all Christian! On the other hand, it seems to be fairly widespread and has affected many Christians. Perhaps most importantly, in at least some areas it seems to be growing.

A "Christian" ghetto is strange also in that it need not be located anywhere specifically, in a geographical sense. Perhaps that is why it is often undetected, unrecognized, or both! But it is, nonetheless, very significant and foreboding.

A "Christian" ghetto consists of people who preach "Christian Power" but who practice false "Christian Separatism." As one should expect, members in this ghetto communicate quite effectively with each other, are often concerned, about one another, and build structures which reinforce their exclusivity. This ability to relate to others, however, does not generally exceed the limits of the ghetto.

A "Christian" ghetto has no physical walls to keep aliens out. Indeed, there may be a high degree of willingness to admit others, provided that they accept the standard ghetto norms and assumptions. Anything that fosters the growth of the ghetto is welcomed; all else is taboo!

A "Christian" ghetto shares with other ghettos an underlying defensive stance. It does not build bridges or seek easy communication with non-ghettoites. In fact, some ghetto members have been known to live beside non-ghettoites for up to 13 years without even discovering their names! That's quite a feat. (Mainly defeat.) Of course, the doorway leading into the ghetto is always open.

A "Christian" ghetto, I suggest, is ultimately a decaying, self-destroying structure. At best only a hollow shell will survive two generations of ghetto mentality. Being self-interested, self-centered, and striving to be self-enhancing, it soon undermines itself.

Then there is the Christian church. Keeping in mind the imperatives of the Great Commission and the Diaspora it reaches out and strives to penetrate. By revealing what transformation means it seeks to produce more transformation. It sees itself not as the essence and source of light but as a mirror. It communicates within itself but its essential communication is with God and with those who do not normally communicate with God. It is out-going, other-directed, and self-giving. The church stresses Christ; the ghetto stresses the ghetto. The church is strong because it admits human weakness; the ghetto is threatened by anyone who suggests that it is weak—yet it is, in fact, weak because it relies on itself.

The ghetto will go; the church will go on to victory.

JUNE 26, 1970

LOYAL OPPOSITION

Elton Trueblood has observed that when a church ceases to be in tension with its times and its surrounding culture, it has ceased to be a witnessing church. Now that we are again in the midst of church convention season it seems appropriate to remind ourselves of where our church stands, or more particularly, should stand.

As we assemble in various places we need to recapture the vision of our responsibilities. As in the days of the early church, our conventions need to face relevant issues squarely. Unless this is done and unless we are willing to change our personal views after careful study and fellowship, it might be better to cancel virtually all of our sessions. After all, there doesn't seem to be much point in sending delegates hundreds or thousands of miles merely to hear reports when these can be distributed at much lower cost to the entire membership.

My point is that something important must happen at conventions, something that would not have occurred had the respective men and women not met. This Christian re-envigoration does not exist "out there" someplace. It must be related to something problematic. After all, if we have nothing urgent about which to confer, why convene? Vacationing with relatives is in itself not a part of the Great Commission.

If we want to make our conventions increasingly valuable—and I believe that there has been major improvement during recent years—we must come to grips with basic issues. We might well ask ourselves: Why is our church not growing more rapidly? Are we really in tension with society or are we limply yielding to an un-Biblical accommodation? Have we got too much of a church super-structure? Should we ask other Christian groups to unite with us in a healthy ecumenicity? What new areas of tension are emerging and how should we cope with them? What does "Christian stewardship and brotherhood" mean at a time when there is increasing economic disparity within the church and society in general? Are we willing to face some of these issues and re-direct our efforts?

If we are, then much ease and complacency will have to go. It is not always easy to listen to critics and agitators but perhaps that is exactly what we need—and not because we want only to show Christian tolerance to some lively dissenter and then get on with the program. Rather, I submit, we need to listen and think because it is good for us. Somewhere along the line I got the notion that church conventions were called in order to reflect Christian unity. It now seems to me that that is not the New Testament pattern. Christians should meet in larger assemblies not only to worship and have fellowship but to deal with differences, to share concerns, and to discover new areas of tension and need. If that is our attitude, then we will be open to prophetic voices and to radical redirection by the Holy Spirit. As we catch up more with the present we may also find that we will have to rely less on gimmickry to attract young people and get them involved.

We are headed in the right direction and we are doing many God-honouring things but the swath we are cutting is still much too narrow and our progress, I fear, is too slow.

APRIL 21, 1972

CLASS AND BROTHERHOOD

Every Canadian city of significance contains both the high-class, expensive churches (the most elite are usually called Cathedrals) and the architecturally unimpressive gospel halls (the larger, better-designed ones are often called tabernacles).

In general, different kinds of people attend these two kinds of churches. If one considers society as a whole one finds almost invariably that the wealthy, those with high incomes, those with much education, and those holding positions of power over other people attend the high class churches. Conversely, those who have limited income, little education, etc., attend the low-class church.

Numerous studies and statistical tables are available which illustrate the general observation summarized above. Evangelical leaders have long been aware of this duality and have tried, albeit with only minor success, to minimize the distinction. Now, however, the situation is rapidly becoming a major, often unrecognized, problem in our own brotherhood.

For more than half a century in Canada we experienced relatively little class differentiation in our churches. Most of our forefathers were relatively recent immigrants, most lived in sheltered rural areas and enjoyed a common way of life. Our church buildings were architecturally similar to the point of uninteresting predictability and our theological assumptions and expressions were likewise almost uniform. We were largely homogeneous; our settlements a collection of lower class and lower middle class enclaves.

But times changed. Since World War II urbanization and assimilation into large industrial and business complexes have put some of us into top executive offices and some of us into the lowest paying manual jobs. No longer are we all farmers (or labourers) more or less on an equal footing. And education, even that which was sacrificially provided in our private schools to perpetuate our distinctives, quickly dispersed us into the full range of professions and power positions.

Amazingly, our brotherhood remained largely intact through the first decades of change. But as language and ethnic distinctives declined, a trend which developed quickly in the 1950s, our church unity weakened. The trend continues.

Today we are a small denomination, now mainly middle class and middle church, but with large segments of lower class and of upper class membership. Sociologically it is an unstable situation. If we follow the usual patterns of identification our non-church class associations will increasingly override our much repeated phrases of brotherhood.

Of course, we may be able to prove the sociological prediction to be wrong but only if for all of us Jesus Christ and his claims come first. And that will demand much.

CONVINCED OR CONVERTED?

In this time of constant challenge and rapid change our churches, and we as members, are discarding many earlier attitudes, traditions, and beliefs. Often this is "to the good." Any dynamic endeavor needs periodic re-evaluation in the light of basic purpose and mandate.

However, some things should not be changed. One of these is our traditional emphasis on conversion. Jesus called people to believe on Him, follow Him, and change their worldly ways. One can call this transformation "conversion." Surely we should continue to follow his example.

Because I believe in the centrality of Christian conversion I am dismayed to see some people apparently substituting the notion of being convinced. Being convinced involves the mind only; one gives mental assent. Thus one can believe that Jesus lives, died, rose again and is preparing a place for Christians without actually being a Christian. It's easy! Satan does it all the time!

A convinced person accepts the Gospel as being true but this intellectual affirmation is without personal meaning. Repentance, confession and forgiveness don't enter the picture. Neither do stewardship, evangelism, or accountability. Nor do Bible study, praise, or prayer.

A converted person is precisely that. He is changed—a new creature! His entire being centers around a new relationship. He has new desires, new priorities, and a new mandate. He loves to be with fellow believers and to serve his Lord. He has moved from Galatians 5:19-21 to Galatians 5:22-25.

I venture to suggest that for some of us this fundamental distinction is blurred. Apparently some people think that because they believe that Jesus lived, etc. they are automatically His disciples. What is lacking, of course, is commitment without which the Holy Spirit cannot indwell the believer.

The result is that more than a few church adherents drift away. It seems that they have no desire to be part of a fellowship and live a life of discipleship. Small wonder! The happy Christian life does not come without commitment. Being convinced may bring many things including outward conformity but it does not bring salvation.

Let us continue to emphasize conversion. We need that thrust much in these days. Or at least so it seems to me.

JULY 13, 1973

DEAR MARTHA

I am writing to you because I assume you will understand what I am trying to say.

It never ceases to amaze me how most members of most congregations ignore church Bible Study and Prayer Meetings. Christians can talk about the importance of prayer and study, they teach it in Sunday School, they sing heartily about it, some even preach about it on occasion, but never come. Not once. Such meetings are for others.

They have time for business breakfasts, club luncheons, long formal dinners, and late midnight lunches but not for an hour of prayer and praise. Maybe they have no praises!

They take time for long holidays, numerous social visits, endless hours of recreating, evening after evening of relaxation, weekly forays to real estate Open Houses, countless hours of home and yard improvements, lots of hours for cottage activity, but there is no time for Bible study and prayer.

There is time for bowling, baseball, fastball, football, basketball, billiards, golf, tennis, badminton, sunbathing, skating, skiing, skidooing, canoeing, swimming, sailing, flying, fishing, hunting, hockey, and calisthenics, but no time for a midweek meeting of Christians. Prayer is for others.

Time is found for house maintenance, car maintenance, dental maintenance, lawn maintenance, beauty maintenance, furniture maintenance, rug maintenance, hair maintenance, shrub maintenance, muscle maintenance, but not soul maintenance.

There is time for PTA, NPA, NDP, PC, SC, LP, service clubs, Pollution Probe, glee club, drama club, chess club, concerts, movies, travelogues, conventions, conferences, retreats, committees, night school, driving school, sales school, finishing school, and overtime, but no time for group Bible study and prayer. Life is too busy; let others do it.

Time for photography, philately, ceramics, mechanics, number painting, other painting, antiquing, sewing, crocheting, knitting, embroidery, needle point, petite point, model airplanes, aquariums, and model trains but not for group prayer.

Time for Tupperware parties, birthday parties, housewarming, housecooking, showers, and raising flowers but no time for prayer.

Time for novels, magazines, TV, telephone, TV, radio, TV, stereo, and talk shows but not for God-talk.

Time to read Dear Abby, Ann Landers, Horoscope, crosswords, gardening, the letters column, birth notices, engagements, wedding write-ups, the social columns, anniversary notices, bankruptcy declarations, divorce statements, and obituaries, but life is too busy for reading God's statements.

Time for the sports page, woman's page, front page, farm page, weather page, comic page, sale page, garden page, grocery page, recipe page, hobby page, financial page, political page, entertainment page, editorial page, fishing page, complaints page, even the church page, indeed almost any page, but not "the Printed Page!"

Year in, year out. It makes one wonder, if not doubt!

BIBLE
STUDY
NOTE

MAY 31, 1974

LEADERSHIP

Frequently, especially around church convention time, one hears complaints about lack of leadership in our denomination. No doubt we could do with better leadership—as we could also do with better followership—but I suggest that the problem is deeper and more complicated than some of us might be inclined to think it is.

Sometimes, and at its most superficial level, the clamour for "better" leadership is nothing more than a desire for silvertongued oratory, new techniques, psychological manipulation, polished entertainment, or charismatic personality. Useful as these dimensions may be, they do not lie at the heart of dynamic Christianity, whether individual or collective.

At a deeper level the criticism about "lack of leadership" may focus on more substantive matters. Quite properly, it seems to me, we can assert that we need leaders who will clarify ethical options and point to the one they believe best, who will exhort their followers while leading by example, who will not compromise on essentials but will be open to change in non-essentials, who will move the church (including the pulpit committee and council) by preaching the full Word, who will not hesitate to tackle controversal issues tactfully, who will diligently teach and train God's troops how to use the items described in Ephesians 6, and who will be willing to become unpopular (at least with some people) as they speak boldly that which the Word clearly sets forth. No doubt many leaders would themselves be the first to admit that there is considerable room for improvement in these areas.

But there is also a third level of the problem. Perhaps it is the most important one. I have in mind the problem of basic theological disunity. How can we expect to have strong leadership if we are not in agreement on what the church should be doing?

Apparently there was a time, decades or generations or centuries ago, when the New Testament norms as understood from an Anabaptist perspective served as indisputable guidelines. Times have changed. Among some Mennonite Brethren the term "Anabaptist" has itself become a subtle epithet. The doctrine of limitless Christian love, or Christian non-militarism which is one of its expressions, is widely rejected. Theologically we have run hither and yon. On matters of church-state relations, civil religion, evangelism (especially child evangelism), evangelism techniques, missions (especially non-foreign), eschatology, the place of discipleship, the peace emphasis, the role of the Holy Spirit, the authority of the Old Testament, the nature and role of a fellowship community, the meeting of physical needs, and the value of ethnic distinctives we have almost as much diversity within our MB denomination as one finds among the whole gamut of evangelical denominations. Little wonder we complain about lack of leadership. How can leaders lead us if we, and they, are heading off in all directions? It's a minor miracle that organizationally we remain united and even love one another!

At this most basic level we need leaders—prophets is a better term—who will fearlessly call us back to those New Testament basics which alone justify the existence of the Mennonite Brethren church. In this time of a largely sophisticated and "professional" clergy such modern prophets appear to be in very short supply.

Some time ago I watched our university basketball team play an exciting, crucial contest. All players knew exactly what they wanted to do and "worked their hearts out," as the saying goes, to achieve that end. The fact that one of them had "C" (for captain) sewn on his uniform was largely overlooked and almost irrelevant. Even the coach on the bench served mainly to make sure the players didn't overwork themselves in the gruelling duel. His task was made singularly easier by the fact that his entire team was trying to move the ball to the same end and every player, as far as I could tell, knew exactly what to do with it when he got it there.

JUNE 14, 1974

DELINQUENT DELEGATES

Sometimes I think that Brownie points or gold stars or green stamps or red ribbons should be given to delegates who stay to the end of a convention. It wouldn't cost very much, considering how few manage to hang in there.

No doubt some of us have thoroughly legitimate reasons for leaving early, such as job commitments. But for many, I suggest, the arguments convince no one but themselves. Permit me to intorduce some of my friends: Jim, Joe, John, Jake, Jack, Jeff, Jean and Jane.

Jim is a fine Christian and a dedicated churchman. He is also an avid golfer. Convinced that one must not separate the sacred from the secular he spends the last two afternoons out on the fairways. He is obviously confused about what the Psalmist meant when he said that our Shepherd would lead us to the green pastures.

Joe, equally diligent and dedicated, is cut from different cloth. He is a fine Christian businessman. Since his business interests include local acreage he finds it necessary to absent himself the second day and to leave a day early. He cannot accept the invitation to the spiritual banquet table because he has bought himself some land. I think I've heard that excuse before!

Then there's John. John is a nice fellow. Although he never says a word at the convention he always thinks hard and votes enthusiastically. He is a farmer and a very good one. After the first day he is tired of sitting. Operating on the principle that the mind can't absorb more than the seat can endure, he leaves a day early. "Let the preachers and deacons settle things," he rationalizes. And besides, the air-conditioned tractor cab is more comfortable and his taped music more soothing than the Bethesda report.

Then there's Jake. He's quite an individualist. He speaks quite a lot and usually makes a lot of sense. The delegates have learned to respect his views. He too takes off a day before the sessions end. He wants to be back home for his twenty-fifth wedding anniversary and besides he volunteered to come and is paying his own way so why should he be required to stay! In short, he can't stay because he took a wife.

Jack's case is similar to Jake's. Only instead of having taken a wife he has bought some cattle—not 25 years ago but a week ago. They're out at a feedlot and he must see them to decide whether to sell before the price drops a dollar a hundred. He'd like to stay, he really would, but he has to sell when the price is right. He changes his booking and flies off quietly. As he takes off into the blue it occurs to him that if he can close the deal quickly, he may not have to reschedule his package tour to Hawaii.

Years ago I would not have mentioned Jean but now she is a full-fledged delegate although she hasn't yet marshalled sufficient courage to speak up. Monday evening and all day Tuesday she takes off to visit distant relatives who live nearby. After all, she tells herself, her husband will tell her what happened, which is probably the biblical method anyway. Thus her church's representation is cut in half.

Lastly there are Jeff and Jane, who are newly-weds. She was made a delegate mainly because her husband, who is a board member, was going in any event. The last day Jane and Jeff are missing. Vancouver, in summer, is such a delightful place to continue the honeymoon. They're off to Little Mountain, Capilano Canyon, and the cedar-crowded paths in Stanley Park.

Meanwhile, back at the session, attendance is down 50 percent. The moderator is disappointed and a bit discouraged, although he doesn't show it. More importantly, God in heaven is noting where his faithful servants are.

SEPTEMBER 19, 1975

CHRISTIAN CLASS CONSCIOUSNESS

People who are destitute, or at least relatively poor in financial terms, tend to develop a sense of homogeneity rather than social differentiation or class consciousness among themselves. Especially is this true for evangelical Christians whose relationships rest on a fundamental sense of equality and kinship.

But affluence produces great changes, or at least so it seems to me. The traditional patterns of general social homogeneity which I recall from my childhood in a Mennonite Brethren setting seem to be dissipating rapidly. Increasingly we seem to be accepting a basically Marxist view of class cleavages if not of class antagonisms.

Or haven't you noticed? We make much about the fact that in Jesus Christ there is neither Jew nor Gentile, male or female, master or slave but somehow our egalitarian emphasis gets lost in practice. As the income, occupational, educational, and general status differentiation grows in our brotherhood, some basically unchristian attitudes and behavior patterns are growing as well.

The wealthy tend to isolate themselves. In home visitation they tend to hobnob with one another, with wealthy non-Christians or with no one. Those whom we might describe as financially poor tend to avoid socializing with Christians who are more well-to-do because they don't want to embarrass anyone or be embarrassed. Especially if they are receiving government assistance, or welfare, they will studiously avoid coming under the glare of those who berate—or pity—welfare recipients. Their lot is bad enough without having to experience additional inadequacy.

The broad middle classes mix quite freely among themselves although even here vocational grouping and exclusiveness is common. Social interaction often rests on shop talk and those experiences which we would have in common even if we weren't Christians. In any event, we feel more comfortable with one another than with the rich or poor. From a purely sociological perspective, that makes sense.

As the years pass and as greater affluence for some and economic hardship for others become more widespread, our Christian unity is sorely tried. The rich go to their spas, stay in fancy hotels at church conventions, and become more aloof. The middle group tends to ignore all others while enjoying their visits with one another and even with unfamiliar families of similar strata at church conventions. The poor can't afford social mingling with either of the other two groups, or so they feel, and thus become even more withdrawn and isolated.

And thus the barriers grow. With fundamentally different life styles, different attitudes, and socio-economic segregation we are experiencing real difficulty maintaining a sense of unity. Such a situation is natural for non-Christians but surely it should not be thus with us. Or have we forgotten that in all the ways that are really important we are basically the same?

Too readily we have bought the non-Christian perspective that what a person has is more important than what a person is, and that a person's economic profession outranks his spiritual profession. To accept one another as brothers and sisters, as one in the spirit, and to relate honestly and easily with those whom non-Christians would describe as "different," that, I suggest, constitutes real Christian "class". More real Christian "class" and less class consciousness is what the church and the world both need.

OCTOBER 3, 1975

WHY I LOVE THE BROTHERHOOD

Frequently this column takes issue with various policies, practices, or trends and it does so in keeping with the notion that one of the highest forms of support, perhaps even of praise, is constructive criticism.

The old Russian proverb expresses the idea tersely: "the yes-man is your enemy, but your friend will argue with you."

Today, however, I would like to be explicitly positive. My involvement with our brotherhood this year at the local, provincial, Canadian, and General Conference levels has greatly reinforced the warm, supportive, and appreciative attitudes I have had about our denomination for many years.

Obviously people do not all agree.

Some people have told me that their reaction to their local church is one of frustration—everything, they feel, seems to be so formal and stilted. Members, they continue, seem to be playing roles. Others have told me that provincial church activity is "for the birds," specifically, I suppose, for ostriches; provincial leaders, allegedly either seem unable to get anything off the ground, they just run around without ever taking off, or they stick their heads in the sand and avoid the issues.

National church endeavors have also evoked rejection from some of my friends. "The bureaucracy," I am told, is power hungry. Presumably every officer and committee seeks to build an empire. "All planning and talking; no doing and acting," I hear.

Following the General Conference sessions some of my friends again gave me the benefit of their views. "Disillusionment" was mentioned more than once. "Preachers seek status," and "We're floundering in security and wealth" were other responses.

My friends are entitled to their views. I have not been frustrated, disappointed, or disillusioned. Rather, each experience has increased my love for my church.

- I love my church because it is part of God's great church. The church is one great body. I am part of that body. How can I reject my own body?
- I love my church because of the many saintly people I have met there. Great men and women, spirit-filled and self-giving, have shown me what it means to have a living faith.
- I love my church because, despite its obvious shortcomings, it still holds the Bible to be its reference point and seeks to be guided by God's Word.
- I love my church because it has taken the Great Commission seriously, even if the starting point has not always been neighborhood Jerusalem.
- I love my church because it has strongly supported sound ecumenical ventures. Whether you look at Bible Societies, the Evangelical Fellowship of Canada, Campus Crusade, IVCF, ISCF, Nurses Christian Fellowship, Teachers Christian Fellowship, Christian Business Men's Committees, the Gideons, and Christian Women's Clubs, or at various relief agencies, Christian community activities almost always includes strong Mennonite Brethren representation and leadership. This phenomenon also extends to churches of other denominations.
- I love my church because it is willing to listen to constructive criticism and to change if a sound case can be made. Witness policies

regarding baptism, foreign missions, the role of women, etc.

• I love my church because it is trying hard to be relevant. In its institutions, publications, and service to others it seeks to scratch where it itches.

• I love my church because it still preaches, even if not always practices, the full Gospel.

• Finally, I love my church because it includes so many people who have shown real love to me. That may be sentimental but man does not live by reason alone.

A SABBATH SURVEY

This week I would like to report on a survey, more or less scientific, dealing with the question of how certain Christians spend their Sundays. In this interim report I shall deal with only 10 categories.

(1) *Grasshopper Christians*—I found these hopping about everywhere, going from church to church, ever restless and always on the move. It seemed to me that these hoppers never stayed in one place long enough to discover what was really going on. However, I managed to find out that their favorite hymn was, "Where ere my fancy takes me, There let me stop and rest, To do a little sampling, And be a little blest."

(2) *Wholly Strollers*—Although I had become quite familiar with this group in Europe, I was surprised to find them in growing numbers in Canada also. These people like to take long meditative walks on Sunday mornings. Unfortunately, their strolls never take them to church. Their favorite hymn is, "We walk for health and not to church."

(3) *Morningside Mennonites*—An odd lot these, many of them make much of the idea of a covenant community but their community seems to function only on Sunday mornings. Rarely do they come to church on Sunday evenings and never on weekdays. Their favorite song is—I can remember the second line only—"Only in the morning, our praise shall rise to Thee!"

(4) *Latter Day Faints*—Here we encounter some very fine people but, oh, what a weary lot, especially on Sundays. Their past years are strewn with good intentions but in actual fact they rarely make it out to the church service. The week has been so hard and they are just too tired. However, they do hum the tune of, "When

Morning Gilds the Skies, My Heart Still Fainting Sighs.''

(5) *Sun-Worshippers*—Sun, not Son. This group obviously is more interested in the creation than the Creator. And their theology is a little mixed up about absorbing light rather than being light. On any bright sunny Sunday morning you can find them stretched out on the back lawn. Their favorite gospel song seems to be, ''Oh Let the Sunshine In, Tan Your Chest and Chin.''

(6) *Seventh-Day Adventurists*—Of all the groups I am describing today, I found this one particularly intriguing. During summer, and even in winter, these people, alone or in groups, spend many Sundays roaming around in the great outdoors. I concluded that they are pursuing the good, but missing the best. Their campfire favorite seems to be, ''Encamped Along the Hills and Vales.''

(7) *A—frame Apostolics*—Closely-related to the Seventh-Day Adventurists, these people are less itinerant, preferring to domicile in their lakeside abodes. Some get up and go to some sort of service but most just get up; rumor has it that a few don't even manage to do that. The roofs of their cottages point heavenwards but since they are totally on vacation from usual routines, these people rarely find their thoughts tending that way. They are pre-occupied with relaxation and cannot be easily moved. Some have been known to sing, ''I'll Go Where I Want Me To Go.''

(8) *Intravenous Independents*—I found these right in their own homes. These are Christians who are fed their Gospel only through a tube, the TV tube. They like the fact that they can doze off without being embarrassed and the fact that there is no offering. Their favorite hymn is, ''Channels Only.''

(9) *Bedside Baptists*—These are people who are usually awake but only physically. They like to lie in bed on Sunday morning, dozing or listening to the radio. Sometimes the programs may be Christian but it

seems not to matter. Their top hymn is, "Come My Soul and Be at Rest," sung slowly and very softly; they also like, "Asleep My Soul to Joyful Lays."

(10) *Sabbath Sleepers*—I located this category right in the church. These people manage to drag themselves to the service, usually arriving late, and with drooping eyelids they manage to nod their way through it. They don't always catch the hymn number although I do recall that some seemed to join in the singing of "Let Me Dream On."

Well friends, there they are, the first 10 groups. I've learned a lot doing this survey, but I readily admit that some of you are obviously much more familiar with some of these groups than I am.

AN UNUSUAL MEETING

How would you react to the following dream? It's not overly exciting, just disturbing.

We were all sitting row upon row in what to me was an unfamiliar setting. A church business meeting, or consensus session, was obviously well underway. The faces somehow did not seem strange or unknown, yet I could not recall any names.

Very quickly, however, I realized that this was not an ordinary church meeting; from time to time a hidden voice interrupted proceedings by speaking out in clear, measured tones. Everyone could hear him well—nobody seemed to know who he was or attempted to silence him.

I first heard him right after Sam had been nominated to be Sunday School superintendent and had refused, saying that he was too busy. As soon as Sam had finished spelling out his excuses, the voice began. In a few sentences it told the startled group that Sam was not busy at all, that Sam had just taken up a night school hobby course and had recently joined a chess club. Sam, the voice said, was not really busy, he just didn't want to get involved in church work because he was spiritually lukewarm. (I was reminded of Revelation 3:16). Sam was dumbfounded and said nothing. Neither did anyone else.

The next agenda item was the treasurer's report. Henry, the treasurer, stated that income was down quite a bit from last year and, in response to a question, said that some families and single adults, including some students, gave very little. Whereupon the voice interrupted him. Speaking quite unemotionally it named about ten people, telling us exactly what each one's total income was and how much was given to the church. Obviously the income figures were higher than had been thought and the contributions lower. No one had given more than 3%. Those who had been named were acutely embarrassed, especially the students. The voice had stated that they seemed to have plenty of money for pizza, and movies, and clothes, and concerts, and holidays but all had given only very little to the church, and two nothing at all. No one disputed the figures given so I concluded they must be accurate.

The third agenda item was the pastor's report. He discussed a number of items; when he got to attendance at the mid-week prayer meeting the hidden voice interrupted again. This time the interruption was long and acutely embarrassing to many people. The voice named all those people who had not attended even one mid-week service all year. In each case it was convincingly shown that the problem was not lack of time but simply lack of interest. Scores of church members, including some esteemed leaders, were exposed. Again, no one disputed what was said.

The last agenda item which I recall involved the election of a youth leader. Four people had been nominated but all declined to let their names stand, saying that they didn't think they had the necessary qualities. After the fourth one had finished his little speech the voice spoke again. He told the first one, a teacher, that what he had just said to the congregation contradicted what he had written about himself on a merit pay application statement he had given his principal earlier that same day. The voice then told numbers two and three that their biggest problems were sheer laziness and self-centredness. Number four was reminded that he was doing very well as scoutmaster and Junior Chamber of Commerce president. His problems, the voice explained, was that he was more interested in money than in people.

Again no one contradicted what was clearly a true explanation. The stunned secretary had long since ceased taking minutes.

Immediately the buzzer rang, the session ended and many people were relieved, some were relieved and embarrassed, and a few were relieved, embarrassed and repentant.

BROTHERHOOD IN THE CITY

With some notable exceptions our denominational brotherhood in Canada has traditionally been rooted in a rural lifestyle. Our unity has been derived not entirely from our Anabaptist Christianity, but has rested in part on common immigrant experiences, on frontier comradship, on the pre-eminence of farming as a vocation, on neighborhood ties, on family connections and on ethnic bonds such as common language and social customs.

But changes have taken place. In earlier times many of our city congregations saw themselves as offshoots from a rural base. That is no longer the case. In previous decades many of our city brothers and sisters managed to retain certain over-riding bonds of unity, despite their geographical dispersion in various residential areas. That, too, has changed.

In sum, the general fact of the matter is that in Canada most Mennonite Brethren now live in the cities, many have become socially assimilated into secular society and many of the earlier brotherhood ties are weak. But to balance the picture it should also be said that fortunately most of our city churches now resemble more closely the New Testament church with its multi-ethnic and multi-racial composition.

Midst all of these changes a very basic question looms ever larger: what does it mean to be a truly Christian brotherhood in a modern city? I suppose that it would be possible to spell out a grand theological prescription, but permit me to shortcircuit that kind of response and simply list some very practical suggestions, not necessarily new.

I suggest that a Christian church in an urban setting (also in a rural setting, though the persistence of some traditional norms there affects the situation) might well be characterized by the following:

1. The congregation should have a Brotherhood Fund which, administered by a small committee, would provide adequate resources for members in needy situations. Such a fund would carry no negative stigma but simply facilitate mutual Christian caring and sharing.
2. When church people move into a new (or different) apartment or house, the congregation provides the needed help. A barn-raising bee becomes a furniture carrying venture.
3. Specific sharing times could be scheduled: after the summer holidays, at Thanksgiving, during the dead of winter, etc. Unless we get to know what people do, we cannot get to know who they are.
4. A senior citizens' assistance program to provide transportation, shopping assistance, social interaction and home assistance could meet many needs of deserving elderly or disabled Christians.
5. An emergency assistance program with someone as near as the telephone at all times, would help people in crisis situations of all kinds.
6. A monthly church newsletter would go a long way in helping to keep the congregation informed about church family developments. We need a better information network—but less gossip.
7. Congregational sponsorship of Missions/Services and MCC personnel can provide a significant bond. Shared responsibilities generate closer relationships.

8. Special emphasis days have an important place. The traditional Harvest Festivals are now seemingly anachronistic and out of place and have largely been abandoned. Let us therefore focus on present concerns. Situations vary but perhaps, stressing a Biblical perspective, we should focus our attention on minorities, apartment dwellers, employees, students, people in various professions, the unemployed, etc.

9. Congregations need recreational and social activities. These must never become central but they fill an important need. In building brotherhood, our gyms may be more important than our "educational wings."

10. We need to cultivate hospitality. How can we really feel close to a fellow church member if we do not know where he lives and have never had our feet under the same table? We need "open door" Christianity.

11. We might well have more Bible studies and other small group meetings in homes. When I have been in someone else's home, even as part of a meeting, a new tie is created.

12. Many congregations would do well to follow the example of those churches with effective small groups, restructured after a while, with numerous shared activities.

The list could be much longer. Specifics in themselves are not important but the nurture and expression of brotherhood is crucial; or is church only a building to which we go?

HOW MANY BANQUETS?

Recently a reader in Alberta sent me a letter which asked, "in an often hungry world, how many Christmas banquets does an average Mennonite Brethren congregation rate?"

The question is apt. However, the answer may not be as straightforward as we probably think. If by the term "rate" our brother means "deserve," the theologically sound answer would likely be "none." Most of us have probably not been so busy building Christ's kingdom that we need a banquet to recognize who we are or what we have done.

Of course, there are many reasons for having congregational Christmas banquets and there are many reasons why people attend. Maybe some people attend to get into "the festive mood," others because "it's traditional," a third group enjoys "a good time," and still others may find it necessary "to break in the new Christmas clothes."

Well, there may be merit or lack of merit in such motivation but surely the important and justifiable reasons lie in other directions. A church Christmas banquet, be it for choir, young people, or old people, other groups or everyone should not focus mainly on food and fun but on a birthday celebration. His birthday.

Who of us has not put out a spread to celebrate the birthday of a family member? Does the Bethlehem Babe not rate at least as much?

In the second place, a Christmas banquet can be an excellent occasion to foster goodwill and congregational togetherness. I have always found church banquets excellent times to get to know people in the church, to relate in a personal way with many of the newcomers and the "regulars" with whom I never find enough time to interact, and simply to enjoy the table fellowship which eating with fellow Christians brings. Many congregations probably need more, rather than fewer, occasions to become knit together as a body of believers.

Of course, the fare needn't be fancy! And it should never be so expensive that the less affluent and the unemployed brothers and sisters cannot afford to come. Setting prohibitive prices can only serve to divide the congregation rather than unite it. If there be those among us who "require" a spread which cost $7.50 or $10.00, I feel it is then incumbent upon them also to pay for those who cannot afford such costs.

However, we must be fair. I know of some people who annually complain about Christmas banquet costs—as well as other church costs in some instances—but who think nothing about eating out at a high-priced steak-house or spending $15 and more to take the family out to the Ponderosa, the Spaghetti Factory, or some smorgasbord.

I can remember some very inexpensive table fellowships in the Main Centre, Sask., church in the late 1930s and early 1940s. Cold chicken or fried farmer sausage, fresh bread, and limp pickles were the main course. (The long ride in a sleigh was an adequate appetizer.) The children drank water and, at least some times, our parents poured cold coffee from two-quart canning jars. Generous pieces of home-made pie or cake rounded out the repast. I thoroughly enjoyed those noon meals in that comfortably crowded church basement. We did not have to buy tickets.

In those days a lot of things were different. We had lots of church services in the holiday season: Christmas Eve, Christmas Day (sometimes twice), the day after Christmas and sometimes even on additional days. New Year's brought another raft of meetings. They did a lot of good for many people. Now, some congregations have eliminated almost all services. That's too bad, indeed, sad. Has Christmas become a time during which we think only of our families and ourselves, rather than our Lord?

We need Christian Christmas fellowship. We need it in worship and at the table—collectively. In our urban settings and fast-paced, individualistic lifestyles we need it more than ever before.

How many banquets do we need? At least some to nurture fellowship. We need banquets which help to focus our thinking on him and which stimulate us to share with others the largesse which has been entrusted to us.

DEAR AUNT TILLY

What do you make of this? At the recent Mennonite Brethren General Conference sessions at Buhler, Kansas, when the names of recently deceased (important) people were read, some were described as ''wife of a missionary.'' I wonder why?

I have attended numerous commissionings for missionary couples. I think I have even spoken at a few, and it always seemed to me that both husband and wife were kneeling, that both prayed, and that hands were laid on both. Believe me, I really thought that we were commissioning both of them. For 20 years I've lived with this apparent delusion!

That we still make a basic male-female distinction is clear; after all, none of the married men who were missionaries and who had died were referred to as ''husbands of missionaries.'' Surely if it were only a slip of the tongue, so to speak, it would have occurred to the person submitting the name, or to the preacher who presided at the memorial service, but no ''correction'' was made.

Now I know that you're not exactly a women's liber, Aunt Tilly, but I thought you would want to know about this sexist discrimination.

Also, though I know no ill was meant, it bothered me when I heard, ''Will the brethren of BOMAS come to the platform?'' (BOMAS means Board of Missions and Services.) It bothered me because of the ''brethren.'' Miss Katie Penner, is a member of the board and not a brother! You know what I mean. I wonder how Miss Penner felt!

One thing more, Aunt Tilly, on occasion the moderator asked, ''Will a few brethren pray?'' (Believe me, I don't intend to pick on our honored brother, it's just that he happened to be presiding when these things were said!) Don't women pray? Don't they pray in public? Shouldn't they pray in public? Does God not want to hear them when others are hearing them also? You've lived much longer than I have, Aunt Tilly, what do you think?

Maybe you can explain something else to me also. If it is proper to describe a woman as subordinate to her husband, as somehow secondary, i.e. ''wife of a missionary,'' thus strongly implying that the real missionaries are the men, then why has it for decades been the practise of our mission board to send out single women but never single men? I would have thought that it would make more sense to send out the women, the supposedly subordinate, or ''weaker'' people only if they were married, and to send out the *real* missionaries, the men, even though they were unattached. Aunt Tilly, as you do your knitting this fall, you could perhaps think about this and send me your ideas? I don't mind if you write

in German but please don't use "gothisch"!

Some people, of course, get carried away with this whole thing. I hear them talk about chairperson, personkind, Mennonite Siblings Church (I just made that up!), alderperson, councilperson, jury foreperson, mission fieldperson and what not. And some are always saying, "his/her" even though "his," in most instances, is a perfectly acceptable pronoun to refer to someone who could be either. You know what I mean: "Every student should bring his books," and sentences like that. Do you think I'm being chauvinistic? I hope not. Let me assure you that I don't want to change mother earth or mother nature, or have all ships and cars become male, or even my country!

Don't wait too long with writing.

Sincerely,
your nephew in Waterloo

A BALANCED VIEW

For the Mennonite Brethren churches in North America, 1978 was largely a year of looking back. The publicity about P.M. Friesen's *The Mennonite Brotherhood in Russia* appeared on every convention agenda, repeatedly in our periodicals, and often in church bulletins.

The massive research and microfilming project undertaken by J.B. Toews and his associate, Bill Reimer, also focussed our attention on our past. Numerous other ventures—publications, seminars, lectures, and research projects—drew our attention to earlier eras.

As an academic with an M.A. in history and a Ph.D in Political Science, I can only commend those who help us to be interested in history and to benefit from a knowledge of our past. We are impoverished if we only look ahead. In the light of the past, the present is more significant and the future takes on new meaning and potential.

Evenso, I plead for a balanced view. The church must not become an historical society any more than it should become a political party, a credit union, a cultural association, a civil liberties organization, or a sanitation league. Of course, members of the church can and should be active in these and many other praiseworthy ventures but the Christian church, as church, is not called to make any of these its highest priority.

For the Mennonite Brethren churches in Canada, at least those composed largely of long-time Mennonite families, a word of caution may be timely. The immigrants tilled the soil and worked in cities. The children went to school. As increasing numbers went on to graduate studies, not to mention professional schools they studied and wrote about their past. That was and is natural. The graduate papers gave way to theses and dissertations which, in turn, have generated scores of books, and articles. The phenomenon is quite logical and understandable.

However, let us remember that our mandate is not to study ourselves. That is necessary but secondary. True, a denomination that ignores history lacks reference points, but one that dwells unduly on history misses the Christian imperative of urgency, both evangelistic and love-service.

Sometimes it seems to me that many of us, myself included, like to write about the past partly because it is safe. Few people get very upset when we discuss interpretations of events. The real complications arise when we turn from discussing the meaning of past events to the shaping of actual events and discussion of actual issues of the present. Often red flags go up all over when new challenges about present problems are spelled out. Yet, if we want to be faithful Christians, we must focus on the present. Therein lies our mission. We can now write histories of foreign missions only because a minority long ago convinced an apathetic majority that foreign missions should be undertaken.

The Christian church, while acknowledging its roots, emphasizes fruits. It remembers the past but the preoccupation is with the present and the future. It glances back, but it looks forward and upward. In 1979, ever grateful for what was done in 1978, let us concentrate on *The Mennonite Brotherhood in the 1980's and beyond.*

"DO NOT FORBID"

Since the founding of our denomination in 1860 the Mennonite Brethren have consistently emphasized biblicism. Our fathers taught us to take the exhortations, commandments, assertions, and prohibitions literally as well as seriously. Such an emphasis on being "true to the Word" is surely the most praiseworthy aspect of our heritage.

Several times over the years I have encountered situations, all dealing with the same issues, which have raised serious questions in my mind. Are we still being "true to the Word"?

The situations which I think of all dealt with the matter of releasing or dismissing pastors and other church-related "employees" who had spoken in tongues.

One particular instance, which occurred a number of years ago, comes to mind most vividly. The church leader in question was a gifted and effective minister of the gospel. For years he had served the brotherhood with much dedication and success. During the time period in question his ministry was perhaps even more fruitful than previously. However, since he had no intention of being secretive about his spiritual pilgrimage, word soon got around that he had spoken in tongues in private homes and in small groups.

No one, as far as I heard, ever accused him of being critical about Christians who had not spoken in tongues, or suggested that his ministry had deteriorated, or that he had at any time done anything in public which might be subject to criticism. The whole basis of the reaction against the good brother involved something he had done in private and which, if anything, had increased rather than decreased his effectiveness. At that point I got involved in the situation, discussing the matter with the minister as well as some of his critics.

The minister, a meek and gentle brother, did not want to create any trouble for anyone and quietly resigned. Doubtless many people who know him still do not know why his term of service came to an end so abruptly. But many people do know and I, for one, believe that the wrong decision was made. Of course, we do well not to have judgmental charismatics or any other extremists in positions of leadership but that is not the issue here; the issue is simply speaking in tongues.

That brings me to the bottom line question. Are we still biblicists? If we are, then by what authority do we forbid fellow Christians to speak in tongues or dismiss them if they do? The Word is clear; "do not forbid to speak in tongues" (I Corinthians 14:39). Why do some of us disobey this exhortation?

Yes, I know that in several instances biblical writers give the gift of tongues a relatively lesser rating but surely the critical fact remains that it is a gift from God! And Paul himself strongly endorses glossolalia when he asserts; "I thank God, I speak in tongues more than you all" (I Corinthians 14:18). Also, "Now I wish that you all spoke in tongues. . . . " (verse 5). If we are still biblicists then how can we possibly criticize and set aside people for doing nothing other than obeying Paul's exhortation and following his example?

I'd like to remind us that we took a position at a General Conference in

1972 in which we said, "We must take seriously Paul's warning not to quench the Spirit and constantly strive to be charitable to those whose experience of God is attended by somewhat unusual phenomena." I, for one, want publicly to dissociate myself from any rejection of authentic, responsible glossalalia. My understanding of the Word leaves me no other option. And to those who have been wrongfully set aside I apologize for not having spoken out sooner.

NOVEMBER 9, 1979

I LOVE MY CHURCH

Much of my life centres around the church: the local congregation, the provincial and national conferences, and the international brotherhood. I belong to numerous organizations but of those only the church, aside from the family, is divinely established.

• My church is a place of worship. Somehow it seems to be easier and more rewarding to worship God in a group than when we do so alone. Many a time corporate singing and prayer or simply listening to the Word has lifted me into the very presence of God. For those memorable times I am thankful.

• My church is a place of learning. For almost forty years I have participated in Bible classes on Sunday mornings and frequently during the week also. What I have learned in church has been of much greater value to me than all of my nine years of university education which produced four degrees, three certificates and one diploma. For all of that Christian instruction, and that which is still to come, I am thankful.

• My church is a place of fellowship. The best people I have ever met belong to my church; they are my brothers and sisters. The fellowship of which I speak is not some superficial conviviality dependent on location or libation (that's drink!) but grows out of the fact that we are united as a body of Christians. We are joint heirs; we love the same Father and we love one another. The people in my church are my friends, the best in the world, and for them I am thankful.

• My church is a place of assistance. In our church we help one another. It's great to be able to help others, be they recently arrived refugees or long-time members who suddenly find themselves in need of help. That help may take the form of physical activity when people move (or at other times), or emotional support when that is needed, or financial assistance, or emergency aid be it a trip to the emergency room when you have no car at home or a night-time crisis in the family and you simply must talk to someone. It's great to be able to assist others; it's also great to know that others are there to assist you and to assist your family if anything should happen to you and for that I am thankful.

• My church is a place where love is shown to others, to people who may not attend any church, who may not know what it means to be a Christian. In the local community, in other parts of the country, and in regions beyond our borders, my church, in cooperation with others, works to spread the gospel of love and to demonstrate practical love. Oh, I know, we should probably be doing more, but much is being done now and for that I am thankful.

• My church is a place of celebration. In a world in which most people seem to be sad and weighted

down with heavy problems, my fellow-Christians and I not only have cause to celebrate but do celebrate. At church communion we celebrate our Lord's death for us and every Sunday we celebrate his resurrection. We celebrate at Christmastime and Eastertime, at Thanksgiving and Mother's Day, at many other times. We have much about which to be happy, and many occasions to celebrate. Wouldn't you be thankful for that?

Our church is a place but mainly it is people, good and godly people. Our church consists of people who have a purpose in life, who in faith and trust can look forward to what lies ahead in this world and the next. We are the family of God! We have a God to love, a gospel to proclaim, a fellowship to enjoy, and a world to serve. What more could we ask?

MENNONITE BRETHREN DURING THE '70s

For Canadian Mennonite Brethren the 1970s have been an important decade. Let me draw attention to five general tendencies, five significant developments, and five specific church-centered changes.

Tendencies

(1) Affluence. Despite the assorted economic problems in the country, the increase of affluence among most Mennonite Brethren continued unabated. The seventies were generally prosperous years. The result has sometimes been a bane, sometimes a blessing.

(2) Individualism. Perhaps economic well-being played a key role but, whatever the reasons, it seems to me that in many of our congregations there now is more individualism than there was a decade ago. The more individualistic we become, the more difficult it is to develop consequential Christian relationships.

(3) Less social cohesion. For at least some of our church members, the matter of church identification has become less central than it used to be. For them church membership no longer serves as the inclusive and integrating framework within which other activities and interests take their place. Church membership thus has become merely one of many memberships and not necessarily the most important. One's closest friends need not be church friends. There is less sense of community among a socially more diverse church "people." Identification with fellow church members ceases to be an overriding fact.

(4) Aloofness; apathy. Among some MBs during the seventies there developed a growing tendency to remain aloof from church involvement. The existence of a pressing church need leaves these people apathetic. The church tends to be seen by them as something apart from oneself; a sense of responsibility is seen as optional.

(5) Political involvement. At local, provincial and national levels the Mennonite Brethren became more active politically. Equally important, the general church attitude towards politics has become more positive. The net result is still uncertain.

Obviously these tendencies are not new; I am simply suggesting that they have become stronger.

Significant Developments

Three of the developments I have in mind involve education; four of the five are positive.

(1) Since 1970 all three of our Bible institutes and our Winnipeg college undertook major building programs. In all important respects these schools are doing very well. And a fifth school, our Quebec Bible Institute, was launched.

(2) Our three high schools have developed impressively. In Ontario, Manitoba and B.C. major campus developments were undertaken. All three schools have increased their ministry.

(3) During the seventies Canadian MBs joined the U.S. MBs in the operation of our seminary. The MBBS in Fresno has already established itself as an important venture even though for many Canadian members it remains remote and far removed from immediate consciousness. That, too, is changing.

(4) After a somewhat uncertain start, including the cancellation of one

Council of Boards session, our conference structure now stands firm. It serves us well.

(5) For better or worse, probably worse, during the past decade we have seen a decline in structural evangelism. What has happened to the fully booked, highly visible conference evangelist? How many churches or communities still have a week of evangelistic meetings?

Church-centered changes

(1) The pastoral system has penetrated everwhere. During the past decade the multiple paid pastorate has gained acceptance.

(2) The transition to English is now virtually complete. German continues as a major language only in churches where older people or recent immigrants predominate.

(3) Women have taken on new responsibilities in the church. A whole "new" dimension of commitment and ability has been at least partially recognized.

(4) Our national church conventions have grown markedly and changed in composition. Husband and wife teams and family units are now commonplace. The sessions have become less formal.

(5) Church discipline has, it seems, declined or at least taken new directions and church membership has become almost a murky concept, at least in some places. Our fathers would not have understood our notion of "releasing" members.

All things considered, the decade of the seventies was a good one for our brotherhood. As we look back we have much cause for gratitude. Much remains to be done but our recent experience should generate both dedication and zeal.

CANADIAN MBS IN THE 1980S

Though the Mennonite Brethren Church is not presently engulfed in any great theological dispute, nor is there any ominous threat to our unity, we do face important issues as we enter the 1980s.

At least six unresolved theological questions remain on the agenda:

(1) How do we come to terms with the charismatic movement? In certain areas attitudes are rigid and feelings run high. Unless there is more moderation, more acceptance of diversity, and more reliance on the Word rather than on an experience, this question may become very divisive.

(2) Where do we stand on dispensationalism; what do we believe the Bible teaches about end times? In recent years we have, to some degree, dealt with this issue by avoiding it. Even so there has been some sharp disagreement among our preachers and theologians. As world political, economic, military, and population crises mount, interest in this matter will surely increase. People will clamor for answers. In attempting to provide answers we must avoid dogmatism.

(3) Do we still hold to any ethical legalism? Should we retain any church rules, thus binding one another, or should we opt for relativism? Should we have only guidelines and norms in areas where the Word does not give us a clear directive? Though there may be a place for some rigid prohibition, we surely should give greater emphasis to relationships. In any event, let us steer clear of tyranny by a majority.

(4) How should we relate to other Mennonites? If I were a non-MB Mennonite I would likely be quite frustrated by now. Most MBs insist on being known as Mennonites, yet, quite obviously, many feel much more at ease with non-Mennonite evangelicals than with other Mennonites. Eventually we will have to decide which is our most important religious identification.

(5) What should MCC be doing? For half a century we have emphasized relief and crisis assistance. Should we expand our ministries to include prevention, land development concerns, broad social needs and "justice" causes? There are some strong arguments on both sides. Let us at least be willing to listen to one another.

(6) Should we continue to separate, in a general way, relief activities and material concerns from evangelism and church development? I have always felt that having separate organizations for welfare (MCC) and missions (BOMAS) was strictly a second best arrangement; a tactical move which we reluctantly accept because of operational exigencies. The Word, as I understand it, does not thus fracture the Christian witness. The Gospel of Life, the Way of Love, is an inclusive message to the entire person. Are we distorting the gospel by continuing this unnatural division?

Additionally I see at least six clear operational challenges for the decade ahead:

(1) We need to become more successful in establishing new churches. Even more important, we should try diligently to find out why we have not been more successful in the past. Maybe we should even hire some non-MB consultants!

(2) We need to work even harder at retaining our young people, especially

at the congregational level.

(3) We need to generate a renewed determination, and more effective techniques, to cross ethnic and other social barriers.

(4) In both Canada and the U.S. we need to develop more understanding for the other jurisdiction, especially at the grass-roots level.

(5) We need to recommit ourselves to retain strong family units; that will be a major battlefront for the 1980s.

(6) We need to focus more attention on the broken homes in our communities. With about half of Canadian families experiencing some sort of collapse we face a great task. It has become our Samaria.

Truly the church of Jesus Christ faces a challenging decade; the needs have never been greater, but neither has the basis for optimism.

LEARNING FROM THE "LEAVERS"

During the past thirty years, ever since many of my high school friends left the Mennonite Brethren church, I have kept some sort of record, mainly mental but sometimes written, of reasons why people left our congregations.

Also, it has been my privilege to study the results of several significant surveys, both local and more general. Reviewing the data, checking my notes, and remembering numerous responses, I should like to suggest twelve main reasons why people left and continue to leave. I am not suggesting that most reactions are correct or even warranted, though many surely are, but I am suggesting that we can benefit from reflecting upon them.

The theologically significant reasons can be described as follows, with a largely impressionistic ranking of items from most frequently to least frequently cited.

1. Disagreement with the peace emphasis, whether it is called "non-resistance," "limitless love," "suffering discipleship," or something else. Many have left our ranks because they see this emphasis as unrealistic and impractical.

2. A perception that we are too ethnic, that too much is made of "Mennonite names," "Mennonite food," Mennonite culture," and "Mennonite heritage." Our widespread fusion of ethnicity and Christianity has turned many people off. These are the people who are impressed negatively by the Steinbach Mennonite Museum and similar valid but ethnic ventures.

3. A belief that Mennonite Brethren are too traditional, too resistant to change. In this category, particularly in certain regions of North America, you will find scores of people who have left us because, allegedly, we resist modernity in music, ethics, "charismatic" experiences, and much more. These are the people who assert that we are too much enamored with our past, too taken up with roots rather than fruits.

4. A conviction that, despite the official Confession of Faith and the pious rhetoric, we are insufficiently evangelical. There is, we are told, too little concern about "the lost." These critics see other churches, schools, periodicals, and missions/service agencies as more salvation-oriented.

5. The allegation that we are too legalistic. Often this criticism focuses on views about mode of baptism, the consumption of alcohol, the use of tobacco, and, at least in times past, on dancing, movie attendance, etc. Church rules, we are told, loom too large.

6. The criticism that we are too evangelical. I have heard this criticism particularly from certain professionally-oriented and "upwardly mobile" individuals and couples. One educator summed up his views by saying, "I don't like altar calls."

7. The criticism that our worship services are too informal, too irreverent. The chatting in the sanctuary and a "social hall" atmosphere are disliked by many people, some of whom drift off to a more formal setting.

8. The allegation that Mennonite Brethren have too much organization and too many conventions. A "conference mentality" and a supposed preoccupation with structures turn some people off.

9. The criticism that we are too

clannish, too closed, too cliquish. Obviously such a criticism was spoken about only certain congregations.

10. The allegation that we are too preoccupied with finances. Although this notion seems not to be very widespread, some people are very critical.

11. The criticism that we are too intolerant. Some "leavers" see us as intolerant of other Mennonites, some see us as intolerant of other evangelicals, and some see us as being intolerant of other Christians generally.

12. The criticism that we are too smug, too self-satisfied.

Of course, there are additional criticisms which could be cited involving views of dispensationalism, acceptance of certain translations of the Bible, quality and type of preaching, and "per member costs," but these items seem to be less frequently mentioned.

My intent in this column is not to assess the validity of each criticism or to emphasize only the negative, but simply to present my mainly impressionistic "findings" and to let the criticisms speak for themselves.

AUGUST 28, 1981

CLOSING DOWN THE CHURCH

Recently a few of my over-scheduled and innovative Christian friends have suggested some intriguing ways in which "the church" should be trimmed back. They have concluded that the church has too many activities. Their arguments constitute, one may say, another application of the "more with less" ethic.

If I understand them correctly, the startling sum of all their arguments is that the church should virtually close down. Oh, they don't say it quite that way but that's what it all adds up to. But let me be more specific.

Summertime, particularly July and August, is really not a good time to schedule church activities. Many people are on vacation. Cottages beckon. More than a few people are away at church conventions. Sunday school teachers and other "workers" need a holiday. The pastor needs a holiday. Choirs disband, clubs disband, youth groups disband. Many people, young and old, are away at camp. Numerous people work long hours at summer jobs. Besides, summertime is a time to be together as families, a time to take weekend jaunts, a time to enjoy God's great outdoors. Instead of trying to limp along and make everyone feel guilty, why not simply close down for the summer?

Next come the fall months; they are very busy. Children are starting school, community activities resume, night school gets underway again as do hobby classes as well as piano lessons, minor hockey, and all the other activities to which the children need to be taxied. The weeks are crowded. Then, when the weekends finally arrive there's more hassle. Non-Christians can at least sleep in and rest on Sunday.

December. What a month! Banquets, rehearsals, credit buying, fashion "parades," programs, extravagance, over-indulgence, and frayed nerves. Why? Who needs it? As far as we know the early church never even celebrated Christmas. Let the church react to the whole extravaganza by shutting down for December. Community and family activities can fill any resulting void. That takes care of six months.

The winter months come next. Times have changed. Energy savings must be given high priority. It is simply poor stewardship to heat huge structures for a whole week when they will be used only a few hours. Let people meet in homes. House activity would be quite appropriate and adequate. The New Testament talks about house churches; let's resurrect that tradition. The long winter evenings and the blustery weekends would be great times to build community in cozy settings. And the money we save could be put to very good use. In addition Christian parents could utilize the opportunity to teach their children at home.

April is dominated by Easter, and Easter was originally a pagan festival celebrating the spring equinox. In our day it is a pagan festival centered on fashions, bunnies, easter eggs, chocolate, and a commercialism almost as crass as Christmas. We need to react. We can react effectively by cancelling the whole thing. "Closed for April." That would get people to think.

That leaves May and June. Situations vary somewhat, but these months are busy with cleaning up after winter, gardening, graduations of various kinds, weddings, home improvements, and what not. Weekends in May and June are great for opening up the cottage, working at campers, tents, and boats, preparing for the holiday trip, Sunday outings to the park, getting winter grime off the cars, and just relaxing at home. Besides, as in fall and winter, there are a lot of good Christian programs on TV Sunday morning. Aren't they good enough?

And that's the way it is! Now, what shall I tell my friends? Shall we close down? More important, what shall I tell myself? More important still, what shall I tell God?

MURMURINGS

The diversity in the conversation is exceeded only by its persistence and regularity. Twelve-year-old Susie explains to her friends why she will not be going to camp with them this summer. She also describes graphically how her kitten is behaving, what she got for her birthday, and why she thinks her parents are too strict about movies and television. As the conversation progresses, sometimes interspersed with subdued giggles, her friends express ideas about the new family in town, the last episode of "Little House on the Prairie," recent books read, and assorted new clothes, both acquired and desired.

Meanwhile, about twenty feet away an older sister in her mid-teens exchanges verbal "notes" with her friends about assorted romantic developments, baby-sitting rates, homework assignments, a TV special on the Beatles, plans for the summer, a Friday "sleepover," and the high school basketball victory. (One of the young ladies was a cheer-leader.) The four friends seem quite oblivious to what is happening in the larger setting. After all, important items can't wait. Who would have thought that James was interested in Chris or that Mary would drop out of school to work full-time at the Dairy Queen? More surprising still, would Melanie really have a big birthday party and not invite either Ruth or Anne?

In the back row, across the aisle, Susie's older brother, just turned 19, is equally preoccupied with his friends. Details about the new motorcycle can't wait. What a bargain! A 1980 Honda 650 Custom, complete with crash bars, fairing, Shoei saddlebags, and two helmets for only $1750. And only 8,000 kms! Jack's description is hardly finished before Tom gives the group his obviously informed assessment of Gretzky's incredible overtime goal the night before. Who would have thought that the Islanders-Oilers confrontation would turn out that way? It was certainly worth staying up for the game. Time is running out so Steve quickly explains where the afternoon contact football game will take place, adding that he'll provide transportation for the other three fellows who live near him. At that point Jim joins them. Jim has spent the year at the Capernwray school in Texas and quickly the conversation shifts to his experiences.

In the row in front of Jack, Barry and Kevin are discussing their continuing search for jobs. Barry has been offered 10 hours a week at the cycle shop at minimum wages but is holding out for something better. Kevin, who has already been looking for work for three weeks, is getting discouraged. He is seriously considering applying for unemployment insurance and going to summer school. He doesn't know what to do.

Five rows further to the front two young couples are busily chatting about their afternoon hiking plans. The weather is pleasant, the trail beckons, and they need to decide who shall bring what. They agree to meet at the parking lot at 1:45. Sue reminds them that they should bring umbrellas—some showers have been forecast—and Jeff reminds Ron that this time he should not forget to bring the canned pop. Ron's forgetfulness last time has not been forgotten.

Across the room, in the section where most of the older couples sit, the environment is no less sociable. Two grandmas pore over their most recent grandchild photos. The semi-blurred prints evoke mutual admiration. Forthcoming visits from "children" are discussed as are several ailments, a new hat, and the latest word about Thursday's car accident.

Hardly less audible, also on the north side, is the exchange of ideas concerning the Conservative leadership race. Mr. Reimer and Mr. Schmidt manage to get quite worked up about the matter. Reimer thinks Clark is getting a raw deal while Schmidt has become an "ABC" (anyone but Clark) supporter. Both wonder whether Jake Epp still supports Clark. Behind them two brethren are animatedly discussing the current gas price war while their wives swap tentative plans to attend the Mennonite World Conference and assess the consequences of Betty's separation.

The murmuring permeates the sanctuary, blending with the quiet organ prelude.

The pastor and the choir enter. The "worshippers" become silent.

In such a fashion some people of God "prepare" themselves for worship.

THREE GENERATIONS

An old adage holds that given the human propensity to squander that for which one has not worked, ''economically'' speaking it is often three generations from shirtsleeves back to shirtsleeves. A similar assessment of Christian renewal movements is probably equally valid; after all, history is replete with examples of significant Christian revivals and reawakenings which lasted only a century or so. In general terms one can describe the three generations as follows.

Generation one—''Immediacy and authenticity.'' This generation is the one which experiences the renewal. Like newlyweds the converts exude happiness and excitement about what has happened to them. They vividly remember their previous situation and readily articulate their joy over having left it.

The comparison with what has been left behind constantly reinforces their commitment to the new life. The vibrancy accompanying personal renewal is readily evident.

This is the generation of discovery. New norms are established, new practices initiated, and new expectations are spelled out. A sense of novelty persists. Routine has not yet become ritual; form has not yet become formalism.

Old things have passed away, all things have become new.

Generation two—''Authenticity and normalcy.'' This generation still hears from the previous generation about the initial renewal of revival and the unfortunate state of affairs which preceded it. But it has not experienced either the previous state or the transition. The fervor of the parents impresses the children. They observe that the renewal was authentic but even as they accepted its relevance they do not get as excited about it as did their parents.

The first generation crusaded for the faith; the second generation defends it. That which is correct and proper must be upheld. The traditions established by the parents must be maintained and passed on.

The religious experience of the second generation is obviously authentic but it is also characterized by a sense of normalcy. To believe the correct creed, to do the right deeds, and to avoid certain practices are part and parcel of belonging to the movement. Most of the group's religious life is predictable; some segments have become ritualistic and formalistic.

Generation three—''Normalcy and formalism.'' The third generation struggles to retain as much authenticity as possible but often the battle is lost. The renewal which the grandparents experienced is all too often viewed as mere history or folklore or both. Rules and practices are generally still maintained but not without difficulty. Numbers are down. Meetings are fewer and shorter. Leadership roles become more formalized and the distance between leaders and the led increases.

With much exhortation and coaxing the ''normal'' structures and practices continue but corners are cut. Members of this generation are easily distracted from their Christian cause. It does not take much in order for them to skip a service, refuse responsibilities, or let financial support sag. Interest in evangelism and discipleship wanes.

Most importantly, this generation is not particularly concerned whether or not their children, that is, the next generation, join the movement. That, of course, becomes the crucial matter. If normalcy and formalism persist, if there is no widespread personal rediscovery among the children, then this third generation will usher in a fourth which will hardly be distinguishable from the first—before the first experienced renewal. The group returns to spiritual shirtsleeves.

Of course, the description is simplistic, but it may be instructive. For our denomination the third generation is drawing to a close.

PART IV

Mennonites

MARCH 20, 1964

MENNONITES AND BI-CULTURALISM

As most readers probably know, a study of bi-culturalism is currently being made by a Royal Commission appointed by the Canadian government. A major aim of this extensive undertaking is to calm the separatist movement in Quebec. A further aim is to determine what rights and privileges should be extended to the various cultural groups in this country. In view of the commission's apparent interest in even minor cultural groups, a number of Mennonite spokesmen have suggested that a brief be presented on behalf of the various Mennonite groups. I, for one, do not support this suggestion.

There are several reasons for my stand. In the first place, there is much disagreement among Mennonite groups as to what our cultural values are and what concessions, if any, we should ask for. Who is to speak for whom? What spokesman can claim to know the interests of all of us?

Aside from the general problem of disagreement there is a further, more basic question of whether we, as Mennonite Brethren, want to be known as an ethnic group; whether we believe that it is the church's mission to champion cultural distinctives. This, as I see it, is the fundamental issue. True our status in history is unalterable, but the image which our church presents of itself to society here and now is a matter largely under our control.

I find nothing in the New Testament which suggests to me that cultural distinctives, as secular goals in themselves, are somehow the responsibility of the church. The Great Commission is, I suggest, unrelated to the perpetuation of any particular language or set of folkways. Our Anabaptist-Mennonite origins involved strictly spiritual, not cultural, concerns. That a spiritual body of believers can degenerate into an ethnic group is understandable in view of later emigration and colonization, and in view of the usual trend toward de-spiritualization among revivalistic groups, but it is hardly cause for satisfaction or pride. I agree fully with Harvey Taves' recent statement that the fact that Mennonites are to some extent an ethnic group is

> "a reproach to us and not a vindication of our Anabaptist principles. It is because we have failed as a church that this has come."

We need to remind ourselves that while cultural differentiation and high achievement are counted as great values in the secular realm, they are "good" only in a relative sense for us since cultural differentiation and separation can be very real obstacles in building the Kingdom.

Historical evidence suggests that any church group which insists on retaining cultural peculiarities must of necessity be largely ineffective in spiritual outreach. This is so for the simple reason that membership in an ethnic group is determined almost entirely by physical birth; it is, by and large, not achievable by a later spiritual conversion.

Some Mennonite groups and many individual Mennonites are making an all-out effort to overcome cultural-secular obstacles. Let us not make their task more difficult. There is a very real and important place for culture in the life of civilized man, but let us not put it on the same level as Christianity, for if we do this, we have set up a false god and are guilty of idolatry.

JUNE 26, 1964

THE WINDS OF CHANGE

These are difficult years for our Mennonite Brethren churches. As I see it, few, if any, other religious groups in history have experienced transition and change in so many areas simultaneously. Listed below are some of the major changes currently taking place. I suggest that each trend or aspect of transition merits careful attention if major trouble is to be avoided.

• **De-ethnicization.** For a long time the MB brotherhood has been both an ethnic group and a denomination. The shift in emphasis from the former to the latter, whenever it has occurred in history, has always been a difficult one. The special danger is that extremists on either side tend to adopt rigid and dogmatic positions when it is an attitude of compromise that is really needed.

• **Language and Culture change.** This is related to the above, yet it is a separate phenomenon. Language and culture are a vital part of one's personality and are at least subconsciously associated with the individual's innermost religious experiences. The major danger here is that antagonisms tend to develop between the older and the younger generations. The danger is particularly great in a situation where large numbers of immigrants from the traditional culture join the group after the period of transition has already begun.

• **Urbanization.** The bright lights of the big city have always posed a threat to young people as well as their elders, who have been reared in a more or less sheltered environment. The tendency seems to be either to ignore the new social and ethical problems or to adopt an unrealistically severe attitude.

• **Dispersion.** No longer do most MBs live in predominantly Mennonite communities. Individuals and families have moved into virtually every town and city and have merged with the rest of society. In itself this Mennonite Diaspora is a good thing—perhaps long overdue—but the problem is that all too often religious values and associations also become dispersed and displaced. A defensive attitude, which results from traditional physical segregation, is in itself an insufficient defense against conformist pressures.

• **Professionalization.** The burgeoning drive for secondary and advanced education has necessarily resulted in large-scale expansion into the various professions. New problems of ethics and propriety have overwhelmed more than a few unprepared "pioneers." In brief, more than a few are finding it difficult to interpret the Christian Way apart from the plow.

• **Class Change.** Widespread prosperity, together with various effects of the above-mentioned transitions, has resulted in a far-reaching sociological transformation. The erstwhile fleeing and impoverished remnant is now generally well-entrenched as solid middle-class citizenry. A man with a cottage at the lakeshore, with two cars in his double garage, with a new promotion at the office, and with an affluent retirement in sight, easily forgets that his citizenship is not on this earth. He is more or less content and wishes not to be bothered—and not to bother others. Personal witnessing does not fit easily into such a situation.

Reviewing the various items

mentioned above, one can say that it is indeed a multiple metamorphosis that our brotherhood is currently experiencing. Almost everything seems to be in a state of flux. Let us be alert to the dangers or the winds of change may blow away the essence of our childlike Christian faith. Few denominations in history have successfully weathered such far-reaching changes.

OCTOBER 7, 1966

ANABAPTISM

The existence of any movement is justified mainly by an emphasis on its distinctive qualities. If there is nothing special about an organization it should probably abandon its own existence and join with larger groups doing the same thing that it does.

Sometimes I feel that the Mennonite Brethren church has shown little evidence of having a special contribution to make. We are in a position to do so but we make so little of it in fact. I am thinking, of course, of the distinctive emphasis which is best termed evangelistic anabaptism.

The unfortunate point of fact is that instead of proclaiming the full gospel of conversion plus discipleship we often tend to minimize the Anabaptist emphasis on discipleship and are even embarrassed by it.

My own experience is a case in point. Although I spent five years in one of our private high schools, attended an MB Bible Institute, and attended an MB church regularly, I left the home community without any notion of the meaning of Anabaptist values. True, I had studied Mennonite history but had never gained an appreciation of our New Testament-oriented heritage. Fortunately, self-study and exposure to various periodicals together with some stimulating presentations at inter-Mennonite peace conferences changed my views.

I suggest that to the extent that we have exhibited a theological identity in the past few generations it has rested largely on social, ethnic, and geographical separatism. That age is past. Unless we manage to teach younger generations the distinctive qualities of our orientation our future is not particularly bright. We may well become little more than a recruiting ground for both narrow fundamentalism or easy-going, "cheap grace," common denominator, evangelicalism.

Professionalism, urbanization, and great social and economic mobility are scattering us far and wide. We can no longer hold our own by being neat little piles of salt at Kitchener, Winnipeg, Hepburn, Coaldale, Yarrow, or Clearbrook. Our young people are moving out, but many are not interested in pioneering new MB churches. They see no point in merely duplicating what the Alliance and Baptist churches are already doing. And frequently their point is well taken.

Our denominational future, and with it our faithfulness in discharging our divine commission, hinges largely, I suggest, on the degree to which we teach and stress the full meaning of a strongly biblical and strongly evangelical Anabaptism. Let us renew our vision and redouble our efforts.

TWO BOTTLES

There were two bottles on the shelf. At one time both contained a uniquely helpful medicine called ''Alpenkraueter'' but times had changed. One bottle was eventually emptied and for a long time simply stood there containing nothing. Then, one fine spring morning, the head of the house—I mean the housewife—was laundering some clothes and was scouting around for some place in which to keep the left-over cleaning solvent. Finding no other suitable container nearby, she poured the clear fluid into the empty bottle and put it on a lower shelf—so that she would remember. The two tinted-glass bottles still looked the same, and, of course, still had the same labels.

As you have probably guessed, a mishap occurred. The twelve-year-old son felt a bit ill one day and decided to try out some of the well-known cure-all he had seen his parents use from time to time. Proceeding to the basement hall closet he spotted the two containers, one only half-filled, and decided to take some. The statement of directions instructed him to take two tablespoonsfull for his particular ailment. He promptly got a spoon and proceeded to fill it. The medication seemed to have a strange smell but, then, medicines often were bitter or strong. Quickly he gulped down first one spoonful and then the other. Hardly had he swallowed the last of it when a terrible burning sensation seemed to grip his mouth, throat and stomach. He let out a cry of agony and his parents came running on the double. His mother immediately knew what had happened.

On the way to the hospital, as she explained the unfortunate turn of events to the puzzled father, she was almost beside herself with remorse. After all, it was her fault. If only she had changed the label. Of course, changing the label would not have changed the content but it would have prevented confusion and, in this instance, a sad ending.

Who says names don't make a difference? Of course they do! A change in the label, or of a name, is of crucial importance when two or more basically different things are called by the same name. The only way to end the confusion and prevent unhappy consequences is to have different things called by different names. Not to do so is to be guilty of a sin of omission. It is not a matter of trying to change the nature of the contents by renaming the container, but rather a matter of renaming the container when its contents or those of other containers with the same label, have changed drastically.

This story of the two bottles came to mind the other day as I was looking out of my office window. Down below, on one of the busiest streets of the city, was a young man dressed entirely in black, wearing a very funny-looking black hat. As the cars zipped by him he was urging his horse to pull the buggy just a little faster.

The view was interesting but also more than a little confusing. My eyes remained fixed on the klippety-klopping black rig till it disappeared into the bustling traffic of a modern city.

DENOMINATIONAL PRIDE

At the 59th session of the Canadian Mennonite Brethren Conference in Winnipeg Dr. David Ewert asserted in his major message that "denominational pride is just as wicked as racial pride." I agree. So do many other people judging by the many oral and written responses. What difference does all this apparent agreement make? As far as I can tell it has changed virtually nothing, at least in the short run. We seem to feel comfortable with the notion that having gone along in theory with a proper denunciation of a sin, we can then continue practicing it. It's sort of like the medieval "sale of indulgences" except that the price is only momentary audio discomfort and some conscience pangs. The sale goes on!

Now for some positive and specific suggestions. On the basis of 1 Corinthians 12, 1 Corinthians 3, John 17 and the many other biblical references stressing unity in Christ I happen to believe that purely denominational boundaries are not part of God's plan for his church. This means that the 16,600 (1968 figures) MB members in Canada are only a small fraction of the Church of Jesus Christ. Unless my logic is way off base this also means that the onus is on us to justify any kind of inefficient undertakings, any kind of organizational "empire-building," and any type of deep-seated or unproductive rivalry with fellow Christians.

Are we doing all we can in cooperating with other Christians in spreading the Good News at home and in foreign countries? (or is real cooperation still limited only to short-term, Graham-type crusades?)

Are we even considering the possibility of joining with other denominations in operating Bible training schools at all levels? Must we necessarily duplicate all the facilities? Is there a peculiarly MB way of teaching poetry, German, Greek, anthropology, spelling, epistemology or pastoral counselling? Could we not share facilities, libraries, most instructors, etc?

Furthermore, I can see no biblically valid reason why we should designate ourselves as followers of Menno Simons. I say this not because of any basic disagreement with his emphasis but precisely because of my very great respect for the Anabaptist emphasis on disciples following Jesus Christ. (There is, of course, the related problem that the word Mennonite has about five meanings, four of which tend to confuse whatever validity the other one might have.)

Why are we often so loathe to dialogue with those who want to interact with us? Is our foundation so weak that we cannot endure exposure or cooperation?

Are we being efficient in the whole area of publications? Is God honored more because our hymnbooks and quarterlies, our service periodicals and information sheets almost all bear an "MB imprint"?

For a small denomination we certainly go a long way to display a name. Our Mennonite Brethren churches sponsor a Mennonite Brethren College located near the office of the Mennonite Brethren Herald. We have had (and have) Mennonite Brethren Bible Institutes, Mennonite Brethren High Schools, and Mennonite Brethren Rescue Missions. Is Menno more important than Christ?

Would we stress our self-hood so much if we knew that the rapture of the Church would occur a year from now? Would we then be so reluctant to cooperate with others who agree with us, or more importantly, with biblical essentials?

Must we wait for events to force us to act or are we prepared to lead? I'm dedicated to work in, with, and through a Christ-centered church—other things are secondary.

Oh yes, one thing more! Please permit me to disagree, if there be disagreement, on the basis of mutual good faith.

A WAY OF LIFE

This week I am inclined to comment on several recent events: the massive "peace demonstrations," the second moon shot, the continuing Middle East crisis, etc. I shall, however, content myself by responding to a provocative and revealing statement which appeared recently in another favorite family journal. In a letter to the editor (November 7, 1969), a reader of **The Canadian Mennonite** observed, "Mennonite Low German is much more than a medium of peasant communication; it is a way of life. By losing this way of life and with it generally our heritage as well, we shall soon see completion of the trend . . . " Because I believe that this view is held by a significant number of people, I would like to state why I think it is both erroneous and deceptive as well as heretical—at least potentially.

In the first place, most Mennonites do not speak Low German, have never heard of it, and likely never will. I disagree with the implication that these people, be they in Africa, India, Indonesia, Canada, etc., are for that reason spiritually deprived.

In the second place, much as I enjoy hearing someone use Low German well—which is usually not in a "spiritual" setting—I see no particular value in stressing the importance of one language in comparison with others. Knowledge of many languages is, of course, highly desirable.

In the third place, as far as I am concerned, "our heritage" is essentially a spiritual one. Our forefathers challenged us to live and teach the true Christian Way, not to be prepared to yield up our life, if need be, for the preservation of a picturesque, colorful dialect!

In the fourth place, "Mennonite Low German" is hardly "a way of life." It may be a localized expression of a way of life and thus a useful tool but let us not be deluded into thinking that some appropriate means of expression, for some people in some places, is the important factor. There is a crucial difference between means and ends and certainly in building the church the former must be well subordinated to the latter.

Finally, I am deeply concerned with the whole matter of encapsulating the Gospel with a heavy "cultural" shell. Is that not one of the activities for which Jesus criticized the religious leaders of his day? Furthermore, how can we have any kind of outreach or impact spiritually if a knowledge and acceptance of a "Mennonite Low German," "way of life" is a prerequisite to acceptance in our denomination? I am convinced that if we try to hitch our spiritual thrust to a particular language or culture, the result will be not the preservation of a spiritually vital way of life but an inevitable spiritual stagnation, a spiritual way of death!

THE MENNONITE RACE!

In the August 21 issue of this periodical a reader shared with us some thoughts concerning ethnicity, assimilation, outreach, etc. I agree with him that we must come to terms with our ethnic heritage but have difficulty accepting some of the observations presented. Permit me to illustrate and respond.

(1) "Being a dispersed people, Mennonite ethnicity is the closest thing to nationality that Mennonites can claim." Hardly! I claim Canadian citizenship as do most readers. Some claim American. No doubt other nationalities are also represented. In any event nationality is a political designation and ethnicity a social one with politicial overtones. It strikes me that Mennonitism (anabaptism, etc.) was originally a Christian phenomenon and to the extent that it has been allowed to become something less than that, the heirs of the martyrs must repent.

(2) "Is the German Baptist apologetic about his German background?" The implied answer is obviously "no" which is, I think, correct. However, I submit that the analogy is false. As far as I can tell the only, albeit crucial, distinction between a German Baptist and other non-Baptist German immigrants (or people in Germany) is the Christian commitment. It seems to me that the analogy would be valid only if one perceived Mennonites as a race. On the basis of widespread evidence, as well as ideals, I reject such a notion.

The hundreds of thousands of Mennonites in Indonesia, India, Congo, etc. illustrate what I mean. In fact their existence also effectively destroys the myth that there is an all-inclusive Mennonite ethnicity. There is, of course, a peculiar European-Russian ethnicity among certain Mennonites, an ethnicity which should be recognized for what it is: an aberration from the original; an obstacle of effective discipleship; a hindrance to evangelism; a self-oriented cultic emphasis; and a source of confusion. Obviously it includes much that in itself is good, but God have mercy on us if we are prepared to cling to the "good" while rejecting that which is "better." (What about "becoming all things to all men"?

(3) The reader suggests furthermore that outreach is primarily a matter of individual responsibility. True enough, but does not outreach involve building Christ's church? Having read the letter in question many times I still do not understand what the reader would suggest to the new converts. I can only conclude that he would either try to ease them into the ethnic group or perhaps send them on to the fundamentalist churches which he criticizes.

Much more should be said in connection with the letter but that must wait. I suspect that the writer's deepest concerns are Christ-motivated and praiseworthy. I say this despite some clear-cut disagreements. Whatever the situation I can certainly agree with his suggestion that we should "rather dwell on the positive aspects of our heritage, and remember that we are Christians with a positive mission . . . "

EVANGELICAL-ANABAPTIST BUT NOT MENNONITE

Sometimes it is desirable to switch from personal opinion to the reporting of a dialogue.

A. "I hear that you're convinced that we should drop the label 'Mennonite Brethren'"

B. "That's right! Does that surprise you?"

A. "Well, yes, in part."

B. "What do you mean 'in part'?"

A. "I don't want to give up a good thing. Besides why do you want to change things all the time?"

B. "I don't want to change things all the time, but I can't think of one good reason why we should keep on calling ourselves Mennonite Brethren."

A. "You know that's not true. A different name doesn't change anything. Right?"

B. "Wrong. By the way, do you want to be called a Fascist or a Communist?"

A. "Why, no! Of course not. People associate those words with ideas I don't support."

B. "Precisely, my friend, that's the point. Most people associate the word 'Mennonite' with quaint culture, good farming, buggies, pacifism, and all kinds of other things, many of which are good, but rarely do they associate it with straighforward Christianity, the way Jesus taught and lived it."

A. "How would you change things?"

B. "I'd drop the word 'Mennonite' from our denominational name. I don't see where it does any good anyway. Menno Simons surely wouldn't want us to be named after him—you know that. And the Bible tells us not to form little groups named after some human preachers. Also, the Bible says that we should be willing to give up things that hinder others."

A. "Do you think that the word 'Mennonite' is a hindrance to some people?"

B. "I know it is; some have told me so. You know yourself that both of us are forever trying to explain it away."

A. "But wouldn't the church leaders object?

B. "Maybe they would. I know some would. But I also know that many pastors and others are playing down the name as much as they can. Some use it only in small print and some have dropped it altogether in the name of their local church. That should tell us something."

A. "Are you suggesting that we should reject our evangelical-Anabaptist beliefs?"

B. "Exactly the opposite. It is because I want to keep a true evangelical-Anabaptist view that I would like to see the name changed."

A. "Would you suggest that we break our connections with MCC, MDS, etc.?"

B. "No, we should keep those connections, just like the Brethren in Christ do."

A. "Somehow you haven't convinced me yet. Do you really think that changing our name will change our attitudes and our problems?"

B. "Well, let's put it this way. Changing our name will, I believe, make it much easier to win people for Christ, and his church, when we get to work in our own Jerusalem. A name change won't in itself mean very much but it might make effective witnessing far more likely. Now people are confused when we brag about our Lord (as we should) and give rambling explanations and excuses about our name (as we have to).''

A. ''Do you know of any group that has tried this?''

B. ''Yes. The Missionary Church is one example and there are others. The people I personally asked were all glad that they had dropped the confusing name 'Mennonite'.''

A. ''It's all very confusing to me.''

B. ''By the way, do you know of anyone who has ever suggested that the word 'Mennonite' tended to scare him off?''

A. ''Yes.''

B. ''One final question, for now, do you know of anyone who was drawn to our denomination by the word 'Mennonite'?''

A. ''Let me think about that for a bit. Well—I guess I have to say 'No'.''

A RESPONSE

Because of the letters appearing in the Herald as well as the considerable response received directly, I shall expand briefly on my July 9 column, "Evangelical-Anabaptist But Not Mennonite." Let me begin by responding to some of the questions raised by brother Victor Doerksen.

Brother Doerksen asks why anyone should associate the name Mennonite with Christianity "more than they already do?" He adds, "my impression is that outsiders make this association to a greater degree than is warranted as it is." I am under the impression that the call to discipleship and the Great Commission are inseparably related to Jesus Christ and the building of his church. I am disturbed—if I understand the argument correctly—that it is somehow seen as satisfactory that we describe our religious convictions as Mennonitism and at the same time we should remain quite unconcerned when "outsiders" don't associate Mennonitism with Jesus Christ! Frankly, I'm baffled. I agree with the second quotation cited above and point to it as additional evidence that the word "Mennonite" is now confusing and has perhaps lost its utility for evangelical-anabaptists.

Another basic point raised in the letter by brother Doerksen deals with "straight-forward Christianity." The writer asks if I know of some ideal group and urges me to name it so that we might join it. I know of no ideal group; I submit that Jesus Christ must be our ideal and that we are under divine orders to strive to be like him. (Matt. 5:48) It is not a matter of joining some ideal group but of striving to become more Christ-like and communicating clearly.

Brother Doerksen makes much of our history and our heritage. To the extent that it contains Christian values I cherish it; some other aspects are desirable but hardly crucial (see Philippians 3:8). If heritage and historical roots are postulated as being intrinsically and generally the best option then according to what kind of logic have we a right to invite non-Christians to leave their un-Christian ways and follow Christ? If historical fact is taken as being crucial, we may have to terminate our attempts to get people to leave their un-Christian heritage.

The letter concludes by inviting me to state that brother Doerksen is wrong in his interpretation of my column. In part I sincerely believe that he is wrong. My intent is not to weaken evangelical-anabaptism but to strengthen it. (Nor am I in favour of withdrawing from MCC or MDS.) In part, if I understand him correctly, he is not wrong. My main concern is not historical continuity, ethnic preservation, or sociological unity.

In general I was sorry to note that none of the criticism I received claimed to be biblical. Not a single letter-writer explicitly took the Bible as the norm. It is strange how we rise so quickly to defend Menno and make so little of what Jesus taught.

I shall close by repeating my basic concern: We will not be faithful disciples unless we let the Holy Spirit work through us, however, even when we are obedient and Spirit-filled we will find that the confusing term "Mennonite" (which has changed in meaning) constitutes an unnecessary additional barrier for which we are responsible.

1874 - 1974

Although my grandparents—both families—emigrated to Canada in the early part of this century, the centennial celebration of the big Mennonite migration beginning in 1874 is of great interest to me. Clearly, those first pioneers in many parts of the old "Northwest," now the prairie provinces, endured much, built a solid economic base for future generations, and kept the faith.

Now we want to celebrate their coming, commemorate their contribution. And this is where I sometimes feel a little uncomfortable. Certainly their early pioneer lifestyle, often a brutal experience, is both significant and interesting. They brought a new strain of wheat to North America, new and better farming techniques, and assorted other innovations. But is that really the important substance of our heritage?

There is a place for recreating those often pictursque homesteads, those reliable brick ovens, the versatile household utensils, imaginative field implements, and the rest of whatever goes into establishing a Mennonite Museum or a Mennonite Village. All these physical aspects were very much a part of early life. But, I ask you, is that really the important dimension of being a Mennonite?

I imagine that many of those early preachers and doers of the Word would be just a little disappointed to note that we are putting so much emphasis on how their congregations churned butter, ground flour, baked bread, wove cloth, machine-pressed laundry, heated horseshoes, slaughtered hogs, made sausage, cooked laundry soap, mended harnesses, or gathered buffalo chips to heat their simple abodes.

Let me not be misunderstood. There is a place for this kind of historical awareness. But I wonder whether that agricultural-ethnic component should be made the centre of our grateful commemoration!

Why not express our gratitude to God in another way? Perhaps a new Missions/Services venture could be launched as a memorial. Since we cannot initiate something in the lands from which our revered forefathers fled, we would have to choose an alternative. Why not Spain? Our centennial celebrations could well generate a small army of new missions volunteers and more than enough continuing support to keep them in that land of special need. Or perhaps our Board would have some other suggestion. My point is simply that we ought not only to be looking backward and ought not only to be focusing on pioneer life.

Our true citizenship is not on this earth and the temple we are building is not one made with bricks and mortar, caulked logs, rough-hewn timber, or prairie sod. Will our centennial celebrations reflect this fundamental truth?

God called them and us to be a peculiar people; how are we defining that term?

WHO IS A MENNONITE?

During the past few months I've heard of several instances in which Mennonite Brethren congregations or smaller groups of MBs have dealt with the question, "Who is a Mennonite?" or, more particularly, "Who is an MB?" I was astonished at what I heard.

In at least two situations the decision reached was that unless a person's parents are Mennonite, he is not a Mennonite. Such secular, totally unchristian, reasoning saddens me. More than that, I find it appalling!

The first Mennonite churches in the 16th century consisted of people who had experienced a Christian transformation, who accepted biblical truths for what they claimed to be, and who then lived accordingly. When, as a result of several Christian renewal movements, the Mennonite Brethren church was founded in 1860, the same standards prevailed, as of course they should, for these are the only biblical requirements for any Christian church.

The fact that non-Christians started making the mistake of calling non-christian relatives of Mennonites, "Mennonites" as well, does not make such labelling correct, nor does it change the requirements of being a Mennonite, specifically an MB.

We had better be fully clear on that point. An MB is a person who is a Christian and who accepts the Mennonite Brethren confession of faith as an adequate or correct summary of what the Bible teaches. That is all that is required; nothing more and nothing less. Jesus never made family background a requirement for membership in his church. If we do so, then we are guilty of playing God and need to repent of our sin.

Admittedly, in North America and some other parts of the world, the word "Mennonite" has some ethnic connotations but that simply means that the term has taken on two meanings: the primary and correct one which refers to people who have accepted a certain Christian belief system and a secondary, technically incorrect meaning which categorizes people according to background and family names. The inadequacy of the second definition becomes fully evident when we realize that most Mennonite Brethren live in Africa and Asia and would not be termed Mennonite according to that definition. To accept that second definition, then, leaves us with the ludicrous situation in which the majority of Mennonite Brethren are not Mennonite Brethren! (Incidentally, this confusion of meanings explains why some of us see much merit in choosing a new name for our denomination.)

In view of all this confusion, some people have suggested that those people who join our ranks but who do not have a Mennonite background should be referred to as non-Mennonite members. I think that suggestion is both silly and unchristian. What sense does it make to speak of a non-Mennonite Mennonite? It is much better, and indeed Christian, to speak of first-generation Mennonites.

I believe that in this whole area of viewing first-generation Mennonite Brethren as somehow inferior, many of us are guilty of much sin. We have placed too much emphasis on birth and not enough on rebirth; too much on things ethnic and too little on

Jesus' ethic.

When the Pharisees of Jesus' day refused to repent and to abandon their condescension and pride, Jesus condemned them. His standards have not changed.

(men′ə nīt′) *n.*

OCTOBER 1, 1976

A MENNONITE BY ANY OTHER NAME . . .

My recent column, "Who is a Mennonite?" elicited a lot of response, virtually all favorable. A few readers, however, raised queries about the whole matter of name change which I only mentioned briefly and which was not directly related to the main point of that column.

The gist of their remarks was that changing our denominational name would solve nothing; after a few years the new name would take on the same connotation as our present one. Some other time I may want to spell out the various theological and other reasons why a denominational name change should be considered; today I want to deal only with the specific question raised by my readers.

Originally the word Mennonite was used only to describe those individuals who had become converted to a particular kind of Christianity. Their relatives who had not experienced the same conversion, no matter how close those relatives might be, were not called Mennonites. Hence there was no confusion. In several European countries where Mennonite Christians and their neighbors today have the same language and share a common origin, the name is still used correctly and distincitions are generally clear.

What, then, has caused all the confusion in North America? Very simply, this. When the Mennonites came here they were immediately seen as different from the general population, not primarily because of their religious beliefs but because of their language and customs. Small wonder, then, that children and other relatives, whether they were in fact Christians or not, were all called Mennonites. Moreover, settlement patterns which often created isolated, closed communities reinforced the faulty perceptions and the faulty labelling. That is how a Christian denomination became an ethnic group.

Other groups of Christians, from Baptists to Pentecostals, and from Quakers to Adventists did not evolve into ethnic units. Either they came here as part of the dominant English cultural group or they arose from within it. That helps to explain why, for example, people can refer to a non-Christian town drunk as a Mennonite, which happened in a town where I used to live. After all, his relatives were Mennonite Christians. He claimed no faith but he was still seen as "one of them." Of course, no one referred to the other non-Christian drunk as a Christian and Missionary Alliance even though his relatives were CMA Christians.

As long as we clung to a foreign language and culture as a central part of our church life we could not expect to be treated as anything but an ethnic group. But now times have changed. Our social indigenization, our acceptance of the English language and the general Canadian culture enables us to make a fresh start.

If we now called ourselves Christian Brethren, as our early forefathers called themselves Mennonites, we would have a clear designation of a Christian denomination just as they did. Our non-Christian relatives would not be called Christian Brethren. Such a change would make it easier for us to counteract the widely held assumption that a person becomes a Mennonite by birth rather than Christian rebirth. In any event the "birth" requirement would obviously not apply to the denomination; it might, however, still apply for several generations to Mennonites as an ethnic group. (The recent and current experience of the Missionary Church here in Ontario illustrates my point.) Of course, if we again migrated to a totally different cultural region, for example, Mexico we would again face the same problem. Then our denomination, including both Smiths and Friesens, might become a new English-speaking ethnic group.

However, as long as our basic language and social culture are the same as our neighbors, we have the option of clinging to a denominational label which because of migration has taken on ethnic qualities or we can choose to stress our purely Christian distinctives. If we want to do the latter we cannot parade the term "Mennonite;" its ethnic connotation is too strong and too widespread.

Thus we see that a Mennonite by any other name is not exactly the same. That other name would allow us to make a new distinction between Christians and non-Christians. That new distinction would enable us to eliminate a lot of confusion and to emphasize our only really important distinctive, our commitment to Jesus Christ.

FEBRUARY 12, 1982

THREE KINDS OF MENNONITES

During the past several decades there has been increasing confusion and unease about the concept of Mennonite identity. Numerous factors played a part in the growing awareness that somewhere there was a problem. Foremost among these factors were: the social impact of World War II; a new concern for authentic community evangelism; the transition from the German to the English language; increased urbanization and social absorption; increased intermarriage of Mennonites with non-Mennonites; increased interest in historical-biblical Anabaptism; a growing interest in genealogy and ethnic roots; and occasionally, some perceptive questioning by a few clergy and lay leaders about the relationship of the church to ethnicity.

Without probing the many dimensions of the problem, let me suggest that in part it grows out of the distinctly different meanings of the word ''Mennonite.'' As I see it, in North America today, there are three categories of Mennonites.

1. ETHNIC MENNONITES

This variety is found across the continent, often far removed from other Mennonites. The distinguishing trait of people in this category is that while they have abandoned—or have never had—any religious commitment, they are still seen as Mennonites, by others and generally also by themselves. These people have traditional Mennonite names, have traditional Mennonite foods, many have recognizable Mennonite lifestyles, and more than a few have retained some of the German or Low German language. Other ethnic traits may include an emphasis on ethnic roots and, for some, a preoccupation with Mennonite painting, Mennonite writing (poetry, short stories, dramas, etc., sometimes in dialect), Mennonite handicraft, and Mennonite lifestyles in Europe, particularly Russia.

Authorities on Canadian (and American) culture and ethnicism recognize the existence of ethnic Mennonites of which this group is a part. Almost any major work refers to them. Thus, for example, *Cultures in Canada,* by Jack Bavington and others (Toronto, 1976), lists Mennonites together with 27 other major cultures in Canada. The list includes: Italian, Portuguese, French, Spanish, English, Dutch, Polish, Russian, Chinese, Inuit, Ukrainian, etc. The list is entitled ''cultures'' and there are no religious

groups mentioned; "Mennonite" is one of the cultures.

Ethnically this category of Mennonites is diverse. I vividly remember that in one town where I lived it included the town drunk—that particular Mennonite died of alcoholism. This group also includes many fine people who, however, want nothing to do with religion, let alone Anabaptism.

Indicative of the self-image of this group is the 1980 comment by a restaurant manager in St. Jacob's, Ontario, "We don't pass ourselves off as being a religious organization. We are Mennonites." *(Kitchener Waterloo Record,* Oct. 11, 1980.)

2. ETHNIC-RELIGIOUS

This category consists of people who generally share the ethnic traits and interests of those in the first category, but they are also religious. They combine traits of "birth" with those of "rebirth," though in various ways. They come in two subcategories and cut across denominational lines.

(a) Ethnicity dominant

This group consists of those who

tend to be inward and backward oriented. They try, through various customs and traditions, to cling to the old ways. However, their religion is authentic and their lifestyle in many respects enviable. Some drive buggies; others drive cars and live in middle class suburbia.

(b) Religion dominant

This group, thoroughly Mennonite in background and ethnicity, tries to minimize, and sometimes hide, the distinctive culture. Theologically they range, in most Mennonite denominations, from very conservative, even fundamentalist, to the liberal. The word "Mennonite" is sometimes dropped from church names. For many, Anabaptist theology is vitally important—they have discovered or caught the vision. For others, the religion need not be Anabaptist. Thus we find thousands of them in Baptist, Christian and Missionary Alliance, Evangelical Free, and even United and Anglican churches.

In both categories with the passage of time, the dominant emphasis, be it ethnic or religious, tends to become even more dominant, though the other, that is the lesser, component has an amazing resilence, reinforced by family and other social ties.

3. RELIGIOUS

This was, of course, originally the only category of Mennonite. In the early decades of the renewal, before the mass migrations, there was no distinctive culture, no ethnic peculiarity. Nowadays this category includes converts and new members having no Mennonite ethnic identity. They are the Clarks, the Joneses, the La Rogues, the Chans, and the Singhs. Many have a real problem; they sometimes feel like outsiders. They identify fully with the religous element, often they are zealous Anabaptists, but they have a "different" ethnic derivation. As one, a deacon in a Mennonite Brethren church, told me, "I am a member of a Mennonite Brethren church but I am not a Mennonite." In a fundamental sense, of course, that statement was correct.

Once we are clear on this three-fold meaning of the word "Mennonite," then we can consider how best to deal with the confusion. If we deny these basically different definitions, we only add to the confusion and make life difficult for the increasing numbers of first-generation Mennonites now joining our churches. They obviously see the ethnicity and sometimes don't know how to cope with it.

As we emphasize religion rather than culture, realizing that God never established the church to nurture culture or ethnicity, and as we preach and practice the true tenets of Anabaptism, we are at least beginning to move in the right direction. After that there are other steps to be taken.

PART V

Christian Ethics

APRIL 10, 1964

WATCH YOUR LANGUAGE

It has recently been drawn to my attention how easily and thoughtlessly many of us use certain phrases and expressions which insult various minority groups. Such expressions as, "He is good at Jewing people down," or, "He's a good Jew" (in the sense of being an adroit bargainer) are deeply hurtful to any person of Jewish origin. Many other expressions involving similar false usage of the term "Jew" could be cited.

Another example of unbecoming language is the rather common colloquial expression, "There's a nigger in the bush" which is used to convey the thought that an offer, agreement, or bargain is simply too good to be true. The thrust of the expression is that there must surely be a catch somewhere. Aside from the obvious fact that Blacks resent being called "niggers" there is the basic issue that the expression constitutes a cynical slur on colored people in general and is therefore greatly resented.

Then, too, there is the reference to someone as "an Indian-giver," that is, a person who gives a gift but then asks for it back again. Equally repugnant is the description of someone "gyping" someone else; taking advantage in a money transaction. But Gypsies are probably no more dishonest than anyone else.

Is it not possible for us to express ourselves clearly and fully without using such vulgar language? Surely it behooves us as Christians to analyze our speech habits and to eliminate that which is unbecoming.

I trust I will not again be guilty of thoughtlessly uttering these and similar offensive phrases. It may not be the beginning of the year, but I have made the resolution never to use them again.

RULES AND REGULATIONS

As a brotherhood we tend to put much emphasis on church rules and regulations. Many of these rules are stressed in pamphlets and in sermons. Lists of rules are generally read to baptismal candidates. We have established rules to govern much of our behavior. Personally, I think that the existence of these rules is, generally speaking, a very good thing. Rules can serve as crutches for the weak and reminders for the strong. I believe that every denomination should have certain binding rules. And yet, I am troubled about some matters in this regard.

It seems to me that often we forget that there are different kinds of rules and that these rules are of varying degrees of importance. Not all of our church rules emanate from God; not all are necessarily binding for all time. Surely it is incorrect and unscriptural to say that a rule which states that ladies may wear jewelry around the neck but not on the ears is of the same order as one which states that the Lord's name is not to be taken in vain.

Many of our rules, such as the one forbidding any consumption of alcoholic beverages, (no matter if the alcoholic content is so low that the drink is less harmful than strong coffee) may well be helpful and justifiable on the basis of observation and experience but they can hardly be traced to any specific scriptural teaching.

Some of our rules are related to a specific culture. This means that as the culture changes we may have to re-evaluate and even change some of them. If we fail to do this we may find ourselves in very uncomfortable predicaments such as, for example, asserting that black trim on cars is holier than chrome, that eyes and hooks are holier than buttons, that still pictures are necessarily holier than movies, that braids are holier than permanents, and that one language is more acceptable in God's sight than another.

The challenge then to us is to realize that each of these two types of rules is important; to realize that we should be highly dogmatic about the one type but not about the other; to discern which rule belongs in one class, and which in the other; to be willing to accept modifications in a culture-related or other less central rule; and, to be willing to subject our own man-made secondary rules and regulations to critical re-evaluation.

DECEMBER 23, 1966

SELLABRATING CHRISTMAS

Let me introduce you to a friend; she may even be related to me (or you). I've known her for a long time. Perhaps you will recognize her from the following description. I should perhaps add that her husband, in his own way, shares her views and habits.

Since last June 25 she has been planning for Christmas. House-painting, window-cleaning, interior decorating, and shrub-planting were all carefully scheduled.

Following the relaxing, rest-filled, summer vacation, things really began to happen in earnest. First there was the headache of re-upholstering the furniture. Then there was the complicated business of ordering the various sewing materials, and while the "wrong" items were still being sent back and forth to Eaton's it was time to begin preparing more detailed shopping lists.

And so the weeks and months passed. Till late at night her nimble and love-motivated fingers prepared gifts. The sewing, the cake baking, both light and dark (but no wine), the cleaning, and the redecorating consumed many hours. After all Christmas comes but once a year and should be celebrated in the right way!

By the middle of November the various kinds of preparation were well underway. As the shopping trips and order forms came and went the total cost of the whole affair kept mounting. Much of the money was spent on everyday necessities but more than a little was spent on non-essentials. Meanwhile, the cakes in the basement were aging (and so was the man of the house as he thought of all the bills).

At last report my friend was still going strong. Christmas 1966 should be a banner year. The freezer is bulging with a full assortment of delicacies, in fact, as I think of the desserts, snacks, and main courses carefully tucked away, my mouth waters. There should be plenty to last through all of the get-togethers and TV programs which are on the agenda.

If 1966 is like last year it will be December 27 before both my friend and her husband will be able to settle down for a few minutes of quiet meditation. And by then, of course, it is high time to get everything ready for all the New Year celebrations. I have a great deal of respect for my friend and her husband (who is also my friend) but. . . .

Oh yes, one thing more, her first name is Martha.

WHERE IS THE PRINCE?

A great party was to be held. A birthday party for a child of royalty. Preparations began weeks in advance. Guest lists were carefully prepared, shortened, lengthened, and corrected. The proposed menu included a vast assortment of expensive delicacies as well as the usual staples. Professional decorators transformed the large dining area into a wonderland of color and sparkle. No effort was spared to make the occasion as festive and delightful as possible. After all, a birthday party, even for royalty, comes only once a year.

Finally the great day came. The hosts dressed the child in his special new costume for the day and put him down for a nap so that he would be well-rested. At the appointed time the guests arrived, and everyone brought some special present. A servant relieved the guests of their coats, hats, and the presents. Ere long all were assembled and the grand party began. A warm welcoming speech was followed by lusty singing, which in turn gave way to informal chatter. Cookies, candy and drink made round after round. The guests gossiped about all the latest news, congratulated each other on various achievements and generally enjoyed themselves. Several commented on the importance of the occasion. A great time was had by all at this very successful party.

One hour passed, then two. Finally it was time to sit down for the banquet itself. The host suddenly remembered than no one had as yet brought the young prince to be presented to the guests. Nor had anyone inquired about him! The guests had all been so taken in by one another and the splendor of the event that they had quite forgotten about him for whom the whole affair was staged in the first place!

Suddenly the people began asking, "Where is the prince?" Quickly the host dispatched a servant to fetch him. A few minutes later the servant returned to ask where the prince had been left. Then the host remembered that perhaps no one had informed the servant-doorkeeper that the young child had been put to sleep in the usually-darkened nearest guest-room. The host rushed into the room and gasped in horror and disbelief. The bed was piled high with coats and wraps, and glamourous finery and expensive gifts. With one lunge he shoved the whole pile on the floor. There he was, with the colorful blanket still covering him to keep out chilly drafts. No drafts had harmed him, but gifts, and furs, and other personal finery had smothered him. Forgetfulness, self-indulgence, and preoccupation had resulted in the death of a prince.

And that was the sad end of a great party, on December 25, in the year of our Lord, in a community I cannot name.

A CHRISTMAS PROJECT

There is probably more lying done in supposedly Christian homes in December than at any other time of the year.

Many of these lies involve Christmas, or at least Santa Claus, and thus are considered respectable or "white lies." Frankly, I am amazed to find how many young parents who wouldn't think of lying at other times, don't bat an eye when it comes to lying about Santa Claus. After all, children are children and are surely entitled to "enjoy their childhood." Here are some carefully considered pointers to help in this venture.

In the first place, parents having determined to lie to their children concerning good old St. Nick, should stick with it. If junior asks how a big man with a bigger middle can come down a chimney, either tell him to take it on faith or compare it to such fantastic ventures as the moon-landing. This may keep him quiet and in any event it will allow you to change the subject.

Above all, don't give up. If some "smart alec" neighbor child suggests that Santa is really only a friend or neighbor dressed up in an oversized suit and stuffed appropriately with a pillow, laugh it off. Tell him that some children get strange ideas about Christmas, etc.; perhaps their parents are to blame for trying to spoil a good time. Show him pictures of Santa. Children love and believe pictures.

When the five-year old asks how it is possible for Santa to be at Simpsons, Sears, Eatons, and elsewhere all at the same time—you've got a bit of a problem. This type of dilemma needs advance consideration or your story will fall apart. Prepare to tell the young thinker one of three things. (a) if he is quite young and naive, tell him that Santa travels faster than you do (it is perhaps best not to make a comparison with horse-power and reindeer-power or sleighs and Chevs); (b) if he is really serious tell him that some of the Santas are really fakes; he'll believe you for a year at least and should clearly respect you for your honesty; (c) if he persists in pursuing the point tell him that all of these pre-Christmas Santas are mere fore-runners and that the real Santa doesn't appear till Christmas Eve. Since reference to Christmas Eve will remind him of his presents he should remain quiet after that. If he doesn't, you may write for further instructions.

Perhaps the best way to avoid trouble is to take adequate precautions. Maybe you should raise some of these questions, and answers, before your youngsters do; that way they will be prepared in advance.

It is also important to repeat one's point. A child learns from repetition. Build up Santa as much as possible. Find as many red-covered knees as you can. Buy color pictures, etc. However, warn the children that sometimes Santa gets his messages mixed-up concerning who wants what for Christmas. It's safer that way, both for budget and reputation.

Since all of these lies are white lies they blend beautifully with the "Spirit of Christmas," at least in those parts of Canada where Christmas is usually white. It may help to sing "White Christmas" often. The more whiteness, the more purity!

Of course, there is another alternative. One can "tell it like it is."

But apparently many people prefer deception to truth.

TRAINING THE FACULTIES

For decades and perhaps centuries evangelical Christians have been plagued by a dilemma; how to achieve and maintain a "correct" balance between freedom in Christ and the legalism of church regulations. Some have stressed Titus 1:15, "To the pure everything is pure, but to the unbelieving nothing is pure" (Williams translation). Or 1 Corinthians 8:7, "Howbeit there is not in every man that knowledge: for some with conscience of the idol unto this hour eat it as a thing offered unto an idol; and their conscience being weak is defiled." The point being made is that it's time Christians grow up, escape the fetters of legalism, develop strong consciences and stop taking offense easily.

Others, again, emphasize the point of going what might be termed the second moral mile. Paul's comments in the last verses of 1 Corinthians 8 are cited as appropriate guidelines. "Yes, the over-scrupulous brother, for whom Christ died, is ruined by your so-called knowledge. Now if in such a way you sin against your brothers and wound their over-scrupulous consciences, you are actually sinning against Christ. So then, if food can make my brother fall, I will never, no never, eat meat again, in order to keep my brother from falling" (11-13).

And thus the unity is split. Some of us, it appears, are perpetual and inveterate offense-takers. We are hurt because someone does something, owns something, etc., which strikes us as being non-Christian. We want rules passed and enforced even though the Bible does not go that far. Specifically, we delight in taking advantage of our apparent right to tell someone that he is offending us. Presumbably, from this perspective, his only option is to yield.

Others of us make much of Christian liberty and freedom. We see ourselves as more mature and wonder how long it will take for the critics to arrive at the point where we are. Of course, we are not proud, we just know that we're right and thank God for it. To prove our maturity we press our liberty just short of licence and obvious abuse. While others appear to be tied to legalism we get all wound up with liberty, perhaps even becoming enslaved by it. What a pity!

Frankly, it seems to me that unless Christians will start looking more in the mirror instead of at the other fellow, there's a rocky road ahead for evangelical churches. Unless we are careful we may be quarreling about non-essentials and forget why we are here in the first place.

Three verses, if applied personally, may help us avoid such a crippling quandry. "But you must see to it that this right of your does not become a stumbling block to others" (1 Corinthians 8:9). "The man who eats anything must not look down on the man who does not do so, nor should the man who does not do so condemn the man who does, for God has fully accepted him" (Romans 14:3). Finally, Hebrews 5:14 may help us all to discern the goal more clearly, "But solid food belongs to full-grown men who on account of constant use have their faculties trained to distinguish good and evil."

MAY 29, 1970

HOW TO DECIDE

More than a decade ago I faced a major decision concerning my future. Several options seemed to be available and, as far as I could tell, suitable. How was I to decide what to do? I could perhaps "put out a fleece" but even if it would have been sopping wet the next morning I probably would not have known what that indicated. Fortunately, an older friend of mine gave me some helpful advice at that time. Over the years I have thought about his comments frequently, especially when others have mentioned their personal "dilemmas" to me. Considering that important decisions must be made by many young people during the coming weeks and months, I thought that it might be appropriate to share some of the decision-making guidelines which were once given to me and which I have sought to develop.

(1) One of the best things to do is to ask for advice and suggestions from older individuals who know the general situation. The better the person knows the questioner, the more likely that his comments will be helpful. However, the older person's welfare and enhancement should not be interwoven with the outcome of the decision. If three or more respected individuals say approximately the same thing, their responses should be considered seriously.

(2) God has given each one of us a mind and expects us to use it. Provided that our general spiritual state of health is good, I see no reason why we should not use our mental ability. There are times when God guides individuals in a way which seems illogical but these situations are not standard. God has given us a mind wherewith to think!

(3) It isn't necessarily the case that because a person wants to do something, God doesn't want him to. The thing that you desperately want to do may be exactly what God wants you to do. For a committed Christian, personal desire may well reflect God's guidance.

(4) There is virtue in letting fellow Christians decide. We tend to be so individualistic in our economic pursuits that we find it difficult to put our future into the hands of fellow members of the body of Christ. But we are part of a body and can hardly expect to be effective when we insist on "going it alone." Perhaps we may some day reach that state of spiritual maturity where, in fullest confidence and openness, we act according to the views of the local brotherhood. This assumes, of course, that there is a real brotherhood and that we are both willing to be known and ready to know.

(5) Patience and prayer form a healthy although at times a frustrating team. We have been conditioned to program ourselves well in advance. God does not work that way, at least not always. One may have to wander for some time with Moses in the wilderness or contemplate the ashes while sitting quietly with Job. Personally, I must admit that it is often hard to pray without preconceived answers in mind. In such situations there is, I suggest, only one solution. With Paul and Peter we must learn to abandon ourselves—to be willing to accept the unknown.

(6) The situation is significant. If there is a need which we can fill, a job that needs doing, there is no reason why we should hold back and

wait for some traumatic directive. We should proceed. If, perchance, we have misread the situation and are tuned in for signals, God will likely put obstacles in our paths. Maybe he has been waiting for us to step forward in faith. He may re-direct us once we get moving or make it obvious that we are doing the right thing, but in any case we have at least indicated a willingness. Often specific statements in the Bible will suddenly take on a new and directive meaning.

(7) God is probably more interested in who we are than where we are. Being and doing are closely related but the latter flows from the former. Maybe it does not make a great deal of difference where I am but it makes a tremendous difference who I am.

(8) Finally, let us not minimize the importance of preparation. It seems to me that very many people make either or both of the following errors: a belittling of formal Christian training in Christian schools and a wasting of time in places of learning whatever kind they may be. We used to hear much about "being fit for the Master's use;" I think that it is high time to reemphasize this truth.

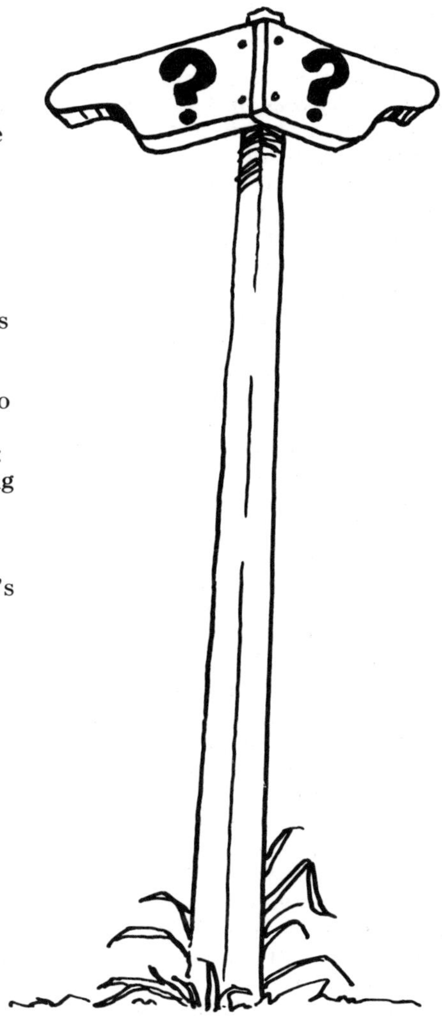

ABOVE THE LAW

Recently I had the opportunity to see Urie Bender's drama, *In Search of a Country,* which portrays the life and times of the early Anabaptist leader, Conrad Grebel. For reasons which the play depicts convincingly, the courageous Grebel did not hesitate to break the law of the state when it unsurped his right to practice biblical Christianity.

As I am writing this, some hundreds of postal employees in Montreal and elsewhere are also claiming that they have a right to break the law. Many Canadians find their arguments unconvincing and condemn their tactics. My concern is that in condemning the irresponsible actions of the defiant and militant strikers, we may also condition ourselves to reject the proper kind of rejection practiced by Grebel, and many others.

Let me explain. There are two basically different stances involving claims about being above the law. The one kind, as reflected by the mailsorters out on an illegal strike is basically self-centered. Its cause is generally personal gain, usually economic. The attitude tends to be one of defiant indifference to others and a refusal to listen to opposing veiwpoints.

Leaders in this first category often do not hesitate to employ intimidation and violence. The aim is not so much to change their opponents' minds as to coerce them into granting certain concessions, some of which may well be warranted. In brief, the issues which presumably justify illegal actions usually involve personal material gain with very little consideration for anyone else, especially those who hold opposing views. The morality of the methods employed is of no great concern.

The second stance which claims a right to live above the law reflects essentially different values. These were reflected in the life of Conrad Grebel and many other biblical reformers—and of course Jesus himself—and in recent times by Christians such as the late Dr. Martin Luther King.

Individuals in this second category break the law, albeit very reluctantly, not for reasons of personal economic gain or other personal external benefits but because of their prior and all-inclusive commitment to a higher moral law. The aim is not to defeat people but to change them, not to hate people but to love them, and not to intimidate opponents but to have them see the error of their ways and change their minds.

These responsible, authentic revolutionaries—using the term in a positive sense—are quite prepared to accept imprisonment, beatings, and even death as the price of obedience to their higher calling or as proof of their dedication and commitment.

Their methods normally eschew all violence and certainly all reprisal. Motivated by love, they love even those who punish them for breaking the law. The force they employ is moral and their ultimate weapon is their own example.

As I listen to my fellow Christians I am inclined to believe that in our eagerness to denounce the irresponsibility of the first category of law-rejection, we tend also to deny the validity of the second. Such a blurring of a fundamental difference probably reflects an unbiblical accommodation to the kingdoms of this world. Conrad Grebel has a very important message for us concerning this temptation.

DECEMBER 12, 1975

CHRISTMAS, 1975

At this time of year all of us are given to at least a little nostalgic introspection and assessment, which is as it should be. We need to pause and to think. As I do so, the following comes to mind.

(1) Despite the talk of recession and cut-backs, etc., the fact of the matter is that at least 90% of us have probably never before had it so good as right now, at least in economic terms. And if that is the case, surely the 90% of us can easily make certain that the 10%, the unemployed, etc., have nothing to fear.

I am constantly reminded that what my parents and grandparents saw as luxuries we take for granted as common necessities. When we don't get what we want, we complain. Our children, observing our widespread insistence on getting what we want, will probably insist that government supply what they want.

The crux of the problem, of course, is that when we complain of the high cost of living we are really griping about the cost of high living. You disagree! Please note.

It's been a standard day. This morning, after being awakened by our radio-alarm, I adjusted the thermostat for daytime comfort. The refrigerator provided me with chilled juice, the electric kettle with decaffeinated coffee, the electric range with cereal while the electric toaster did its thing. An FM station, via cable, brought me a fine Christian program. The evening brought some extra work but also TV news, some piano background, a reading session in the study, writing materials spread out over the dining table—with appropriate electric lighting, and refreshments from the deep freeze. I could go on and on, as could almost all of you. But note, of the 14 items mentioned above, my parents, typical middle class people in a rural community, had not a single one when I was a lad 30 years ago. How quickly we forget.

(2) Which brings me to the second thought. I am utterly amazed at how thankless people tend to be. Even Christians catch the disease. It seems that the more we have, the more we want, and the more we get, the less we express gratitude to God and man. Thanklessness, I suggest, is one of the commonest sins of today, both outside the church and within it. Hopefully things are different where you live.

(3) The third (unrelated) thought that comes to mind is that urbanization, sophistication, and television are rapidly destroying the traditional pre-eminence of church services at Christmastime. That saddens me. Not that I think we must always have formal church meetings or that I minimize the value of family activities or even solitude, but because it seems to me that Christmas, in many instances, has

become less Christian. Corporate worship has been crowded out by ski trips, Walt Disney movies, basketball tournaments, snowmobiling, Ice Capades, shopping sprees, hockey games, trips to the city, TV specials, home remodeling, academic research, house parties, furniture refinishing, snow-trips, piles of presents, holiday relaxation, and sleep.

(4) Fourthly, I find myself overwhelmed by all of God's blessings—the personal and family matters, Christian friends, our church fellowship and the larger brotherhood. And much, much more.

(5) Lastly, I am reminded that the years are rushing by. My father used to remind us, ''Kinder, es bleibt nicht so.'' (Children, it will not always stay thus.) He was right. It didn't. Nor will it. Therefore let us celebrate wisely, fully, thoughtfully, and thankfully. And let us not forget that we are, of all people, most fortunate.

WHO DECIDES?

As modern governments get involved in establishing sets of minimal moral standards in many areas, sincere Christians must be very careful not to let the world's standards become our standards.

That which may be good enough for a largely secular society is, in many cases, not good enough for Christ-followers.

In certain sectors of public policy we have long ago recognized the existence of basic ethical tensions or even of fundamental disagreement. For example, we don't accept government (or societal) norms as our norms in areas such as super-patriotism, militarism, vindictive punishment, or exploitation of "third world" peoples.

Further, in matters such as education of our children, desecration and pollution of the environment, and overseas relief we don't simply say, "What the government does, or wishes to be done, is good enough for us."

Fundamentally, it is important to stress that all people should recognize that not everything which the law permits, e.g. gossiping, is morally right, and that not everything which it requires, e.g. paying minimum wages, is morally sufficient.

By and large, the law addresses only matters of external behaviour which are serious threats to the general well-being of society. But Christian sensitivity and responsibility go far beyond that point.

We acknowledge that governments do not and cannot and should not attempt to address all moral issues in a specifically Christian manner. Accordingly, we believe that Christians do not derive adequate moral guidance from the necessarily minimalistic and pragmatic edicts of the state.

(1) *Divorce.* Just because the law now allows for relatively easy divorce does not mean that if we act in accordance with that law, we are still holding to what is right!

(2) *Abortion.* Just because many governments are making abortions, for larger categories of women, both legal and accessible, does not mean that our views should necessarily change.

(3) *Fornication involving "freely consenting adults."* Governments and society now generally view such behaviour as acceptable, but God's directives have not changed.

(4) *Pornographic books, movies, magazines, and television.* Our society is awash with such trash. Much of it is published and propagated legally. But that fact should not become our benchmark for what is right and proper and good.

(5) *Sunday laws.* Rapidly we are approaching the time when the Lord's Day is virtually like any other day. A largely sub-Christian society will ultimately have its way, but let us not allow it to decide our lifestyle for us!

(6) *Charging what the market will bear.* In a largely free enterprise society it is legal, in many pursuits, to "charge what the market will bear," and thereby exploit people. Such actions may be legal, but that does not make them morally right.

(7) *Giving nothing to charity.* According to the laws of our land it is quite legal for us to ignore our needy, even destitute, neighbors. But that fact does not make such indifference right.

Christian morality, we need to remind ourselves, is not based on legality. In a free society, the reverse must also be true.) Let us not take our moral cues from an essentially sub-Christian "Caesar." Our behavior should not be conformed only to the minimal moral standards which a pluralistic and largely secular society sets for itself. Christian standards are higher. "Be ye not conformed to this world, but be ye transformed. . . . "

Are majorities right?

SEPTEMBER 9, 1983

ARE MAJORITIES RIGHT?

Sometimes; sometimes not! However useful it may be as a decision-making device, majority rule has its limitations. Just because 9 people out of 10, a 90 percent majority, agree to defraud the 10th person of his earthly possessions hardly makes such action right.

Throughout history majorities have many times been in error; their mistakes stand as constant reminders of how often and how easily masses of people have been swayed to make wrong decisions. The classic examples are well-known. In antiquity Socrates paid the ultimate price for misjudgment by the majority. In later years Galileo shared a similar fate. The victims have been legion.

Modern majorities have sometimes acted equally unwisely. The masses cheered Hitler and Mussolini. For centuries most Western societies broadly supported oppressive racism. During World War II the majority of Canadians and Americans endorsed the bigotry meted out to their ethnic-Japanese fellow citizens. In country after country, majorities have clamoured for blood, shouted for war, and thoroughly endorsed desecration of the environment.

Down through the ages the established church has hardly fared much better. The blood of many martyrs amply attests to that fact.

Even more important for us, majorities in evangelical churches have also at times been in error. At various times a call for renewal, a challenge to stewardship practices, or an exhortation to take certain biblical teachings seriously has triggered majority wrath. In recent years, even in our ranks, the proper practice of some spiritual gifts has at times precipitated ostracism by an unthinking majority. With much pain some of our brothers and sisters have discovered that wisdom and propriety are not always exhibited in majority decisions. They would identify with the old adage that on many issues insight does not suddenly come to the many.

Of course, decision-making by majority rule has its place, especially concerning lesser issues. It is one of the best ways of deciding whether or not to pave the driveway and of establishing times at which meetings shall begin.

But on major issues, on key questions of substance, let us not hide behind the veneer of majority decision. Let us build consensus rather than suppress legitimate, sometimes prophetic, dissent. After all, tyranny by the majority is just as reprehensible as tyranny by the minority.

If in the secular realm the power of the majority needs to be constrained, then the faithful church has good reason to be doubly cautious. The verities of the Word and the working of the Spirit, for example, are not dependent on majority votes. Therein lies an important lesson for the church.

Are majorities right? Sometimes; sometimes not! Therefore, let us be cautious on what kinds of issues we rely on numbers only.

PART VI

Practical Christianity

RACE AND THE GOSPEL OF LOVE

"The first opponents of slavery in North America were religious leaders and groups in Pennsylvania—Quakers, Mennonites, and Dunkers." This is how Anson Stokes and Leo Pfeffer begin Chapter 12 of their fascinating study, **Church and State in the United States,** Harper and Row, 1964. The authors go on to state that no other groups were "as fearless and active." The love of God, it appears, compelled these people not only to take sides but even to assert leadership on the important moral issues of the day.

What has happened to this commendable zeal? Why have we so little to say to crass injustice? Have we no responsibility to speak out when our Indians, Blacks, etc., in both Canada and the United States, are mistreated, cheated, kicked and beaten? Why are there so few Mennonite Brethren voices raised in the land? Oh yes, we shouted loudly some years back when for a short time we lost the right to vote but now that we are not involved, that it is not our skulls which are cracked and bleeding, we are strangely silent.

Somewhere along the line something has gone wrong, sadly wrong. Perhaps it is that we have allowed the anti-Social Gospel fanaticism of certain fundamentalists to undermine our total commitment. I think this is part of the story. Then, too, it seems that as we have gradually moved well up the socio-economic ladder we have tended to forget what it feels like to be the object of derision and prejudice. We, who come to a large extent from an earlier persecuted minority, now join the self-righteous throngs who by-pass the bleeding wayfarer lying on the road. True, there are some who stay back with the Good Samaritan but they are all too few.

Lastly, too many of us seem to think that the acceptance of biblical non-resistance carries with it a prohibition against all verbal involvement. I cannot accept this view. The fact that I am not willing to shed human blood does not mean that I should not criticize evil. In fact, I tend to take an opposite view. Perhaps those of us who believe it to be un-Christian to hit back have a special responsibility to spell out the Christian doctrine of love. This may even involve joining the marches!

In any event, it seems to me that many of us are grieving our Lord by our safe and smug silence.

MARTIN LUTHER KING

Martin Luther King has come and, all too soon, he has gone. Now that the official eulogies and orations have ended and the burning, looting and killing have hopefully come to a halt, it might be well to reflect briefly on the life, the teachings, and the death of a great man.

King was simultaneously a stark realist and a dedicated Christian idealist. He realized that it was futile to attempt to achieve full freedom for Negroes by resorting to violence. Reliance on force would only trigger a backlash of further social suppression by the overwhelming majority of whites. He was fully aware of the fact that most people are actually or potentially racially prejudiced but, just as importantly, he also knew that most people are at least superficially committed to an intellectual, sometimes religious, acceptance of racial equality. Consequently he appealed to consciences in an attempt to change both emotions and actions. He shamed us, cajoled us, accused us, and pleaded with us. He did his utmost to get the White Establishment to accept his views without producing resentment or hatred. His contagious enthusiasm, irrefutable logic, and self-sacrificing diligence resulted in an amazing degree of success.

But perhaps King was attempting to do too much, perhaps he was aiming for the impossible. His insistence on brotherly love, justice, and non-violence were surely Christian, but is it realistic to expect a primarily non-Christian society to live by Christian standards? The months and years ahead will probably indicate the extent to which King's hopes and aspirations were feasible.

Every society needs spokesmen for its conscience, people who point to evils and means of overcoming them, but it also needs those who state unequivocally the call not only to act Christian but to become Christian. King attempted to act in both roles, and that is no easy undertaking. No doubt some will say that he pressed for the former cause at the expense of the latter, but let only those point an accusing finger who have expressed more truly Christian love than he did.

If King's life was a strange phenomenon in this largely loveless world his death, more particularly the reaction to it, was even stranger. Never before has the United States granted a "private citizen" a more momentous farewell. From East to West, and North to South, the great and the not-so-great either stiffened their lips or wept openly. Whether the groundswell of emotion was mainly one of sympathy, shame, anger, or fear is hard to tell. Perhaps it was all these and more. But there was also a great irony in the whole affair. A society which is still largely opposed to the doctrine of full equality for which King became a martyr mourned massively for him with whom they disagreed. Perhaps people wept because weeping served as a satisfying substitute for the acceptance of black neighbors. Who can tell!

Whatever additional significance there is in King's life and death it at least confronts everyone, and especially those of us who call ourselves by the name of Christ, with the question whether we have been true to His example in the increasingly crucial area of race relations.

MAY 31, 1968

THE BREAD OF LIFE

Last night I watched a TV program I shall not soon forget—a one-hour "special" describing the conditions of hunger and starvation which exist in various areas of the U.S. The shocking picture of the one-year-old child who, because of starvation, weighed less than he did at birth; the sad-eyed mother who reluctantly told the reporter that all her school child had had for breakfast was "some gravy;" the eleven-year-old girl who had been arrested for prostitution to which she had turned to get money to buy food; the gaunt Indian mother on a starvation-plagued reservation who has lost eight children, all under one year of age; and the month-old infant who had survived almost entirely on water for six weeks are scenes not easily forgotten.

Although this particular program focused on the problem in the U.S., no doubt similar situations could be found in supposedly affluent Canada. As far as I am concerned, programs such as the one I saw last night should be required viewing for all middle and upper class Christians in both countries.

Especially for my friend "X." A few weeks ago "X" informed me that he was "against the Mennonite Central Committee." After some probing I discovered that the reason why my friend did not support the MCC was that it supposedly stressed proples' physical needs rather than their souls. Of course, if he would have investigated the matter for himself he would have discovered that our venerable service agency is concerned with the total needs of suffering, sinful mankind.

As the revolting scenes passed across the screen I remembered "X"—and hoped that he was watching—but I also remembered what Jesus said when confronted with two groups of people, those who had provisions, and those who were hungry: "Give ye them to eat!" By parable, by assertion, and by personal example, our Lord repeatedly reminded his followers that mere words are insufficient in the face of dire physical needs. Let us not forget the desperately needy as we climb up the economic ladder, rung by comfortable rung.

I have resolved to increase my material and prayer support for our missions and service projects, including the MCC.

Brother "X," are you with me? I wish you would have been last night!

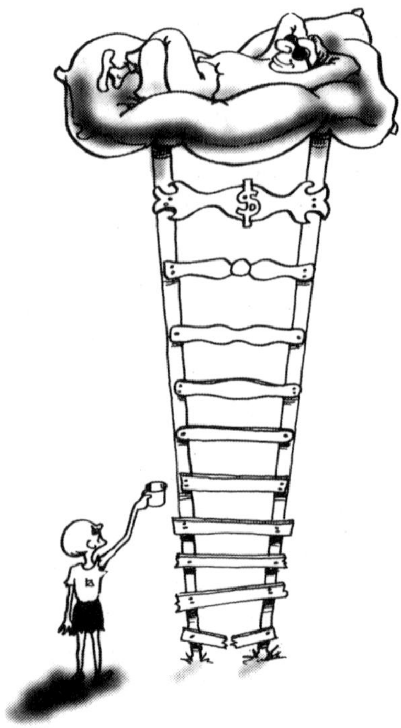

. . . AN EXPERIENCE

It seems to be a part of human frailty that we talk more about our problems than our successes, more about what we "need" than what we have, and more about what we think God should do than about what he has already done.

This week I should like to relate an answer to prayer which has strengthened my faith; perhaps it will also encourage others.

For our last year in California we needed a house which would be for rent from August or September until the following July. In April we began to enquire about possibilities but nothing suitable seemed to be available. By May we began to check the "want ads" but somehow I felt that God would answer our prayer some other way. I checked only two houses and entered only one of them. Perhaps it was somewhat strange but I had the firm assurance that we would have a suitable place at the required time. I then stopped checking the advertisements.

Suddenly, one day as some of us were walking about a block from the college, the answer came to me. On the lawn of a house was a sign "For Sale." The house was occupied at the time by our friends, the Elmo Warkentins. An enquiry revealed the fact that the home was owned by a family in another city and that the Warkentins would likely move to their new place in August or September. Elmo emphasized, however, that as far as he knew the place was not for rent. I, nevertheless, was convinced that we would rent this house for the next year and took my family over there to see it. We discussed various aspects of the house and mentally placed our furniture at appropriate places.

In the meantime I telephoned the owners. The response was clear and firm—the house was not for rent. I was a bit taken aback but had the inner assurance that we would live there. Several times I telephoned and always the answer was the same. From the Warkentins I learned that several families were seriously interested in buying the house.

As the days passed I became even more sure that we would live at "the Townsend house" and made arrangements for a truck to move our furniture, first to some friends' house while we went on a trip and then to "our new place."

Soon only a few weeks remained till arrangements had to be finalized. Still the house was not for rent. It became rather embarrassing to tell friends that we neither had a house rented for the following year nor were we busily checking all leads. We had, however, arranged for several fellows to help us move.

Then, not unexpectedly, the situation changed. The house was sold. The new owner was a widowed relative of the previous owners and upon an initial enquiry informed me that she intended to move into the house herself—if she could sell her farm. However, even if she couldn't sell, she didn't want to have small children in "the Townsend house." By now things were looking at least a little brighter.

A few days later I telephoned the new owner again. She said that she had decided to rent the house but only for one year. She still wanted no small children in the place but agreed to meet me to discuss the matter.

We met, chatted briefly, and

although I had not raised the point, she stated that she would rent us the place for one year beginning about September 1 and that she had changed her mind about the matter of the children. I suggested that we draw up a lease or some other type of written agreement but she commented that if we belonged to the same church to which the Warkentins did, that would not be necessary.

We rented the house for a sum which was certainly not high but was her stated rental and lived there for the desired term.

Some might insist that we were lucky but we remember the episode as another vivid reminder that God answers prayer.

A BROTHERHOOD FUND

A few weeks from now many of us will be celebrating the birth of Jesus Christ by taking stuffing from inside a turkey and putting it inside ourselves. And in other ways.

One of the ways in which we can try to reflect the love exemplified in God's greatest gift is to establish a brotherhood fund. I'm convinced that for most if not all of our churches the existence of such a fund would be highly beneficial for all who are involved. It does not necessarily replace governmental or community welfare services, but is an immediate expression of love.

Here is a specific suggestion. The church council or the larger body should select a 3 person committee, preferably consisting of the church treasurer and two other members one of whom should be a woman. One of the latter should be chairman. While monies designated for this fund should be channeled through the treasurer and the membership should be aware that the fund exists, the committee should generally function without much publicity. Its records should not be made public although the pastor and perhaps a few other church officials should have access to information if they deem it necessary. The committee decides.

Basically such a fund operates in the following way. It is brought into existence when the church is reminded that the idea of Christian brotherhood has important economic consequences. Those of us who have regular and adequate incomes have both the opportunity and responsibility to assist our fellow Christians who are needy.

With the accumulation of designated gifts the fund is launched. The purpose is to provide assistance to our brethren who find themselves in difficult financial straits. I'm thinking not of people whose business investments went sour but of those who have problems providing for essentials.

As people genuinely need help they are cheerfully given it without fanfare or public evaluation. The small committee functions quietly, quickly, and effectively. The onus for getting help to those who need it rests partly on the committee members as well as on other members of the congregation who make it a point to be sensitive about material needs. But it also rests with those who deserve Christian sharing. Christian brotherhood includes grace to receive as well as grace to give. Indeed, the former may be more difficult than the latter but Christians, by definition, must be capable of doing both.

But, you might say, many who really need help don't want to accept "charity." They don't have to. It is generally taken for granted that those who receive help will return the funds if/when they are able to. The details of time are mainly the concern of the recipients. No doubt some will return more than they were given. That's how brotherhood works.

Such a fund differs from the traditional "Armenkasse" (Fund for the Poor) in that everyone is seen as a potential giver and receiver. There should be no embarrassment in becoming involved in such a revolving fund. With a minimum of "means testing" and no publicity we function as the New Testament exhorts us to function. As the committee indicates a general need for funds, we give. When we individually find ourselves in difficulty we call on the rest of the brotherhood. When we are able, in turn, to help others, we do so by returning that which was given to us. The committee is the intermediary.

We are living in days when personal economic well-being can change unexpectedly, suddenly, drastically. We often emphasize that we are a brotherhood. If we mean it, then this time of economic recession calls for a new form of expression.

A CONGREGATIONAL MORTGAGE

Granted, it may be an outlandish idea, but at a time when increasing numbers of our fellow church members are in danger of losing their homes because of mortgage defaults, it at least warrants consideration.

Perhaps the fundamental issue we need to confront is whether a congregation has any responsibility to assist in a major way someone who has become a victim of our ever-widening recession. What is the responsibility of continuing income earners to those who are suddenly without income? Is it enough to take some meals and grocery hampers to the needy family or should we do more than that?

I suggest that before our present economic malaise has run its course, at least some of our congregations will have to face the question of basic economic sharing. The issue is not a communal lifestyle but a communal responsibility for the essentials for living.

Some of us are in the midst of paying off a mortgage, some have finished, and some are just beginning the many years of monthly payments. In a normal situation, especially given our dubious penchant for hyper-individualism in financial affairs, that is an accepted fact and creates no great problems. But present times are not normal times—unexpected financial casualties are becoming more frequent. What is a Christian response?

One option involves a partial pooling of our financial resources in terms of mortgage payments. A "congregational mortgage" would include all the personal residence mortages being paid by members of the church family. Those members with regular incomes would contribute to the mortgage fund an amount somewhat exceeding their own mortgage payments or, if their mortgage is paid off, a reasonable contribution. "Reasonable" would be defined in terms of income. If everyone contributed in this manner, it should be possible for all involved to keep their homes.

Of course, as soon as those who benefit most once again become employed they would be expected to contribute generously. The guideline for every family unit should be to give funds to meet its own requirements and as much extra as is needed in a fair distribution of additional obligations. All families would continue to live in their own homes and basically handle their own finances. The new dimension resulting from the operation of a congregational mortgage would be that no one who suddenly became unemployed would face the prospect of also losing his home!

Of course, helping one another can take many forms. For some people the initiation of a congregational mortgage would be too big a venture. Doubtless in certain cases a massive enlargement of a congregation's brotherhood fund or assistance fund could meet the need. But the advantages of a congregational mortgage are not to be minimized: there would be no explicit designation of a family as a charity case; there would be easy changes in contribution patterns; and the congregation would develop greater unity, sense of community, and a new awareness of joint responsibility. If a congregation would choose to go this route, a special administration committee would presumably have to be established.

Admittedly there would be some problems. What about mortgages assumed by homeowners as a means of raising funds for business ventures? How would one deal with a mortgage on a lavish, or at least unjustifably expensive home? These are only some of the difficult questions that would have to be faced.

But these hard problems do not vitiate our Christian responsibilities. We cannot easily avoid the issue: what is the responsibility of those of us with continuing employment to our fellow believers who, through no fault of their own, are suddenly without employment and face the loss of their homes? We can invoke all kinds of arguments involving renters, unemployment insurance, and welfare but after having stated them all, there remains an important residue of responsibility derived from Christian kinship. How extensive such financial assistance should be is a question which a growing number of our congregations will have to ask themselves. I cannot tell you what constitutes a perfect response to the problem but I am convinced that it does not consist of aloofness and indifference. ''He who has a job and a home and seeth his brother in need. . . . ''

CHRISTIAN ENTREPRENEURS

Over the years it has become customary, in certain Christian circles, to come down rather hard on our brothers and sisters in the business community. Doubtless some carefully considered and ethically consistent criticism has its proper place. In business, as in other pursuits, not all to whom God has entrusted particular gifts seem to be worthy stewards.

But let us not be one-sided in our assessment; there is another side to the story. Many of our business brothers have been key people in the ministry of our churches. Indeed, during my almost 30 years of denominational involvement, in a variety of settings, I have increasingly recognized the vital role which many entrepreneurs have played in Kingdom building. This other side of the story needs also to be heard.

It is time that we thank our businessmen. Time and again they have contributed generously, sometimes sacrifically, to Christian causes.

I am speaking of the people who for years have been at the top of my lists when it has become my "privilege" to help raise funds for our Seminary, for our College, for several Bible institutes, for several high schools, for several camp purchases and development programs, for a local church building program, for Inter-Varsity, for several evangelistic crusades, for emergency help for needy families, for foreign students, for destitute immigrants, for assorted endowments, for several debt retirement campaigns, and for the Brotherhood Fund. Almost without exception our Christian businessmen have "come through."

From the time I first sold a ¼-page ad in the MEI yearbook (to a kindly Clearbook merchant who cheerfully invested $7 in a commercially dubious venture), to the evenings last week when I was part of a telephone emergency "blitz" for a Christian school, I have rarely encountered anything but good-will and support.

The track record of most of our entrepreneurs, those enterprising people who have been willing to take some risks, who have created many jobs, and who have quite properly realized a profit, has been commendable.

For example, if a certain generous manufacturer had not made a substantial donation, the sod-turning ceremony which preceded the construction of Ebenezer Hall at MBBC in the 40s might never have take place, If a handful of big-hearted merchants had not put their money "up front" in the 1950s, Columbia Bible Camp in the Fraser Valley might still be only a dream. If a group of service-oriented Manitoba business and professional people had not contributed notable sums, Camp Arnes would certainly not have become what it is today.

Further, if some well-to-do brethren had not added their gifts to the many small and medium-sized gifts as they came in, the "half-million dollar" Camp Crossroads property in Ontario might still belong to a Jewish estate. If some prosperous Clearbrook-area businessmen and land developers had not purchased the beautiful acreage of the "new" MEI, the expansion of that school's ministry would probably not have occurred. If some generous businessmen in Canada and the U.S. had not committed major sums, then our first-class Seminary would surely not have been able to build the B.C. Lounge, the Manitoba Room or the Ontario Room. Without the vital interest of one California family, the Hiebert Library at Fresno Pacific College would almost certainly not have come into being. The CBMC International would not be what it is today if a certain successful businessman had not generously supported its work. Similarly, a large Mennonite community in South America would not today have a much-needed public meetingplace if a certain prosperous Canadian brother had not recognized the need and then met it. The list could be made much longer.

In thanking our supportive businessmen, I am not suggesting that they are better because their gifts are bigger; I am rather insisting that just because their resources and gifts are bigger, these stewards should not be seen as less virtuous. God's standard requires cheerful and proportionate giving from us all, be the gifts large or small. God can make much out of little or little out of much.

Let us thank God for brothers and sisters with entrepreneurial skills. Let us acknowledge that their faithful service is as important as any other faithful service.

A VERY PRESENT HELP

"Not a chance!" was the response of the ticket agent in Salt Lake City airport when I enquired about space on the next flight to Seattle. Late and delayed flights and an unusually large crowd of Friday evening commuters had created general congestion and confusion in the airport.

There we were, a family of six, apparently unable to continue our flight as planned. Meanwhile, relatives were enroute on a 100-mile trip to Seattle to get us. We could not inform them of our problems.

I checked again. This time the overworked agent was even more frustrated and short-tempered than before. I needn't even bother to keep on trying, he asserted. The waiting lists for all flights out were already hopelessly long and besides, additional flights were arriving late so that bookings would be even more fouled up than ever.

We turned back towards our pile of luggage. The walls and ceiling of the building were beginning to look very familiar. What now? We prayed. Some might say that our prayer was selfish but does God not desire our welfare? Does he not invite us to make our needs known to Him? "God," I said, "you can get us out of here and to our destination on time. I don't know how, but we'll leave that up to you." ("Not a chance!" echoed the agent's verdict.)

The milling, shoving crowds seemed to be swelling by the minute. Long lines of would-be passengers snaked from the waiting rooms into the corridors. The weather was hot—passengers shouted, tempers flared. Little Bonnie, aged 3, fell asleep; I got a headache.

We waited. I asked again. Suddenly the agent's tone changed. "Go to gate 12," he informed us, "There may be room." There was. Without even bothering to issue us boarding passes the attendant hurriedly waved us aboard. The six vacant seats were quickly filled and we took off. I can still not explain, in human terms, exactly how it came about that a plane which was over-crowded somehow had six vacancies.

As we were winging our way to Seattle I was again reminded that God is a very present help in time of trouble, big or small trouble.

WHEN DO WE COOPERATE?

At a time when Christian interaction with other groups is widespread, many Mennonite Brethren and other evangelical Christians are asking, "When do we cooperate with whom?" Here are four unofficial guidelines which may be of some assistance.

(1) *The degree of immediacy.* The question here involves time. The less time we have to assess a situation, the less responsible we are for the consequences of what appeared at the time to be a right decision.

For example, suppose that you are driving along a remote country road during a blizzard. You encounter a truck stuck in a snowbank. Another vehicle is stopped alongside. A man flags for help. It is very cold. You stop. You get out. You see a shivering child on the seat of the truck. The two men are working hard. You and the driver of the van put your shoulders to the stuck truck. It finally moves free. The grateful driver honks his horn and drives off. So does the driver of the van. You feel good; you have done what you could.

Only later, when you are stopped at a police checkpoint on the highway, do you discover, to your utter amazement, that the driver of the truck was a kidnapper, that the shivering child was being kidnapped, and that the van driver was the kidnapper's accomplice. All things considered you acted properly. You encountered an immediate problem, you made reasonable assumptions, and you did what you thought was right. You are to be commended.

(2) *The degree of urgency.* You are out on an early morning jog in the fog. As you round a corner you suddenly see a house on fire. The fire trucks have not yet arrived. Two people are manning garden hoses. Half a dozen others have formed a bucket brigade from a nearby creek to the burning bedroom. More bucket passers are needed. You quickly join in; the buckets move faster. You recognize the man behind you as a well-known local agnostic, indeed, he heads the local unit of the anti-Christian "Freethinkers Association." You take the buckets from him as fast as you can. You remember that two Sundays ago in Bible class you criticized him and his group. You perspire as you hurry. You don't ask whether further down the line there might be any other bucket brigaders who reject the incarnation, the efficacy of prayer, or the authority of the Bible. You manage to keep the fire under control until the firemen arrive. In sweating alongside the agnostic you have put discipleship into practice; you have honored God. Your witness has been authenticated. There are times when the "fruit of the Spirit" intermingles with the humanitarianism of scoffers.

(3) *The nature of the activity.* A big religious rally is being planned in your town. Certain clergymen have decided that since most people don't come to church, the church must go to the people. A broadly ecumenical service in the park is arranged. Your church is asked to participate. The dominant planners and the scheduled speaker are modernists, having openly rejected the virgin birth, the doctrine of the atonement, and the need for personal salvation. You decline; you have acted wisely. To participate would be to send confusing signals. To participate would be to undermine your decades-long ministry. To work with an agnostic to douse a fire is one thing;

to stand alongside unbelievers in a compromised attempt to preach the Gospel is quite another.

(4) *The scope of the involvement.* Two spokesmen for a respected political party ask you to join. After some thought you agree and you pay your fee. You enjoy the activity and contribute good ideas. Soon you are asked to stand for office. You wonder what you should do. Two concerns are on your mind: How will your action affect your fellow church members, especially those who do not share your political persuasion? How will your additional involvement affect your prior and more basic commitment to Christ?

When the nominating committee enquires about your decision, you state the following. You are prepared to stand for office provided (a) that there is no presumption that your congregation is involved and is somehow even unofficially identified with the party and (b) that you will pursue this new venture only to the point that it does not undermine your higher calling to Christian servanthood. To the extent that you can express your Christian views in the new position you are prepared to do so. Your conditions are acceptable. You stand for office. You are elected. You probably did the right thing.

In the months and years ahead many vital issue will face us: the ominous nuclear threat, rampant militarism, glaring social injustice, pressing neighborhood needs, pressures for so-called Christian ecumenicity, pressures for "good works"/"process" Christianity, and many others. Perhaps these guidelines will be of some help.

PART VII

Stewardship

SEPTEMBER 19, 1969

GOD'S CALF DIED

This column is being written 30,000 feet above the waving grain fields of the prairies. It is a bit hard to believe that many people in these areas will apparently be hard-pressed for cash because of declining grain sales and prices. Our churches and our missions programs are already feeling the effects of this situation. Should they? Is the situation really all that serious?

In the first place, most of us aren't farmers and don't even reside in grain-growing provinces. Should we not be able to take up some of the slack? In the second place, even in the prairies people are, generally speaking, hardly destitute.

My "spies" tell me that many of our members are "living better" than ever before. More of us, in the prairies and elsewhere, are spending winter vacations in the South, travelling to Europe and the Holy Land, buying better and more cars, and paying substantial income tax.

Most of us seem somehow to find the funds for the things that we really want. Therefore I am prepared to assert that if we are really dedicated to the cause of missions and services, to name one crucial area, the funds will be found as they were found during the depression years.

Indeed, not only the funds will appear but also the needed personnel and the general support. What I cannot quite figure out is that while most of us now earn our living in relatively well-paid professions, trades, businesses, etc., we tend to blame the unsold wheat for the red ink!

I would hazard the guess that if we totaled the actual incomes of all of our members we would find that they are at an all-time high, even after allowing for inflation. I also suspect that many of our members are giving proportionately less to the church than previous generations did.

Statistics can tell strange tales. If we look at simple increases in contributions and expenditures we may be falsely impressed. The more significant figures, I suggest, are the proportionate ones.

I believe that the needed money "is there" for all of our church needs. Those of us who are not directly involved in the grain crisis may, however, have to dig a little deeper. But for many of us there is still plenty of digging room. The "hurting nerve" is still well covered.

If we really believe that we must cut back on church work during these prosperous times what do we expect to do if and when hard times come?

Which reminds me of the story about the man whose cow had two healthy twin calves. He was so grateful that he decided to give one of the calves to God. The identical calves grew rapidly and were indistinguishable. Then, unfortunately, one got sick and soon died. The farmer was sad because, as he told his friends, "God's calf died." Is it God's wheat that is unsold? Does the decline in grain prices include all of the tithe? Does a salary increase of 5% following a request for 10% mean that half of our tithe is not available? Is the tithe, or general church support, the first part of our financial scheme to suffer?

MEET BROTHER BOB

Periodically some of my friends amaze me. Consider the case of my long-time friend, Brother Bob.

A bit odd, almost eccentric in some respects (for example, one of his hobbies is to try to discover the salary of every Mennonite Brethren pastor in Canada) he is nonetheless an all-round decent and respectable chap. The kind of fellow who would gladly share his sausage with you at an MCC relief sale. He is fortyish and financially secure. He lives with his family at Coalwinkburn, a small town 50 minutes from Wincalgina, Saskaltoba.

Now it happens that friend Bob, along with about five million other Canadians, stay up to catch the latest news on "The National" at 11:00 p.m.

One night, not long ago, slouched in his recliner, with one eye on the toast and tea he was munching and the other on Lloyd Robertson, Brother Bob's attention was caught by a news clip in which the Prime Minister urged every Canadian to save energy, beat inflation and revive the sagging Canadian economy.

Bob thought of his Inco and Block Brothers shares and perked up his ears. Mr. Trudeau proceeded to list various specifics and as he did so several ideas came to Bob's mind. (Bob's no Rhodes Scholar but in some areas he thinks very well—and fast.)

"Less driving," said the Prime Minister. Bob immediately thought of all the trips he made to church during the week. He never had been enthusiastic about going to church Sunday evening so why not have the family stay home. That would save 12½ miles. Besides, it wouldn't hurt the family to also sacrifice a bit. Doing one's part was, after all, a mark of Christian citizenship.

Of course, Bob was already contributing to the Government's national energy conservation program by driving to town for only one hockey game a week. As it happened, he was also making his gasoline go farther by resigning from the church library committee—albeit for other reasons—whose monthly meetings he never had enjoyed anyway.

"And we must spend less," intoned the P.M. This was just what Bob liked to hear. At last someone was talking right. Quick as a flash Bob thought of his church contributions. That was one area where he could force himself to spend less, $30 a month less. It would not really be all that much but $360 a year was at least something. If everyone cut back that much, who knows, it might make a real difference!

"Less electrical consumption," said Mr. Trudeau. Another good point, thought Bob. He and his wife had recently been hosting youth groups often as well as a lot of new church people, and the electric bill showed it. Many lights had been on all evening and there had been extra time for the range and dishwasher. Yes, he and Laura would be prepared to cut back there, also.

"And less spending abroad," concluded our eminent leader as he pressed the point of balancing Canada's international trade deficit. Bob thought a moment and then it came to him. He and Laura were to leave for a three-week holiday in Europe shortly. They were planning to make a three-day detour to visit a small MB church over there and present the leader with a three digit sum towards the local church building fund. But for the sake of national solvency they could easily deny themselves those three days—they would give their friend only $50 (by mail).

Then Bob took his Alpenkraeuter and went to bed. He was tired, but felt good somehow. After all, he had made some big decisions, at least for him. As I said, some of my friends never cease to amaze me.

MENNONITE MILLIONAIRES

At almost all times and in almost all places this set of words used to be a contradiction in terms, but not now. By overt and subtle means my liaison brethren and I have concluded that at present, in Canada, there are approximately 30 Mennonite Brethren men who have become millionaires or, in a few instances, perhaps even multimillionaires. I consider myself fortunate to count at least ten of them as personal friends.

No doubt there are many reasons why these brethren have become wealthy, mostly within one generation. Rising real estate values, shrewd investments, aggressive marketing, expert management, adroit enterpreneurial activities, some "good fortune," and a lot of hard work have all played a part.

But my concern at this moment is not to analyze what has happened or to contemplate the pressures and problems which wealthy Christians face, no doubt these are great, but to assess what this recent phenomenon of wealth means to our brotherhood.

In the first place, I am interested in the matter of millionaires because, while their numbers may be relatively few, their situation differs from that of thousands of fellow-Mennonite Brethren only in degree. We may have "only" thirty or so millionaires but we have very many wealthy church members. Consequently, the stewardship of wealth involves many of our members.

In the second place, while our preachers and educational institutions often dwell on denominational distinctives, philosophies of education, the pros and cons of various ecumenical thrusts, strategies in missions and evangelism, aspects of church membership, and assorted other matters such as situation ethics, the role of women, and political involvement, the greatest ethical and spiritual test we now face may well be that involving our individual and collective wealth. If that is so, then our greatest battleline involves the handling of our vast possessions with our millionaire brethren in the vanguard, in the thick of frontline action. Our greatest ethical trials, thus, may not be associated with what our preachers and educators and other "professional" people say, but with what our wealthy trend-setting brethren do.

Since those who are rich tend to set patterns for the rest of us, I am constrained to spell out some questions, knowing full well that their relevancy is not limited only to those who have surpassed some conventional yardstick of weath.

* How are Christian millionaires different from non-Christian millionaries?
* How are Christian millionaries who are committed to principles of brotherhood and discipleship different from other Christian millionaires?
* Do you ever feel that giving money is a substitute for personal involvement?
* Do you see your status of wealth mainly as reward for your efforts or mainly as opportunity for service?
* Has your great wealth made you more or less sensitive and responsive to the plight of poverty-stricken people at home or abroad?
* Do you feel any special sense of responsibility when our missions and other conference treasuries are in the red?

Maybe we all should remind ourselves of three basic truths:

* We can't take wealth with us but we can send it ahead.
* If Christians become rich, we become rich for a purpose.
* To whom much has been given, of him will much also be required.

THE DOUBLE STANDARD

Some of us are a strange lot—right? We will sit three hours on a hard wooden bench,or even on cold concrete, to watch a football game. The outdoor air conditioning may cause our knees to knock, our noses to drip, and our teeth to chatter, but we don't complain. Indeed, we gladly part with two to ten dollars for the "privilege." But somehow we complain that a one and a half hour church service in a comfortable room, with comfortable seats or padded pews, is "too long."

We will readily drive 25 or 30 miles to patronize new or well-known steak houses, but manage to keep a straight face when we explain that a five or ten-mile drive to church is "simply too far" to "come out much."

Some of us spend $200 on annual golf club memberships, not to mention the considerable green fees, but balk at an annual $10 per member subsidy for our seminary or a $20 subsidy for our college.

Some of us cheerfully lay out $1000 or more, sometimes much more, for a good home stereo set and absorb continuing expenditures for records, tapes, etc., but zipper up our pockets when we are asked to chip in $100 for a new church organ or piano.

Many of us hesitate not at all to take on a $40,000 or $60,000 high interest mortgage for a fancy new home, but come up with a fainthearted, "Sorry, no funds available," when asked to contribute (pledge!) a few hundred dollars over a three-year period for our college building program.

Without batting an eye many of us regularly take out the family for a $15 to $30 Sunday or week-night dinner at the Ponderosa, the Chicken Chalet, Long John Silver's or Mother's Pizza, but can scrounge up only a single, measley $2 bill for a special offering to help alleviate a starvation crisis in Bangladesh.

Some of us easily spend $800 for a fast motor (the old one is still good but not big enough), or much more than that for a flashy boat, yet actually manage a worrisome wrinkle and frown when informed that this year's church "norm" is $80.

And then there are those of us who shell out $2,000 per person to tour Africa, but have relatively little left for our brothers and sisters who labour there as missionaries.

Others of us spend about as much visiting the assorted Mennonite shrines in Europe, from Witmarsum to Zurich, but become obviously inconspicuous when our Mennonite high schools and Bible institutes ask for scholarships or operating funds.

The illustrations could go on, but maybe we have already seen ourselves in one or the other. We seem to have funds for virtually everything we want, let alone "need," yet our church budgets—local, provincial national, international—are, in many cases, struggling hard. Why?

Of course there are also many who give very generously—like the brother who annually earns $9,000 and gives over $3,000 to the church. They know who they are; they are worthy examples. And those of us who give too little, who live and give by a double standard, we know who we are too. So does God.

DECEMBER 7, 1979

SHARING GAINS

Most of us, I suppose, grew up with the notion that while tithing was an Old Testament requirement, it remains a norm for Christians even in the twentieth century. Many dedicated Christians would not think of allocating their weekly or monthly paycheck without first subtracting the tithe from the top. The practice is surely commendable.

But perhaps we need to extend the concept. That idea came to me last summer as I had occasion to interact with people in the five "western" provinces. Tithing in terms of salary or wages is commendable but for some it may be insufficient—at least if their expansion of assets gets turned into cash.

The fact of the matter is that some church members today have become wealthy because of capital gains.

- I am thinking of a certain farmer who never was particularly well-to-do but now finds himself owning 14 quarters of land worth $90,000 a quarter—debt free! Should he tithe only on his annual income or does God deserve a tenth of the million dollar profit the owner stands to make when he sells?
- I am thinking of the land developer who, during the past eight years, has seen his "land bank" increase in value five-fold. Even after costs are paid, he stands to make tidy capital gains.
- I am thinking of investors who have made substantial, in some instances huge, profits. Various individuals invested in gold, gems, works of art, real estate, stock market shares, and a host of other items. More than a few of these have done very well financially. Should God not be given a share of the gains?

Maybe you think that the answer is obvious; why even discuss the matter? Well, on the basis of what I heard last summer the matter is not at all obvious to some people. At least a few of those who make major capital gains do not see those funds as income. They may well give a tenth of their usual income but this one-time, or infrequent, windfall is placed in a category by itself. The fact that even the government taxes 50 percent of these capital gains seems to be overlooked. Let those whose tithe involves all of their basic income be an example to the rest of us.

During the next decade or so many of our church people will likely come into large sums of money because of capital gains profits. Will our churches, educational institutions, mission ventures, and aid projects feel the effect? When some hard-working farmers and businessmen suddenly become millionaires will our missions treasurer know the difference?

In many of our congregations a true picture of income goes much beyond salaries, wages and government cheques. Because of that, there should not only be changing patterns of giving but also substantially increased giving when capital gains are liquidated. God, I suggest does not keep separate books for income from wheat sales and income from land sales.

Micah 4:13 exhorts godly people to "devote their gain to the Lord, their wealth to the Lord of the whole earth." "Gain" includes capital gain; would you not agree? Let us this Christmas season consciously expand our practice of stewardship, financial and non-financial.

WESLEY ON WEALTH

During the current economic recession, when increasing numbers in our congregations are experiencing unemployment, major financial setbacks and even bankruptcy, it may well be the case that those of us who are not personally hurting are tempted to develop all sorts of rationalizations to dilute ethical norms. For example, several times in recent months I have heard fellow Christians observe that the recession was having a negative effect on their charitable donations.

Presumably the validity of their conclusions were supposed to be obvious to all who heard the comments! Well, to me such validity was not at all obvious. I have had then, and have now, great difficulty seeing why donations should be reduced for the people in question.

Several of them have "cost of living" clauses built into fairly generous professional salaries and it is almost certain that all of the complainers are doing at least as well financially this year as they did last year. Despite that situation they were using recession arguments to "explain" or justify reduced giving. It doesn't add up. These fortunate people, enjoying both job security and good income, should be increasing their giving rather than cutting back! Yet there they were, repeating various concerns and problems which, in fact, did not apply to them at all!

About two centuries ago the great evangelist, John Wesley, uttered some wise comments on Christians and material well-being. They are still worth considering: "I fear, wherever riches have increased, the essence of religion has decreased in the same proportion. Therefore I do not see how it is possible, in the nature of things, for any revival of true religion to continue long. For religion must necessarily produce both industry and frugality, and these cannot but produce riches. But as riches increase, so will pride, anger, and love of the world in all its branches. How then is it possible that Methodism, that is, a religion of the heart, though it flourishes now as a green bay tree, should continue in this state? For the Methodists in every place grow diligent and frugal; consequently they increase in goods. Hence they proportionately increase in pride, in anger, in the desire of the flesh, the desire of the eyes and the pride of life. So although the form of religion remains, the Spirit is swiftly vanishing away. Is there no way to prevent this—this continual decay of true religion?"

The great preacher raises some basic questions, questions which for many of us are as relevant even during the present recession as they were for the Christian folk of the 17th Century.

Is there then no answer to the dilemma Wesley poses? I shall not attempt to spell out a full answer in this column but surely a partial answer involves a thorough understanding of stewardship. Some Christians seem to think that Christian stewardship consists of making sure that our gifts go only to the worthiest of causes; some seem to think that the real issue involves giving the tithe. Both responses are laudable but inadequate.

Under God we are stewards of all we possess. The distinction between tithe and non-tithe is of no great consequence. The same Christian stewardship principles apply to both.

To all of us, but particularly to those

not negatively affected by the deep recession, Wesley's words on wealth constitute a continuing sober warning and a relevant reminder. May they constantly remind us of the inclusive scope of our stewardship responsibilities.

PART VIII

Labor And Management

SEPTEMBER 20, 1974

STRIKES

On this Labor Day, 1974, the country is plagued with labor problems, especially in the area of transportation and shipping. In part labor's problem is understandable, the employees are caught in an inflation squeeze which puts them in a situation where their actual take-home pay is declining. While their position may still be enviable from the perspective of those who are unemployed, those affected don't see it that way.

Several aspects in these strikes are particularly annoying. For one thing, in most cases the strike doesn't hurt the managing decision-makers, national, provincial, or city governments, one bit. The grain-growing farmers and the thousands of city commuters are the ones doing the hurting and there's nothing they can do about it.

In the second place, it seems that laws don't matter much any more. An illegal strike is treated just like any other one. If you or I exceed the speed limit or refuse to pay our taxes we invariably must take the consequences. But increasingly unions, at least many union leaders, place themselves above the law.

Consider the case of the Montreal subway strike. The weeks-old walkout was a breach of contract and totally illegal from day one. Eventually the authorities started talking about fines and soon began imposing them. Up to this point about $3-4,000 in fines has been levied. Now that item itself has become a strike issue. The union spokesmen insist that the workmen will not go back until all fines are cancelled, all collected fines returned to the lawbreakers, and written promises given that no legal charges will be pressed. My guess is that the union will win on every count.

In Toronto the provincial government has gone a second mile—in the wrong direction. Originally the city-wide total transit strike was legal but that presumably changed on August 31 when in a night session the provincial legislature passed a law forcing the employees back to the jobs they left on August 12, granted them a retroactive 12% increase, and provided for binding arbitration on all issues including additional immediate wage increases. The law also provided for heavy fines, up to $1,000 a day for each striker and $10,000 per day for the union itself.

But then government spokesmen undermined themselves and betrayed their public trust. Provincial Labor Minister John MacBeth announced that, "We are not interested in prosecuting." The government, he said, was not interested in prosecuting the law-breaking workers. True to his word, the government has levied no fines. Several days have passed. The union has finally decided to conduct a vote to decide whether or not they will obey the law. It makes one wonder who is really the government.

Little wonder that respect for law is everywhere declining dangerously. Governments themselves are leading the way by encouraging massive flouting of provincial statutes. In time to come, when public law-breaking becomes so widespread that governments can no longer control the situation, I trust they will recall their present dereliction.

We should note, in passing, that this present law-breaking cannot be put in the same category as Martin Luther King—type lawbreaking which is done for conscience reasons, in the name of a higher moral law, with the lawbreakers willing to take the consequences without malice or hatred.

THE NEW CONSCIENTIOUS OBJECTORS

For almost a generation young men in Canada have not had to grapple with the fundamental question of whether or not they are willing to take up arms in defense of their country and it is unlikely that the present situation will change soon. But this does not mean that for Christians the phenomenon of conscientious objectors is passe. Indeed, the contrary may well be true. I suggest that we may be entering an age in which conscientious objection, as an unavoidable expression of the Christian ethic, will involve a high percentage of obedient Christians and will relate to many areas of life, areas totally unrelated to direct military activity. The dilemmas, I submit, may soon be rising around us in such magnitude that the automatic association of conscientious objection with military matters will quickly disappear. The new conscientious objectors may include the following:

* the nurse who loses her job at the city hospital because she refuses to participate in an abortion operation. Because of her refusal she loses not only her job but finds that she is black-listed at other hospitals and thus finds it almost impossible to get employment as a nurse. She also loses certain fringe benefits.
* the high school teacher who refuses the federation's instructions to call in sick when he is in good health and consequently finds himself either railroaded out of the teachers' federation or simply subjected to so much abuse that he gets out of teaching on his own volition. He too, loses not only his job but also various benefits.
* the letter carrier who insists on making his rounds, according to his contract, even though his union has called an illegal wildcat strike. When he returns to his car to drive home from work he finds his tires slashed and the windshield broken. His safety is in jeopardy but since he is a Christian he hates no one.
* the longshoreman in Vancouver whose union card is lifted because he refuses to participate in a fake "study session" during working hours, a "study session" which, in fact, is nothing less than an illegal walk-out.
* the dairy farmer who, despite the directive from the national head-quarters of the dairymen's union to which he must belong if he wants to ship to the fresh milk market refuses to dump his milk on the ground as a protest against supposedly inadequate prices. He loses his shipper's permit. He soon has much milk and no money. His neighbors and his cows don't understand.
* the proprietor of a small electrical firm who refuses to sign up with a union whose methods he cannot condone. He loses his business and almost his shirt but not his Christian friends.
* the employee in a box factory who refuses to participate in a one-day sympathy strike. Her employer has treated her more than fairly. Why should she strike against him because of a strike involving another firm? The union, which represents employees at both firms forces her employer to fire her or risk a long strike. She becomes unemployed. The letter of regret from her employer doesn't pay the grocery bill.
* the construction worker who stays on the job even though his union orders him to "walk off" because the lumber yard truck drivers are non-

union. A week later his union forces his employer to lay him off.

* the plasterer who continues to plaster even though his union tells him to quit because the sand is brought in from a non-union pit. Ten days later he is looking for work—the sand has not blurred his vision but his clear vision has taken him away from his sand.

* the conscientious young student who, while completing his time as an articling associate to become a chartered accountant, suddenly finds his hopes shattered. He is summarily dismissed when he refuses to falsify an income tax return. Subsequently his own income tax return shows very little income.

These are ten examples; there are many others. The relevance of Christian conscientious objection has suddenly become very immediate and very personal.

STRIKES AND STRIFE

As this is being written, large segments of the labor and professional sector of society are in turmoil. In Toronto, and elsewhere, the high school teachers are continuing a two-month strike; in Manitoba the physicians are in a battle with the provincial government, and across the country the pulp and paper workers have been out for months. And that's only a small part of the total scene.

Where does all of this leave the committed Christians who find themselves caught up in this malaise of confrontation and manipulation? Do we simply keep quiet and go along with the majority? Do we have nothing to say when group leaders brashly declare that should the government legislate them back to work they will conduct a vote among this group to decide whether or not they will obey the strike-ending legislation? Do we nod approvingly when our negotiators demand exorbitant increases in one year, rationalizing our support on the grounds that since the banks are ripping off the public we have every right to follow their atrocious example?

What has happened to our supposedly biblical distinctives? Do we condemn destructive violence only when it involves the military battlefield, a situation comfortably remote from virtually all of us? Does loving our brother, neighbor, and enemy apply only in a purely individualistic setting? Is all-out economic warfare more acceptable than military warfare? Is class hatred more acceptable than racial hatred? Is it morally right to strike—thereby causing high school students to lose a year—just because such action has been legalized? Have Christian physicians a moral right to break their Hippocratic oath simply because a government refuses to pay them more than six times the average national income?

Whatever happened to conscientious objection? Have we relegated its relevance solely to military matters?

Fortunately some of our brothers and sisters, as evidenced during the last postal strike, are ready to stand up for their convictions. But many of our number seem to be aimlessly drifting along with the crowd in a state of ethical confusion.

We need to deal with this matter; it's much bigger than a series of totally individualistic options. The faithful and concerned Christian community needs to speak, to act, and to be mutually supportive. There are Christian guidelines and directives. We need a major national, if not continental, peace conference to help us understand how our distinctives, or how the biblical teachings, apply to the new kinds of warfare.

THE WORK ETHIC

It used to be assumed that where Christianity, especially Protestantism, was the main religion, there one would also find the so-called "work ethic," the eagerness to work hard. Well, at least in certain parts of this country the work climate has changed. People are still plenty eager to get ahead, to "earn" a high income, but there is much less evidence that they want to work hard.

Several events illustrate the point. Some time ago I had occasion to call a plumber, one who lived only a few blocks from our place. He drove over, looked at the problem, and observed that he couldn't correct it that day. His total time in the house was about three minutes. As he left he stated that the bill for his inspection was about $17 and that he wanted to be paid immediately. I questioned the figure but he was insistent. I paid him and that was the end of that business relationship.

The second incident involved a day I spent at a certain large office. The lack of work output on the part of certain secretaries shocked me. The work day, I use the term loosely, began at 8:30 a.m. They arrived on time. Then followed some beauty treatment, small-talk with other secretaries, personal telephone conversations, and sheer dilly-dallying. By about 9:10 the typewriters started typing. Forty minutes later it was time to get ready for the 10:00 o'clock coffee break. By about 9:58 the office was dead.

The coffee must have been very hot that day, or perhaps the gossip was torrid. In any event the lovely ladies did not return to their desks till after 10:30. Then followed more small talk. By about 10:50 the typewriters were going again. But only for an hour. At 11:50 it was time to go for lunch—walking on company time, of course. After the one-hour break the dear things were back, about ten minutes late. More small talk and socializing and comments on clothes, children, parties, income, and what not.

About 1:20 typewriters sounded forth again—for over an hour! By 2:45 it was time to get ready for the coffee break. The coffee must have been even hotter. Nobody returned till about 3:25. Typewriters banged away, intermittently, because more gossip had to be shared. By 4:25 it was time to quit. Everyone left. I calculated a total of 4 hours and 15 minutes of work in what was counted as a 7 hour work day.

The third instance involves a larger group of people. I have before me the specific demands of the Canadian Union of Postal Workers. In addition to the proposed basic hourly rate of $8.25 the news story listed the following:

- a 30-hour work week for 40 hours of pay;
- a substantial shift premium on top of the basic hourly rate ($3.63 for evenings and nights, $22.00 per hour for Saturdays and $33.00 per hour for Sundays!);
- paid wash-up, rest break, travel and lunch time totalling 3½ hours of the six-hour work-day, according to post office spokesmen. Some Toronto CUPW leaders stated that these paid non-work times would total only two hours and 10 minutes of the six-hour day. The *Kitchener-Waterloo Record* calculated that the actual working time for the 40 hours of pay would be 12 hours for the entire week!

Of course I know that not all plumbers are rip-off artists, or that all secretaries goof off almost half of the day, or that all union demands are so outlandish! Most working people are reasonable. And yet, it seems to me that the work ethic is becoming ever more anemic. Many people, apparently, simply don't want to work anymore.

Surely we Christians have a major responsibility to be the kind of diligent, reliable, and thorough workers which our society needs. In this area, too, we need to be salt and light.

PART IX

Education And Science

DECEMBER 1, 1967

"THOSE WITH IMAGINATION DRINK"

The November 1967, number of *Maclean's* carries several articles on Canadian universities and unversity life. Unfortunately, the otherwise informative and respectable reports continually lend aid and comfort to the seamier side of student pursuits. Thus, in a critical survey of the 20 best universities, the writer finds it necessary to cite the student "pubs" or drinking places as one of the half-dozen key campus traits. I wrote that off as being irrelevant, although the specific details might well be factually correct.

But what really bothers me is the repeated inference that it is only stupid and naive students who shun "residential beer bashes," etc. The point is perhaps illustrated best in the brief critique of the University of New Burnswick which reads, in part, "students are provincial and conservative; those with imagination drink in the Lord Beaverbrook Hotel."

It is a bit unsettling to realize that the author of the descriptions, a professor of philosophy at Toronto, would be so unfair as to imply a close correlation between imagination and imbibing. It has been my observation at a half dozen major campuses in three countries that it is the second-rate, unimaginative students who try to make a frustrating university existence take on meaning via alcohol.

Another theme running through several of the articles is that no campus has really "arrived" until it boasts a sizable hippie colony and a tribe of rebels who rebel for the sake of rebellion. At least one author appears to lament the fact that most Canadian campuses are "pre-Berkeleyan." It is one thing to argue that student idealism is a healthy and necessary response to an intensive and unjust social Establishment, but it is quite another to imply that immorality is admirable if somehow associated with an assault on the status quo.

A student should be a thinker and a critic, and a campus is the proper place for an analysis of all ideas. It is the most logical center of social criticism. But the impact of crusading campus idealism is almost totally undone when presented as wanton destruction, rejection of all authority, sexual immorality, and drug addiction. This is especially significant in view of the fact that, increasingly, students seem to be replacing the Church as the conscience of society. They have a great opportunity, but unfortunately many are destroying their impact by the methods they employ.

Finally, it would appear that the *Maclean's* articles distort the campus picture by their failure to point out that the entire "New Intellectual Left" is essentially negativistic. One searches in vain for positive proposals. Rejection of institutions, leaders, programs, and traditional views abound but hardly a word is said about acceptable alternatives. Therefore, while we, and especially our studying young people, do well to listen to campus questions and criticisms and can learn as we listen, we will unfortunately only be frustrated, if we look to Berkeley-type reactions for meaningful answers.

FEBRUARY 2, 1968

THE MOSES MENTALITY

Life magazine recently carried an interesting account of how a hospital orderly posed and practiced as a medical physician for several years. Despite his apparently very successful service to townsfolk of Groveton, Texas, "Dr. R. L. Brown" (Freddie M. Brant) was immediately arrested when it was discovered that he had never attended medical school. Now things are back to their usual lawful state in the sleepy little town; "Dr. Brown" is in custody, law has prevailed, and the fine folk are again without medical help.

There may be reasons why, in the practice of medicine, it is at present better to deprive people of medical help than to have them served by a self-taught practitioner, the way all people were served before formal medical schools were established. Personally, I doubt it. It would seem just as fair, even in medicine, to evaluate a person's qualifications by his performance as by his formal training.

Be that as it may, what really troubles me is that a similar kind of thinking seems to be sweeping our brotherhood with reference to formal educational requirements for pastors and preachers. Increasingly we tend to evaluate our spiritual leaders not by what they can contribute, and are contributing, in Christian leadership, but by their academic qualifications.

Let me not be misunderstood; as one who has spent more than nine years at various universities, I need hardly be convinced about the advantages of formal education. Evenso, there is something very unsettling, even disturbing, in the spreading assumption that our omnipotent God can work his will only through the finest of polished, varnished, intricately decorated, and high-priced vessels made of doubly-refined clay. What is happening to the simple, pure earth?

It seems to me that we are prone to forget that God worked just as effectively through fisherman Peter as through Ph.D Paul. He needs both, and he needs each as much as the other.

By putting undue stress on formal education, we are, in effect, limiting God. We are saying that his strength lies, at least in part, in our own human strength. But as I recall, my Bible says something about him being great through our weakness!

Moses, you will remember, argued that because of his human inadequacy God would surely not be able to do much through him! He was applying sensible human standards to an infinite, almighty God. Let us be on guard lest we too fall prey to such a "Moses mentality."

By the way, have you heard about the deeply spiritual and otherwise successful pastor who was "fired" because his B.A. and B.D. degrees were earned at non-accredited colleges? I haven't either, and I hope we never do!

STUDENT INACTIVISM

From time to time a columnist gets some very interesting and provocative letters; unfortunately there is not enough time to answer each response individually. In any event, here is a written reply to some remarks directed to me some time ago. The subject matter involves student financial support of our churches. There are numerous reasons why post-high school students should not put dollars in the offering plate; here are some of the major ones.

In the first place, many students—perhaps most—have no trouble bringing their expenses up to their income which means, of course, that there is nothing left to give! (And who can do without pizzas and pepsis!)

In the second place, if one does not support institutions financially then one is freer to criticize authority. After all, it doesn't seem quite right to be constantly knocking "the Establishment" while being part of it. Also, one gets more kicks out of kicking than out of standing for something.

In the third place, since many students have no single church home, whether they are members or not, they have no obligation. Having no permanent ties, one need not be too concerned about establishing financial responsibilities. It might even be desirable to let the "away" church think that one supports the "home" church or vice versa. But that's not a very good idea.

In the fourth place, a student is a student. He is preparing, not participating. He is training for life rather than being part of life. Financial support can come when Christian maturity has been achieved.

In the fifth place, tithing is both "legalistic" and traditional and therefore properly suspect.

In the sixth place, what a student gives to "his church" is no one else's business (and will snooping columnists please mind their own!).

In the seventh place, many students don't agree with missions, evangelism, MCC, or church building programs and therefore are they not entitled to support what they can endorse wholeheartedly?

In the eighth place, some students are, indeed, so poor that all they can give to the church is two cents! And who wants two cents worth of anything? Isn't that a mite too small?

"THE EMERGENCE OF MAN"

The following letter was recently put in the mail:

The Editor
"The Emergence of Man" Series
Time—Life Books

Your advertisements about the new series, The Emergence of Man, and the first volume, *The Missing Link,* are currently being read by countless thousands, perhaps millions. The ad raises many questions, indeed, its unqualified assertions are academically irresponsible.

Unabashedly you transform the theory of evolution into total fact as if its gaping holes and logical contradictions had suddenly disappeared. They haven't.

You blandly assert, "It is two million years ago. On an African savanna, a strange creature browses for food. He looks something like an ape and also like a man. He walks on two legs—yet his forehead is low and sloping, his jaw thrusts forward. He doesn't know it—but he represents a giant step forward in evolution. For he is the "missing link" between ape and man." Apparently your ad writers have conclusive evidence unknown to scientists. They continue.

"Today, that creature who first ventured to raise himself above the other animals no longer exists; he has become you." They may speak for themselves but I resent them assigning ape forbears to me.

When they assert, "And yet you share, with every creature that ever lived, the same origins—the same accident that led to the spontaneous creation of the first single-celled algae 3.5 billion years ago," they are totally in the realm of speculation. Any responsible scientist knows that. By the way, who created that first single-celled algae, as you yourself phrase it?

John H. Redekop, Ph.D
Professor

I, for one, feel very strongly about such high-power, glossy distortion. Readers of this periodical would do well to prepare themselves for this unwarranted onslaught against belief in God as Creator. I can just imagine certain anti-Christian educators having a real hey day with this material. What a pity and what a shame! In the name of science, speculation masquerades as if it were science. In fact, it is the opposite.

SETBACKS FOR EVOLUTIONISTS

Two headlines recently caught my attention. On December 9 the local paper ran a five-column headline story, "Existence of 'missing links' doubted." In the news story Dr. Niles Eldredge of the American Museum of Natural History in New York stated that transitional types of life probably never existed. Echoing a long-standing Christian creationist observation he noted that if it were true that higher forms of life gradually evolved from lower forms, a standard "scientific" belief, there should be adequate fossil evidence. But, as he put it, all of the fossil evidence to date has failed to turn up any such missing links.

However, rather than admit the bankruptcy of the evolutionist view of how man came to be, Dr. Niles Eldredge suggests a "new" interpretation, an "alternate" theory he terms "punctualism." He suggests that there may have been "sporadic leaps" forward producing higher forms of life interspersed with long periods without significant change.

Exactly why this view should be believed is not explained. The Second Law of Thermodynamics states clearly that in all energy transformation there is a tendency for some energy to be transformed into non-reversible heat energy. Thus the energy in our total life system slowly runs down or "wears out." That is termed the Law of Entropy; it flies in the face of all evolutionist arguments but particularly contradicts the "punctualist" hypothesis.

However, we should not be surprised at evolutionists' ready resourcefulness; they are a determined lot not about to admit failure. Note the following:

- In 1856 several partial skeletons of "Neanderthal Man" were found in Germany. Belief that they represented the missing link was scuttled when it was discovered the Neanderthal man's brain apparently was as large as that of modern man and that his tools and lifestyle were more advanced than those of some 20th century primitive tribes.
- In 1891 there was the "big find" of the "Java Man," an imaginary ape-man "recreated" from the top of a skull, a thigh bone, and several teeth. Later, most of the teeth were proven to come from the common orangutan and the other bones probably from a pigmy.
- "Piltdown Man" was found in an English gravel pit in 1908. Scientists raved about the great discovery. "Reconstructions" appeared in most large museums throughout the world. The Encyclopedia Britannica called it the second most important of the fossils in showing the evolution of man! When I was in high school it was paraded in the textbooks as proof that the Bible was wrong. However, in 1953 it was discovered that the whole thing was a fabrication growing out of personal rivalries. Scientists now generally agree it was the greatest anthropological hoax of the century.
- Then there was "Nebraska Man". Actually he was nothing more than a tooth but this was all that many so-called sophisticated scientists needed. Presumably he would still be discrediting the Bible if it hadn't later been proven that the tooth belonged to a pig.

And so it goes on with all of the rest. Each "find" has been false. Yet scientists cling to evolution and, worse still, inflict it on young students as if it were proven fact. What is more, an amazing number of Christian scientists seem to parrot the same lines about man being an evolved animal.

The second headline appeared December 11 and was spread across the entire first page in bold red letters; it said: "Venus data upsets ideas on how solar system formed." The Venus information apparently destroyed the theory that earth and Venus have a common origin. "It's a totally unexpected result" said Harvard's Dr. Michael McElroy. "It certainly is back to the drawing boards" said Michigan's Dr. Thomas Donahue. What all of this means to me is that supposedly convincing scientific theories about origins are going to impress me even less in the future than they have in the past.

We must be careful not to let the creation-evolution debate become our central concern; but we must also be sure what we believe, why we believe it, and stand up for what we believe.

JANUARY 1, 1982

THE INTOLERANCE OF SOME SCIENTISTS

I never cease to be amazed at the intolerance and narrow-mindedness of certain academics who reject the basic scientific requirement that all theories and evidence warrant consideration. Of course, not all scientists are close-minded; increasing numbers are honestly open to options which for them are new. But the disease of intolerance, often masquerading in the guise of academic freedom or sophistication, remains widespread.

At the time that this column is being written, in mid-December, the battle is on again. Here is some background information.

Last March the Arkansas legislature passed a statute entitled, "The Balanced Treatment for Creation-Science and Evolution-Science Act." Though in some respects novel and revolutionary—only Louisiana currently has such a law though other states are considering it—the actual requirements of the allegedly ubiquitous law are really minimal and very logical. It simply requires that if a school teaches the theory of evolution it must also give "balanced treatment" to the creationist view. Given the fact that the theory of evolution is only a theory and that vast numbers of the tax-paying citizens of the state hold the creationist view, such a requirement can hardly be termed burdensome. As a matter of fact, the true scientist should not have to be coerced to investigate and present all major options. It is, after all, in the nature of his profession to investigate various explanations and to search for truth wherever he can find it.

Unfortunately, however, large numbers of scientists don't see it that way. They and their representatives are flocking to Little Rock, Arkansas, in a desperate attempt to get a U.S. Federal court to overturn the law. Apparently, despite all their protestations about the open-mindedness of science and the vaunted scientific method, they can't live with competition. For many the "blind" commitment to the *theory* of evolution is so total that anything which suggests an alternative can't be tolerated. In this connection it should be emphasized that the Bible-believing creationists, who are often ridiculed by assorted academics for supposed narrow-mindness, are quite prepared to have the two views presented; it is certain educated scientists who are opposing the more inclusive study.

What has happened, of course, is that many biologists and other scientists, in Arkansas and elsewhere, despite the acknowledged fact that evolutionism is only a theory, have come to accept it as law.

No one, of course, is asking the evolutionists to change their minds. The only requirement which the new law stipulates is that they acknowledge that their own *theory* is not the only one and that they explain what the other one is. And that is more than they are willing to do. If they are so sure that their evolutionism is the only valid view, then why not, in the name of true science, let it be compared to other views?

Not surprisingly the American Civil Liberties Association, an organizational which in my younger and more naive years I also supported, has joined the fray on the side of the evolutionists. This same outfit has for years defended Marxist professors on the grounds of academic freedom, despite the fact that where Marxists come to power there is no academic freedom. But now the ACLU's double standard is again obvious. Its spokesmen oppose the Arkansas law because creationism is associated with Christianity. Quite apart from the fact that the Arkansas law does not require the inculcation of religious beliefs, one can only conclude that the ACLU finds the religion of Marxism acceptable but the Christian religion not.

Is the theory of evolution really so logical and compelling? In a major 1981 text, *Biology, The Science of Life* (Goodyear Publishing, Santa Monica), the authors, Robert Wallace, Jack King, and Gerald Sanders come up with some real dandies. For example, on page 489 they assert that "The bright petals, attractive scent and sweet nectar of flowers are undoubtedly an evolutionary response to insect pollination. . . . Somewhere along the line, an ancestral plant 'discovered' that it could attract bees by smelling like one."

Perhaps it is this kind of compelling logic and strict scientific evidence which the complaining evolutionists find to be so much more acceptable than the simple Genesis narrative that "in the beginning God made heaven and earth."

APRIL 23, 1982

MORE ON SCIENCE AND CREATION

My January 1 column, "The Intolerance of some scientists" continues to evoke extensive response, especially as transmitted to me directly. Much of it has been supportive and constructive, some has been critical. Be that as it may, I would urge respondents to send their statements to the editor, rather than to me, so that they can be considered for publication.

Since there are numerous indications that the issue will remain topical, let us consider a few aspects more fully. However, before proceeding further I shall, for obvious reasons, do something which I have never done since I began writing this column in January, 1964; I shall summarize my personal educational background in this area.

For years I have read widely in the literature. One of my two major undergraduate fields at UBC was in biology. While completing my M.A. at the University of California (Berkeley), I studied the history of science under Thomas Kuhn, probably the best American expert in that field. During three years of doctoral study—I completed a Ph.D. in 1965—I took several courses in scientific methodology.

Thus, while I acknowledge the well-intentioned and balanced comments by several readers, I can assure them that I am quite familiar with the various usages of "theory" and "law" in the physical sciences. I still stand by my January 1 statement that "evolutionism is only a theory." Granted, for most biologists it functions as a standard operating principle but it remains a theory, not a law. It has not been demonstrated to be valid. Indeed, in terms of the basic distinction between law and theory which many scientists accept, it cannot ever be demonstrated to be valid. Conversely, the law of gravity is scientifically verifiable. Granted, in an ultimate sense it, together with other scientific laws, may not be "provable," but it can be confirmed by testing. The spherical shape of the earth, once vigorously disputed, is clearly demonstrable. That is no mere theory. The theory of evolution, still disputed, is, in contrast, definitely not demonstrable. It cannot be tested even though some biologists believe that ontogeny (the life history of an individual organism) recepitulates phylogeny (the evolution of an animal or vegetable type).

At this point let me remind some critics of the once commonplace Dalton Atomic Theory (not to be confused with other atomic theories). For more than a century most scientists fully accepted Dalton's theory that an atom was indivisible, and found it to be a very useful operating principle. However, their faith in Dalton's assertion proved to be unfounded when scientists split the atom and produced the atomic bomb. Dalton's theory was only theory, not law.

Of course, there are certain theories, such as the theory of relativity, which are fully accepted as valid. Certain primary, or high-level theories have universal acceptance because there is no contradictory evidence. While there is obviously evidence of categories of evolution, the theory of evolution, taken as a whole, remains at best a second-level theory, one which is rejected by more than a few reputable scientists.

One other point must be made.

Several respondents object to having the creationist perspective explained in class because it is not sufficiently ''scientific'' and because the instructors, in the main, do not accept it. These critics are doubtless committed to honesty, openness, and a serious search for truth, but in this instance they have, I suggest, missed the point.

In high school and university education a teacher does not explain only that which he believes; he discusses and explains other viewpoints also. For example, for two decades I have taught courses dealing with political theories—as a standard practice I have explained Marxism and Soviet Communism. I include these not because of their intrinsic rightness, let alone any personal commitment to them, but because they are significant. They may be mainly inaccurate but they are widely-held alternative explanations of political phenomena.

Though I think that Marxism and Soviet Communism rest largely on false assumptions, I also believe that my students should understand these ideologies. To that end I assign writings by Marxists and bring in Marxist lecturers.

If I followed the logic of certain readers, I suppose that I should teach no Marxism or communism whatsoever. Since I do not personally accept these ideologies and since I judge them to be mainly in error, presumably I should simply ignore them. Fortunately most social scientists, while rejecting these ideologies, do not take such a narrow-minded stance.

Some ''creationists'' may ask for other norms but some of us ask only for the following. We want instructors in biology to explain the creationist view, and to do so without condescending arrogance. They do not have to believe it, let alone assert that it is science, but they should expose students to it. They should also add a few of the reputable creationist readings to the course syllabus. Surely a scientist's ego would not be destroyed if he acknowledged the existence of another prespective! Let him delineate his personal convictions but as a responsible academic he should both welcome and provide a variety of ideas, particularly ideas held by some leading scientists and accepted by tens of millions of people.

PART X

Christianity And Politics

GRATEFUL CITIZEN

Mennonite Central Committee (Canada) deserves to be commended for the continuing effort to witness of Christ to a spiritually and materially needy world. The recent news release delineating plans for 1967 revealed a deep concern to extend the impact of relevant faithfulness. Many of the items merit comment but two especially caught my eye.

Mennonite and Brethren in Christ churches are encouraged "to hold appropriate Centennial services on June 25, 1967, to commemorate the founding of the Dominion."

The leaders decided to "send to the Canadian Government early in the year a letter expressing the Mennonite and Brethren in Christ churches' appreciation for the freedoms they have enjoyed in Canada during the last century."

For years we have been quick to ask favors and services of the government. We have asked for exemption from military service, for assistance in immigration, for the right to form special societies and associations, for the privilege to affirm instead of to swear, for intervention on behalf of separated families, and much more. Generally we have been served well and expressions of gratitude are truly fitting. However, it seems to me that several basic facts and principles should be kept in mind.

(1) On a matter of technicality, we should avoid reference to "the last century," since some Mennonites came to Upper Canada following the American War of Independence, 1775-1783, and were treated well.

(2) While we express our gratitude for freedoms we should also inquire concerning ways in which the historic peace churches might render positive assistance to the government.

(3) Expressions of gratitude should perhaps be transmitted not only to the national government but also to the provincial, city, municipal, and (where applicable) county authorities as well, for many of our freedoms and benefits are more directly associated with these lower levels of civil authority. I would not be too surprised if some officeholders, especially at the lower levels, would be shock-stricken at the receipt of gratitude instead of complaints, criticisms, and tax gripes.

(4) While it is appropriate that we express our grateful sentiments to the current office-holders it is important to remember that basically we are grateful for our political-governmental system rather than merely the current incumbents. Our freedoms derive at least as much from the system, including the opposition parties, traditional customs, etc., as from those men to whom this precious heritage is currently entrusted. In expressing our thanks, let us not forget to thank God for our liberal-democratic system.

(5) While it is quite proper for church groups to conduct centennial services it is, in my opinion, inappropriate to make nationalistic patriotism a part of the Christian creed. I hope that we will never sink so low as to start thinking and talking about Christian-Canadianism. No state is intrinsically Christian. We are grateful for our Canadian political system because it is generally free, fair, and flexible—not because it is "Christian." (Nor would it be Christian if we printed "In God We Trust" on our coins.)

(6) Our expressions of thankfulness should avoid any disparaging of other

free societies. As I am writing this I am hearing the lyrics of "Where in the World But in America Can You Sing True Freedom's Song?", broadcast by a supposedly Christian radio station. Such pharasaical pomposity is, in my opinion, unbecoming to Christian citizens.

(7) This matter of gratitude for political freedom is serious business. Only a tiny fraction of the world's population is truly free. We are among the privileged few.

Let us be sincerely thankful that we do not live in a nation in which government is oppressive and arbitrary, or in a country with a Communist government, or in one in which partiotism tends to become a religious cult.

DEFINITIONS OF "SOCIAL-POLITICAL INVOLVEMENT"

As sure as the change of the seasons, and almost as frequently, the pros and cons of social-political involvement are reviewed, revamped, restructured, reinforced, reapplied, reevaluated, or simply repeated in this and numerous other Christian periodicals. That is as it should be. But sometimes, unfortunately, the exchanges and discussion seem to confuse rather than clarify the nature of the debate. Part of the problem, I suggest, is that people use the same terms but here, as elsewhere, mean quite different things. The result is that arguments miss each other, that people are accused of saying things they did not intend to say, and that answers are given for questions which were not asked.

Listed below are several definitions of "social-political involvement" which I have encountered in recent years. They are, clearly, not mutually exclusive, that is, a person can identify with more than one of the following.

(1) Some people define S.P.I. as an alternative to true Christianity. Thus, assuming that a person is concerned about overcoming evil, it is held that he has two opinions: either he gets involved in social-political affairs or he presents Christianity as the only correct antidote to evil. These are the alternatives!

(2) A related, yet essentially different definition employs the same categories but not the same relationship. Thus the argument is advanced that the more Christian a person is, the more he will get involved. The latter is an expression of the former; S.P.I. is a barometer of Christian maturity.

(3) A third definition is that S.P.I. means that a person makes politics a profession. Such a commitment, supposedly, is deplorable. (Even if Christian politicians "deserve our support.")

(4) A fourth definition of S.P.I. stresses institutional activity on the part of churches. This approach has its roots in the Social Gospel controversy of yesteryear. People who employ this definition often hold that the church has no business addressing itself to social or political issues—its only function is to "be the church."

(5) A fifth definition sees S.P.I. as essentially anti-evangelistic. Involvement in society may be a good thing but since, at least so the definition assumes, S.P.I. deals only with bodies and not with eternal souls, it is always second best. Some argue that because of its appeal, S.P.I. is a constant threat to creedal and practical orthodoxy.

(6) A sixth definition, and the one with which the present writer chooses to identify, defines S.P.I. as love in action, as Christian faith made practical. It holds that S.P.I. is a part of the larger phenomenon of Christian discipleship, in that, together with a more narrowly defined soul-concern, it constitutes an attempt to follow Jesus' example of expressing concern for the whole man. S.P.I., thus defined, is both personal and institutional, although the former is of primary significance. Put simply, it is God's love expressed through his followers to suffering, alienated, and lost fellow-man. It involves concern with social and political problems, although not necessarily, or even normally, through social-political means. The emphasis is on the object, not the method. That, in brief, is a

definition of S.P.I. with which I at present feel comfortable.

Maybe, as we explain what we mean, the areas of assumed disagreement will shrink markedly.

AUGUST 13, 1971

LEGALIZING MORALITY

As far as I can tell, most of our church members in B.C. were delighted to see the Bennett Government try to eliminate advertising for tobacco and alcoholic beverages. Many would like even stricter laws. Some, however, feel that the B.C. Government is trampling on freedoms and believe that the law should be rescinded. Similar feelings were aroused a few years ago by the so-called "Hate Literature Bill" produced by the Ottawa Government. More recently Christian periodicals carried numerous pro and con articles dealing with federal law changes concerning drugs, censorship, abortion, divorce, homosexuality and other social problems.

It appears that in general Christian leaders and writers in our day take one of two basic views. The dominant view among evangelicals seems to be that the governments should react to evil by passing more and more laws against it. Some nostalgics look back longingly to the prohibition era which existed in Canada during and after the First World War. The other view rests on the premise that "You can't legislate morality." Numerous times I have heard Christians argue the issue vehemently.

I venture to say that the dogmatic debaters in both camps have overlooked a basic fact. It is not the immediate aim of governments to legislate evil, prejudice, etc. out of existence but to control overt acts. The intent is to deal with behavior rather than directly with attitudes which may prompt such behavior. Thus one can demonstrate that although certain restrictive laws do not make people more moral they do greatly reduce evil behavior. The alcoholic is not intrinsically better if he is banned from driving an automobile but the roads are obviously made much safer thereby. A similar case can be made for much so-called restrictive legislation. The crucial point to be kept in mind is that in a free society the government's main aim is not to make people Christian (or more Christian) by legislation but to counteract action which they consider evil or destructive. Over time some laws may enhance morality but the responsibility for dealing with evil thoughts and attitudes, however defined, is left to the home and to voluntary associations including churches.

One writer recently noted that certain laws on race "demonstrate that, if legislation cannot eliminate prejudice, it can greatly reduce prejudical behavior." We do well to keep this observation in mind when we are tempted to ask government to put our ethical views into law or when we are inclined to be cynical about laws aimed at evil actions on the grounds that "you can't legislate morality."

RUNNING AWAY

In recent weeks a number of respected churchmen have alluded to the presumed desirability of total withdrawal from politics—from any kind of political involvement. As I mentioned to some of them, I not only think that such a stance is intrinsically un-Christian but also that it is a practical impossibility.

For example, we may decide not to vote but that does not alter the fact that our action (mistakenly called inaction) has influenced the outcome. Failure to support the greater good, or lesser evil, results in proportionately more support for a less acceptable candidate. And since we had an opportunity to influence the outcome, we are just as much responsible for it as if we had voted. Perhaps more.

In general, concerning elections and policy formation by public officials, inaction by citizens constitutes a major determinant of outcome. Many unfortunate ideas have prevailed because good people were silent. The bulk of German Christians during Hitler's regime remained silent as ruthless policies of Jewish extermination were implemented; their silence not only made the gassings easier but was taken to mean acquiescence. At least in the early years they had ability and opportunity to speak but partly because they were too other-worldly, and partly because they were too worldly, most said nothing.

Interestingly, despite numerous protestations of political aloofness, most of us have not hesitated to insist on justice for ourselves. Indeed, often we have begged for special privileges. We even seem to be offended if the Prime Minister does not find it possible to meet with our spokesmen annually. Ought we not to be more concerned when the governments we helped to elect act inhumanly or unjustly toward others?

Whether we like it or not, ever since Pentecost the Christian church has been a factor of major political significance and has greatly, for good or evil, influenced countless ethical policy decisions. The option of being politically irrelevant is simply not available.

Nor ought we to seek it. At a time when almost half of our total national income flows through government treasuries in some form of taxation or levy, we can hardly claim to have exercised responsible Christian stewardship by ignoring what happens to that half of our income. Have we nothing to say about public priorities?

Lest I be misunderstood let me hasten to say that the proclamation of the good news of salvation is our first responsibility but that does not mean we have only one responsibility. Not everything which Jesus instructed us to do bears directly on personal salvation. Love knows many forms. The imperative to give a thirsty person a cup of water and the example of the Good Samaritan are cases in point.

In our day much oppression and suffering can be alleviated only by government either because it is itself the culprit or because it is the only agency which has the capacity to deal with the particular evil. On the other hand, much of what governments do is worthy of our encouragement and support. In either instance a symbolic running away is not the answer.

Some contemporary Christian leaders still try to kid themselves that they can somehow avoid any kind of public accountability; they think they can remain totally neutral. Maybe they are deceiving themselves. What I see in many instances seems to be a blind endorsement of the status quo from which they benefit economically. Many have become quiet chaplains of their political and social systems. To come to terms so easily with an essentially un-Christian society strikes me as being less than laudable.

THE DOUBLE STANDARD

The inconsistency of government decision-making sometimes amazes me. Consider the following.

A few weeks ago a major Canadian sports organization planning to host an international competition was informed by our national government that if South African athletes would be attending, then Ottawa's financial assistance would not be forthcoming.

The Canadian government's reasoning, of course, was that they did not want to give the impression of supporting Apartheid, an authoritarian form of racial segregation practiced in South Africa. Unfortunately Ottawa's policy involves straining at a gnat while swallowing a camel or at least a bear—Chinese panda or Russian grizzly!

Now I hold no brief for racism, least of all the crass form inflicted on many non-whites in South Africa and have said so in print long ago. But let us not lose our perspective or sense of proportion. Why does our government, in our name, single out South Africa but ignore much worse segregation and persecution elsewhere? Or have our Ottawa politicians not heard about the salt mines, Siberian prison camps, Gulag Archipelago, Chinese torture chambers, and the mass liquidation of Christians on the Chinese mainland? One can at least visit the black "reserves" in South Africa (which in some ways are similar to our own red "reserves"), but where are the Christian "reserves" one can visit in Russia or China?

Assuming that our government acted out of sincere moral indignation, I suppose we shall shortly hear the first of a long series of pronouncements. In press release after press release Marc Lalonde or Allan MacEachern or even Pierre Trudeau himself will no doubt regretfully announce that hockey teams from communist countries and ping pong players from Peking are not welcome in Canada. Additionally, these spokesmen presumably will also have to disinvite many countries currently planning to participate in the 1976 Montreal Olympics.

That will be no easy task. The list of countries in which either official racism or dictatorships exist is a long one. It includes all of the Communist countries, many of the Arab countries, a score or more of Black African and Latin American countries, and such other assorted states as Australia, Afghanistan, and Rhodesia. Maybe Ottawa, given its abysmal record concerning our native peoples, should even disinvite itself!

But my biggest bone of contention involves the double standard with reference to the Soviet Union. Does our government really believe that there is more freedom in that vast republic than in South Africa? Does it think that Christians fare better under communism than blacks do under Apartheid? Does Ottawa know what happens to evangelical Christians in Russia who carry on public evangelization, even of their own children? Brother Vins and other survivors of persecution could readily provide the answers. Oh yes, we now have detente and the situation has improved in the USSR but the prisons for Christians have not yet been transformed into museums. The sickle is still used more as a sword than as a pruning hook and the hammer more to squelch opposition than to forge freedom.

Has consistency no place in government policy on moral matters?

Our Christian concern for justice and human dignity, and our sorrow when Christians and others are oppressed, compels us to speak up on their behalf.

GOVERNMENTAL DUPLICITY

While I firmly believe that the Christian church should not become pre-occupied with constant criticism of governments, I believe just as deeply that there are times when Christians should speak out. To be constantly silent in the face of corruption, deception, or duplicity is to be immoral.

The time has come, I suggest, for Canadian and American Christians not only to assert gratitude for freedom of expression but to utilize it once again. Duplicity and double standards must be challenged.

Consider the following inconsistencies. The U.S. government, and particularly State Secretary Kissinger, seems to be very anxious to bring about so-called majority rule in Rhodesia, South West Africa, and South Africa. In itself such a goal is fully commendable; racist apartheid policies should have been rejected by all civilized people long ago.

But why do Kissinger and company never press for majority rule in Uganda where President Idi Amin seems to be even more capricious and ruthless than any white government in southern Africa? And what about the many other black African undemocratic states where small minorities suppress large majorities? Then, of course, there are the communist countries of which one can hardly say that majorities are in control! When will we hear about them? I, for one, would be more impressed by Kissinger's pleadings for majority rule in southern Africa if I would hear him make equally strong self-determination speeches for the oppressed millions in Eastern Europe.

The Canadian governmental duplicity, while of less global significance, is even more blatant. Last spring, when the UN-sponsored Conference on Human Settlements was hosted by Canada in Vancouver, the Canadian government decided to welcome one and all, even the terrorist Palestine Liberation Organization. Since it was the host, the Ottawa government argued, it was obliged to accept the guest list prepared by the U.N.

However, a few months later, Prime Minister Trudeau invoked a totally different kind of logic or illogic. Although Canada and the International Olympic Committee had agreed earlier that the Canadian government would not interfere concerning the participation list, Trudeau and company suddenly started interfering. Representatives from Taiwan were kept out because Ottawa did not like the official name of the country. The nongovernment, terrorist PLO was welcome; law abiding citizens of the established government of the Republic of China (Taiwan) were not. What hypocrisy. As a citizen of Canada I resent such dishonesty and duplicity in the government which ostensibily speaks for all of Canada.

Concerned citizens should let their governments know what they think of such shoddy policies and practices perpetrated in their name.

AUGUST 10, 1979

PRAYER BREAKFASTS

During the past 15 years I have attended numerous prayer breakfasts, including civic-political prayer breakfasts. Sometimes I have come away with mixed feelings because the affair seemed to have an artificial quality about it.

Of course, I am totally in favor of morning meetings during which local, regional, provincial, or national leaders meet to seek God's guidance in their service to fellowman. These leaders and public servants carry onerous responsibilities and stand in need of all available help, human and divine.

My problem lies not with those affairs in which committed Christians honestly seek guidance in a publicized setting. Rather, my problem lies with those meetings, (I recall a few vividly) in which I got the distinct impression that prominent politicians participated only for political ends or out of a sense of duty. Those sessions bothered me. I don't like to see Christianity exploited or demeaned that way.

I don't wish to name names but let me say that I have less than profound respect for political leaders whose only apparent interest in any responsibility to God is uttered at the annual bacon bash. All year there is not the slightest indication of any interest in specifically Christian standards, at least not as related to public office-holding, and then, wham, one gets the full annual dose in about one hour!

Does God somehow have different standards for people who shunt him aside, provided they have won an election or hold some other prominent community position? I know of no basis for such a view. I submit that God cares not one whit about all the human recognition. We might feel thrilled if a mayor, premier, or prime minister who is hardly even a nominal Christian deigns to read one of the lessons but I don't think God is impressed even one iota. He does not give advanced standing to a politician, or a quarterback, or a millionaire, or an astronaut, or a beauty contest winner for those achievements. Why should we?

Let me know of a prayer breakfast—and there are some—where the participants, be they politicians or others, speak with integrity about seeking God's will and enablement and who demonstrate otherwise that their Christian concerns precede and outlast the flapjack affair and I shall support it wholeheartedly. But of empty words from bigwigs who hardly know Genesis from Jonah I have had enough.

The organizers should select the tone-setting participants with God's standards rather than press coverage in mind. Is such a suggestion too restrictive; is it asking for too much?

ELECTION 1980

At the time that this column is being written, in early February, nobody can predict the outcome of Canada's general election. And many Canadians seem not to care much who wins the day. Their favorite past-time nowadays seems to be heaping vilification and derision upon the major party leaders.

Unfortunately, those very same party leaders and some of their advisors have themselves contributed to public cynicism and apathy by their own irresponsible personal attacks. Concerned citizens should not hesitate to let these would-be public leaders know how we feel about such repugnant behavior. I have.

But let us not get carried away with negative feelings. Our political situation is more complex and consequential than the superficial partisan skirmishes of the day. The profound advantages of citizenship in a free and open society are not at issue in any one election.

And that is really the key point. The greatness of our free political system, and of others that are similar, lies not in who is elected but in how the system works. The crux of the matter is not who is campaigning but that there is a free political campaign. Similarly, the quality of the system is not measured mainly by the quality of the candidates but by the extent to which parties are free to field candidates and by the extent to which voters are free to vote as they please. (Additional dimensions of our excellent system are that individuals can on their own be independent electoral candidates and that voters can choose to refrain from voting without living in fear of any kind of disfavor or reprisal.)

Of course, over time, the good quality or relatively mediocre quality of political leadership in a free society has its consequences, but with reference to our overall free way of life the negative consequences are not very significant and generally short term. As long as we have free choice at election time, as long as our politicians respect our collective free choice, as long as the losers allow the winners to rule, and as long as the winners continue to arrange for free electoral choosing every few years or so, our free political system is secure.

Moreover, given the fact that our rulers must constantly consider the ways in which their present policies will influence their next assessment by the voters, it follows that, on balance, they will tend to pursue moderation and seek to please the majority by governing wisely. Unwise, unresponsive or irresponsible rulers will, before too long, presumably be replaced by an existing opposition party or by a new party more in line with voters' sentiments. The bottom line, then, in any free society, is that the system will likely continue to be free as long as large numbers of voters continue to express their electoral preferences and the political leaders and parties abide by the results. The continuation of the process, rather than any one set of results, constitutes the genius of the system.

Given the truly fine quality of Canada's political system it behooves all Canadian Christians to be filled with deep gratitude. The spirit of I Peter 2:12-17 and I Timothy 2:1-4 should be widely evident among us. Let us thank God for our free political system and, as we are instructed, let us ask God to give wisdom and direction to those who are temporarily entrusted with its operation. Significantly, with reference to an election campaign, it is quite consistent to thank for the system, pray for those in charge, and simultaneously vote for someone else to take over. Why, even in our church settings we pray for our leaders and are thankful for them even as, in our annual meetings or delegate conventions, we choose other leaders.

May God help us all to be better informed and more thankful citizens. Let us be alert, responsible in our criticisms, and more supportive of that which is right and righteous. Surely God requires that of us.

SEPTEMBER 11, 1981

EVALUATING GOVERNMENT

There is a sickness in society, a malaise whose symptoms include indifference and irresponsibility. In recent months, even years, this social illness has been particularly evident in the upper echelons of power. It has struck more than a few corporate executives, labor leaders, bankers, and government officials.

While indifference and irresponsibility is lamentable wherever it is found, let me focus at this time on government. After all, because it is the most important of all power centres in the land, its inadequate leadership is especially consequential.

Let me not be misunderstood. My criticisms, which are meant to be constructive, grow out of a deep gratitude to God for our open society, our generally free political institutions, and the people who make the whole thing work. Nonetheless, our basically good system is currently in dire straits.

My central point can be summarized as follows. The government of Canada, like all national governments, has the unique responsibility to govern the country but increasingly it seems unable or unwilling to do so. In short, our government is not performing its tasks adequately.

My concern does not involve minor details or the passing specifics of any particular public policy. The very basic role of government itself is the issue.

Let me hasten to add that the problem is not partisan. The brief P.C. interregnum provided no indication that the Clark Conservatives had any clearer sense of government responsibility or would, in actual fact, perform any better than the present Trudeau team.

Let us consider some specifics; more could be cited:

1. Government has the God-given responsibility to rule. Ruling involves leading, assisting, educating, informing, protecting, providing key services, regulating, planning, licencing, persuading and, in upholding the public's interest, having the last word in a public crisis and enforcing it.

If governments are unable or unwilling to rule, to uphold and enforce the public will, then they are inviting defiance, insurrection, and eventually anarchy. At the height of this year's catastrophic postal strike Prime Minister Trudeau stated that he opposed legislating the CUPW members back to work because they would probably not obey anyway. What an atitude for a prime minister! Who is in control of the country? Does our government allow itself to be blackmailed into capitulation? In the event, that's exactly what happened! Small wonder that many citizens are appalled.

2. Government must practice fiscal integrity. The country looks to governments to lead the way. What do we find? In recent years there has been incredible waste and inefficiency, fully documented by the Auditor-General, and massive deficits. Not surprisingly, the Auditor-General wrote that government spending was virtually out of control. Governments are failing us; we deserve something better.

3. Government has an obligation to perform certain services. Since time immemorial, for example, governments have assumed responsibility for postal services. But wait, times have changed in Canada.

On July 30, 1981, Postmaster General André Ouellet observed that if the postal strike was causing business to go bankrupt "they'd better get something better." But what can the public do? Government has the monopoly!

If the government is really unable to deliver the goods, literally, let them at least have the decency to permit private enterprise to set up an alternative. The government's attitude strikes me as being incredibly irresponsible.

4. Government has a responsibility for the needy in society. The present astronomically high interest rates and rampant inflation are causing much hardship and suffering. While the politicians look after themselves, countless thousands are losing their livelihoods and their homes, some are suffering from medical neglect, and one hears increasing reports of people going hungry. The government seems to have adopted a policy of drift. In this richly endowed land governments have a responsibility to do better than that.

5. Government has a God-given mandate to provide the type of environment which will enable the church to do its work. That is its most important task. The fact that most governments in the world do not seek to carry out this mandate or may not even acknowledge it, does not alter the fact.

All governments, including ours, need to be informed and reminded periodically. Government, too, is accountable to God. Perhaps, as governments contemplate their awesome task under God they will take their role more seriously.

As Christian citizens let us do our part. Let us pray for those in authority, let us be model citizens, and let us commend when we can and criticize when we must!

DECEMBER 4, 1981

ON CRITIZING TRUDEAU

During the past several months I have received numerous letters, not to mention phone calls, urging me to "expose" Prime Minister Trudeau. Some of the letters were accompanied by an intriguing assortment of newspaper clippings and other printed material.

The "evidence" included incredible rumors, some statements and experiences taken out of context, some totally unwarranted inferences, as well as some well-founded criticisms.

If I believed even half of the presumably damning evidence, I should at this very moment be nervously rushing to the nearest port of exit before the curtain falls on freedom in Canada, once and for all.

As regular readers of this column know, I have over the years and even very recently expressed strong criticism of various political leaders in Canada as well as elsewhere. Obviously, there was enough to be critical about: gross dishonesty, unbelievable neglect of those most needy, reckless militarism, irresponsibility in spending public monies, budget mismanagement resulting in grotesque deficits, nauseating exploitation of Christian symbols and slogans, spineless acquiescence to bullying by big business and big labor, and the incorporation of racism in immigration policies. The list could be long.

Of course, I have also expressed commendation, involving Canadian and other political leaders, when the situation seemed to warrant. Let us never forget that we owe much to our political leaders, in countries such as Canada, who continue to work diligently, be it in government or in opposition, to perpetuate one of the most open and free political systems in the world.

Many of the respondents I have in mind seem to have a totally one-sided view and that is, of course, their privilege. What I find both disappointing and disturbing, however, is an apparently widespread readiness to rush in with shrill accusations in the name of Christian righteousness. Of course, within very broad limits, our free society allows us even that indulgence. But surely, as Christians, we owe it to our God, our government, our church, and ourselves to exhibit integrity, responsibility, and good grace. Having some knowledge also helps.

Let me share with you some common allegations made against Prime Minister Trudeau, the most frequent object of vilification. The use of quotation marks designates actual quotation from letters.

1. Trudeau is secretly cooperating with Levesque in promoting Quebec separatism.

Many readers confuse two quite different matters. It is true that Trudeau is pushing hard to promote the French language and culture across Canada, perhaps more than many of us wish to see, but such a policy is *not* pro-separatist, indeed, its goal is exactly the opposite! The two pro-French stances are basically different.

2. Trudeau's proposed constitution, "is similar to that of Cuba, Russia, El Salvador."

Not so. There may be many flaws in both the original Ottawa proposal as well as the more recent Ottawa compromise, but both retain the basic ingredients of a free society. It is irresponsible to suggest otherwise. Neither document either spells out or would allow for, the establishment of oppressive dictatorships such as presently exist in the Soviet Union or Cuba.

3. Trudeau is "an unscrupulous Communist."

I respectfully disagree and urge my fellow-Christian critics to look at the evidence. True, in his younger years Trudeau hobnobbed with Communists and espoused democratic socialism, which is quite different from communism, but he has never espoused communism or ruled like Communists do.

4. One letter refers to "dictator Trudeau." Trudeau did indeed use a heavy hand during the 1970 FLQ crisis and has been insensitive on other occasions, but a dictator he is not. Dictators don't hold free elections, don't accept electoral defeat and step down (as Trudeau did), don't accept the existence of an independent judiciary, and don't allow for free press. This particular letter-writer probably owes Trudeau an apology.

5. "Once Trudeau's constitution takes effect only the French will have government jobs." The writer adds that even now the French have most government jobs. Wrong on both counts. The first is an obviously wild generalization; the second is simply not supported by statistics. (Incidentally, the racist tone of several letters was disquieting, to put it mildly.)

6. Sometimes the animosity had a broader target.

"There is only one alternative and that is for the four western provinces to get Independence from Ottawa. The Good Book says, 'be ye separate and come out from among them.'" Let the merit of such a separatist perspective be what it may, the above argument certainly rests on a novel interpretation of the biblical passage in question.

This column is not meant to be any defence of Mr. Trudeau or of his policies. In my view he has handled some things well, others not. I, for one, happen to think that this country would have been well served if Mr. Trudeau would have carried out his retirement from politics as announced in 1979. But that's not the issue. The issue before us is irresponsibility, hatred, bigotry, name-calling, and character assassination. Such responses coming from those who name the name of Christ, who are committed to follow his high ethic, to love as he loved—even to love the enemy—can hardly be termed God-honouring.

SEPTEMBER 10, 1982

WHAT SHOULD WE EXPECT FROM GOVERNMENT?

During the next several months this column will, in the main, focus on various apects of Canada's current political, economic, and social malaise. Virtually all of us are caught up in at least several elements of these difficulties and we do well to remind one another of some basic realities and guidelines.

More and more we are seriously affected by the ominous crises of the day and unless we are alert we may almost unknowingly find ourselves affirming exploitation, condoning injustice, and reinforcing animosities.

Since the size and significance of governments have increased immensely in recent decades, we should probably begin this series with a review of what our governments should properly be doing, at least according to this observer. Here is a partial list.

1. Within broad limits governments should protect freedoms and provide a climate of freedom, including freedom of religion.

Three aspects of this role warrant special note. First, the crunch usually involves freedoms for unpopular minorities. Not only because it itself is often an unpopular minority, but for sound theological reasons the faithful church should stand with governments in protecting the basic rights of all people.

Second, such a stance means that certain freedoms will be extended to error as well as truth. Many Christians find it hard to accept this fact and need to be reminded that in this age of grace that is exactly how God himself deals with mankind. Up to a certain point, freedom includes the right to do wrong.

Third, when a government commands the church to disobey God's mandate by requiring some form of state/emperor worship or by forbidding religious practices which according to any reasonable criteria hurt no one, it is stepping beyond its jurisdiction, it should be thus informed, and should accordingly be disobeyed. Where there is conflict, we obey God rather than Caesar.

2. Governments have a major role in restraining evil. God gave governments this mandate for two main reasons. First, ever since civil authority was initiated with the "mark of Cain," God has expressed his compassion for fallen man by authorizing the institutionalized restraint of evil among those who choose not to live a godly life. Accordingly, governments are to be commended rather than criticized for establishing responsible agencies for the restraint of evil and evil-doers. Second, God has authorized governments to restrain evil and maintain order because such an arrangement facilitates the task of the church in carrying out the Great Commission.

3. Given their ultimate control over society, governments, even though functioning at a sub-Christian level, have a major responsibility to ensure that society is made increasingly fair and humanitarian, that elemental needs are met for everyone, and that human dignity is protected and enhanced. After all, every person is made in the image of God; each life is highly valued. In this role the church can cooperate extensively with governments.

4. Governments should not become arbitrary or unpredictable on basic issues. Governments should not

exceed restraints which the constitution, formal or conventional, has placed upon it. Procedures should be fair, reasonable and generally open to the press and public.

5. Governments should themselves be subject to the laws which they make and enforce. A contradictory example undermines legitimacy and weakens public compliance.

6. Governments have a responsibility to address themselves to the pressing issues of the day such as the nuclear threat, acid rain, organized crime, racism, starvation in the midst of abundance, bureaucratic bungling and waste, appalling prison conditions, etc.

7. Governments should actively seek advice, suggestions, and criticism and as much as possible, be responsive. The church, in turn, should not hesitate to speak out on key issues, always reminding governments that ultimately they are responsible not only to society but also to God.

SEPTEMBER 24, 1982

ARE THERE GUIDELINES FOR GOVERNMENTS?

In last issue's column we reviewed some goals which citizens should reasonably expect governments to pursue. In this column we want to look at some general ethical guidelines which should be followed by governments in fulfilling their duties.

Of course, we must be very clear about the fact that we are focusing on governments in free societies. Concerning dictatorships of various kinds—be they military, monarchical, religious, party, personal, or some combination of these types—there is not much to talk about. As people in more than two-thirds of the world's countries currently know from first-hand experience, dictatorships operate without the constraints of accountability. They are, by definition, arbitrary and unpredictable. Though some dictatorial governments try to increase their popularity and "permanence" by implementing relatively enlightened policies, they are nevertheless still "a law unto themselves."

These guidelines are written with the Canadian political system in mind; with minor modifications they are relevant also for governments in other free countries. As we proceed to spell out some individual items we should remind ourselves to be perpetually grateful to God for the great privilege of living in a free society. Our criticisms, constructive in intent, should always be expressed with gratitude. As the great Sir Winston Churchill once observed, the liberal-democratic political system is indeed "the worst, except for all the rest."

(1) The public interest takes precedence. Governments are constantly tempted to initiate policies and procedures which enhance the well-being of their own political party or of some small but powerful pressure groups rather than the general public. More than a few times Canadian governments have been

self-serving in their conduct of government affairs. Granted, our system requires that some rewards be given to party activists who keep our whole free system functioning, but governments, whether national, provincial, or municipal, have no right to "milk the public purse" or secretly feather their own nests with ill-gotten gain.

(2) The long-term is more important than the short-term. Understandably, elected governments are much inclined to look no further than the next election. But short-term considerations should not take precedence. When they do, then massive troubles result. Future generations are loaded with a mountain of public debt, proper planning for future needs is ignored, the physical world is polluted, pressing crises involving small minorities are shunted aside, and necessary but politically unpopular decisions are postponed. Planning only for tomorrow usually creates big problems for the day after tomorrow.

(3) Procedural integrity is essential. In free countries governments know that they hold office only "in trust." The constitution in question, whether written or unwritten, sets forth rules and restraints which they must respect. Thus, they must call elections at certain times, or by a certain time, and must abide by the results of an election. Fortunately, the Canadian record in this regard is very good. Much less impressive is our governments' record involving the notion that governmental authority is not personal but is derived from the office with which the current office-holders have been temporarily entrusted. Our government leaders frequently forget that truly praiseworthy governments operate as servants rather than as masters.

(4) Proper and efficient use of time is important. Quite rightly many Canadians are critical of governments for wasting a lot of time. Incidentally, opposition parties play a key role here. Sometimes they are the greatest time wasters of all.

(5) Proper decorum is important. Clearly it is eminently better to have a shouting match than to joust with weapons but juvenile, even childish, behavior is surely deplorable. Dignity has always reinforced credibility.

(6) Mutual respect should be the norm. Neither side of the legislative chamber has a monopoly on good sense or good ideas. Both substance and reputation would be enhanced if government and opposition treated one another with more respect and acknowledged the quality of obviously good ideas, even if they had originated "across the aisle." To belittle, denounce, and reject everything that the "other" party does is a failure to practise good judgement and is an insult to the public.

(7) Public disclosure and procedural "openness" are praiseworthy. Governing by secret decision-making should be kept to a minimum. Our governments are much too quick to hide their deeds.

As Christian citizens we have a duty to be informed about how our governments carry out their mandate and a right to require that certain ethical guidelines be followed. If we all remain silent then we can hardly blame our rulers for concluding that we have nothing to say about how they should rule us.

GOVERNMENT AND CHURCH COOPERATION

Historically, Anabaptists have generally described church-state relations in a way which emphasizes the difference between church and state. Given their theology, the type of state which they knew and their own widespread suffering at the hands of the state, their negativism made a lot of sense. More often than not, state officials exploited their citizens, suppressed freedoms, and relentlessly persecuted dissenting free-thinkers such as Menno Simons and Conrad Grebel.

It is hardly surprising, then, that from the 16th century to the 20th, our forefathers saw the state as evil and almost without exception rejected political involvement.

But times have changed. Granted, the political realm remains essentially sub-Christian, but its activities have now been extended to include vast new areas of generally praiseworthy activities. Accordingly, I am arguing that the same theology and view of service which caused the early and later Anabaptists to opt for withdrawal should cause us to opt for selective involvement and conditional cooperation.

I am not suggesting that the church, as church, should make cooperation with government its first priority. The church has a pre-eminent "higher" calling. But various church agencies and—if warranted—even the church itself, need to take the whole matter of cooperating with government very seriously.

Modern governments in free societies are vastly different from those who martyred many of our forebears, as they are also very different from the dictatorships which still dominate most of the world. Our governments now undertake numerous service tasks, many of them initiated by the Christian church itself. As individuals we know this and are even involved increasingly in both the political and administrative aspects of governing, but as a church we seem still to cling to outdated views.

Of course, for decades, if not generations, we have not hesitated to request governments to do special favors for us. We have petitioned for exemption from military activities, we have sought special migration privileges, we have asked for permission to have "block" settlement patterns, we have urged reluctant officials to grant us special educational and linguistic favors, and much more. A full listing of benefits which we have requested for ourselves would indeed be a long one.

But somehow we have largely deluded ourselves into thinking that when we interact with politicians concerning benefits for ourselves, such activity is not political. As any student of politics knows, whatever such petitioners may think, such attempts to influence policies is standard political activity. Politicians and administrators encounter it every day.

My plea is that we bring our attitudes into line with reality, that we become more other-oriented in our attempts to influence government policies, and that we recognize new opportunities and responsibilities for what they are. In short, we need an extended application of the principle of Christian servanthood, always keeping in mind that we have a mandate to practice such an ethic of love and compassion in all situations that permit it and to avoid these situations that do not.

In Canada, in recent years, there have been some excellent examples of "church"—government cooperation involving Mennonites. Let me cite ten specific examples; several involve MCC (Canada), some involve other church agencies, while some involve congregations or denominations:

(1) Immigration arrangements, including the family re-unification program. For more than a hundred years Mennonites in Canada have worked closely with various governments. The result has been mutually advantageous.

(2) Allocation of surplus commodities. At various times Canadian (and U.S.) governments have made available surplus commodities, especially food items, for distribution to needy people throughout the world.

(3) Granting of CIDA funds to MCC and Missions/Services. For several years the Canadian International Development Agency has made substantial "third world" development funds available to MCC and our Missions Board.

(4) For some ten years or so, various provincial and national governments have matched, i.e., doubled, certain sums raised for foreign relief. Thus both charity and tax dollars were put to good use.

(5) Refugee sponsorship. This experience, centering on Indochinese refugees, is well-known and has generally been a very successful joint venture.

(6) Services for Native peoples. Though limited in scope, some fine examples of joint assistance to Native Canadians have occurred.

(7) Assistance in the construction and operation of various types of health-care facilities.

(8) Assistance in the establishment and operation of the Food Bank.

(9) The availability of government grants and loans to student studying at some of our secondary and post-secondary schools. In addition, some provinces designate some funds to the schools directly.

(10) The availability of grants and loans for construction and operation of retirement centres.

Numerous other examples could be cited but even this list makes the point. In many areas the church can work with government. While we must be careful not to develop dependency or to accept reprehensible conditions, let us recognize the many opportunities, let us utilize them wisely, and let us be thankful.

CRITICIZING GOVERNMENT

In the previous column we saw that many governmental activities deserve our wholehearted support, indeed, increasing numbers of programs involve church-state cooperation. But there is another side to the matter. At times responsible Christian citizenship requires us to be critical. While integrity causes us to be candid, Christian tact and an awareness of our own inadequacies dictate that we maintain a balanced perspective.

Further, it is important that we distinguish between criticism of the political system and criticism of the office-holders of the day. We can quite properly point to the weaknesses in leadership and failure in policies without minimizing our gratitude for and support of our free political system.

Additionally, the criticisms cited below are not intended to be partisan but are examples of general categories of inadequacy.

(1) *Financial mismanagement.* No private firm could last a year if it operated like most of our governments do. It seems as if many leaders simply don't care how badly the numerous departments and agencies are run. The national Auditor-General made the point bluntly in his 1976 annual report to parliament: ". . . co-ordination and guidance by central government agencies of financial management and control practices" in most Crown corporations "are virtually non-existent." Many of us had suspected it all along. Nobody seems to be minding the store. Subsequent annual reports are hardly less severe. Indeed, each year's litany of woe and almost unbelievable government neglect is enough to make a person both angry and depressed. Why doesn't the government clean up its act? Why are the very reasonable recommendations of the Auditor-General not implemented?

(2) *Waste.* The examples are almost endless. Why did the national government spend a billion dollars to build Mirabel airport in the 1970s when scores of experts told them that the 50 km distance to Montreal would make it largely useless? At present the hardly used airport loses almost a million dollars a week, depending on which set of calculations one believes. You and I make up the difference.

Provincially the situation is no better. On June 17, 1981 an Ontario cabinet minister and two assistants chartered a flight from Toronto to Thunder Bay, so that the minister could make a speech there. The cost was $3,985. However, that day the regularly scheduled airlines provided 7 different flights to the same city at $287 per person or $867 for the three; $3,124 was wasted. My files contain hundreds upon hundreds of similar examples.

(3) *Abuse of trust.* When a cabinet minister at great cost relocates a major regional headquarters to his own riding, as our minister of defence recently did, we should be outraged. Is there no respect for decency and fairness? Time and again government officials utilize their power positions for personal gain. Responsible citizens should not remain silent.

(4) *Excessive expenditure.* My files are thick; here is one recent case. According to news accounts, Edmund Clark, a senior Ottawa bureaucrat, will be taking a year off to work with a private firm in France. His government salary and benefits will continue at about $90,200, he and his

family will get an educational grant of $20,000, a housing allowance of $20,000 and assorted "other items." How can our government expect us all to tighten our belts if it throws money around that way?

(5) *Accumulation of debt.* Again, the facts are depressing. The national government's cumulative deficit has tripled during the past decade to more than $120 billion. That's more than $5,000 for every man, woman and child in the country! And that sum will increase at least $20 billion this year alone! National debt interest costs have doubled in the last ten years and presently consume about 20% of every tax dollar collected. Provincial and municipal debts are also skyrocketing. And we are ready, with about 42% of all income being taxed away, approaching a critical disincentive and crisis point.

(6) *Indifference to urgent needs.* What are our governments doing about the acid rain that is killing hundreds of lakes? What is being done to achieve justice for Native peoples? What is being done to alleviate utterly appalling and over-crowded prison conditions? Issues clamouring for attention are many.

As Christian citizens we have a duty to let ourselves be heard. Complaining to governments must never become a first priority but neither should it be entirely overlooked. After all, the money being spent—and sometimes wasted—is our money and we cannot easily shirk all responsibility for what is done or not done. After all, opportunity plus ability creates responsibility.

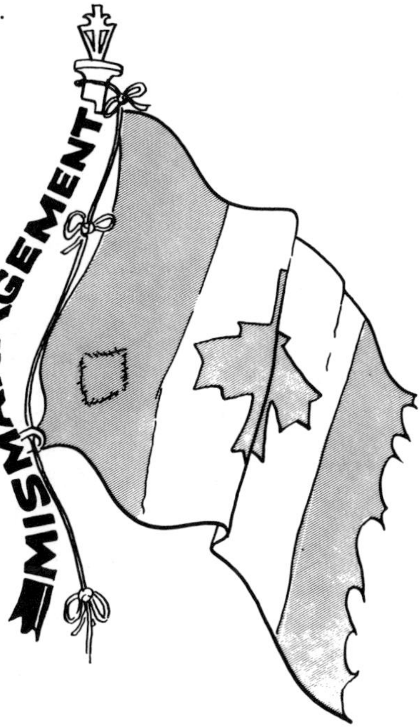

WHAT SHOULD GOVERNMENTS EXPECT FROM US?

In the first column in this series we asked the question, "What should we expect from government?" In this fifth and last item in the series we ask the reverse question. The query is important not only because our perspective must be balanced, but also because in many countries government has replaced the church as the most important single factor influencing individuals.

(1) Governments should expect citizens to be law-abiding. This first principle is sound but we must allow for exceptions. We try to obey all laws which do not conflict with God's requirements. Thus our submission and obedience are always conditional. When we find it necessary to disobey the law, we are prepared to take the consequences—as Martin Luther King and many others have done.

(2) Governments should expect us to be informed. I am frequently surprised to encounter Christians who feel that they have no obligation to find out what is going on in their community, their country, or the world! How can we come to grips with the matter of being good neighbors, in the various arenas, if we maintain ignorance about our neighbors and what is being done to them?

(3) Government should expect Christian citizens to be their most perceptive critics. Precisely because we hold to Christ's higher ethic we have a basis for addressing all sub-Christian performance, including our own. Accordingly, even as we obey a law we do not like, or as we disobey a law which requires us to act in a God-displeasing manner, we urge the governments to change their ways and their priorities. The issue at hand may involve racism, prejudicial immigration regulations, corruption in the bureaucracy, the nature of foreign aid, militarism, desecration of the environment, and much more.

As we seek to be responsible Christian critics, we should realize that governments will likely not be much impressed if the only issues about which we protest are those which are self-serving. If we, in the name of responsible Christian citizenship, advance only our own cause and ignore the pressing needs of others, then our credibility is largely gone. All other groups look after themselves; if we do nothing more, then how are we different? Let the excellent work of the Citizens for Public Justice, formerly the Committee on Justice and Liberty, be our example.

For governments, the nature of Christian response should be an important indicator of the moral level of government policy.

(4) Governments should expect us to support them in their morally sound undertakings. We are often quick to criticize—are we also quick to voice approval when praiseworthy ventures are undertaken? A personally written letter can have great effect. If, for example, you agree with government policies aimed at curbing alcoholism and drunken driving, or at enhancing religious freedom, why not let the authorities know?

In particular we should cooperate with government, and support them as we have opportunity, concerning those situations where both church and government are seeking to resolve the same problem. Issues dealing with immigrant sponsorship, foreign aid, emergency relief, and assistance to Native people come to mind.

(5) We should be thankful. Although our political system with its freedoms and opportunities is more important than the quality of the current office holders, we should thank those incumbents who help to keep the system going.

(6) We should pray for those who rule over us. The biblical injunctions are clear. We shall pray for our rulers even when we do not like how they rule, for then, precisely, they need more understanding and wisdom.

(7) Finally, we need to remind governments that ultimately they, too, are accountable to God as individuals and as a governing body. There is a Prime Minister of prime ministers, a President of presidents, a Lord of lords, a King of kings!

Obviously, governments should expect differing kinds of response depending on whether the response is personal, congregational, denominational, regional, or even ecumenical. There is a time and place for each. We need to discern what is timely and appropriate.

Governments have a right to expect certain things from Christian citizens; are we meeting those legitimate expectations?

A CITIZEN'S LAMENT

God, on this national Remembrance Day I feel like complaining, and I think I have good reasons to feel this way. I know we're supposed to be thankful for our leaders and our governmental system, but that's not easy.

Lord, you know the details; you know the left and the right, not to mention the wrong, better than I do, but let me say something anyway. When I look at our political system, the one which we are to remember today and for which you tell us to be thankful, I'm depressed. I see problems, contradictions, injustice, and neglect. I look at our governments and I'm disappointed about the past, concerned about the present, and alarmed about the future. But let me be more specific.

- Our political leaders often make promises which they don't keep, especially at election time. I just can't believe them anymore. They're like certain salesmen I know, and some neighbors, too. They often say one thing and then do the opposite.
- And often they waste a lot of time. The way those loud bells were kept ringing day after day made no sense. At other times it's less noisy but just as petty and pointless. You'd think they'd stop talking when they run out of ideas but they don't!
- Wasting time is bad enough, but wasting money, lots of money, is worse. I don't know, God, how closely you read the Auditor General's Reports but if you'll scan the last two again you'll know exactly what I mean.
- Worse still, they spend money that they don't have—billions of dollars. The deficits are staggering and there seems to be no end in sight. Don't they realize that someday somebody has to pay the bills? I'm trying to be grateful, Lord, but it's hard.
- Then, too, they seem always to be fighting. They can't seem to agree on anything. Why are they always in opposition and constantly bickering? Can't they get their act together, decide what's good for the province or the country, and do it?
- It's also sad that many really important things never get done. Some people who desperately need help don't get it. I guess they don't have enough political clout—or votes.
- Oh yes, I'm also upset because so many big shots abuse their position for selfish gain. You'll remember the shenanigans that went on when the Montreal Olympic facilities were built. Well, the disease, in question, chronic avaricitis corruptitis politicus, is not limited to Montreal.
- Also, often our lawmakers don't do what the majority wants. Don't they believe in majority rule? Why do they ignore us? Who do they think they are? Who do they think feeds and clothes them?
- One other thing really bothers me; they seem always to cater to the wealthy people, the powerful groups. Why do they ignore the little people?
- Finally, I'm angry—I think it's a case of righteous indignation—because they talk peace but prepare for war. Why? Don't they know what a nuclear holocaust would mean? We need ploughshares and pruning hooks and emergency relief for refugee camps but we're getting bullets and bombs and cruise missiles.

When I look at this list of problems I get perplexed. What is a Christian citizen to do? Surely, Lord, you can see why I feel as I do and why I'm writing this lament. Together with many other right-thinking, God-fearing citizens I'm going to act. Next time there's a local or provincial or national election we'll throw the rascals out. I'll make use of my freedom not only to tell them what I think but to vote for somebody else.

Come to think of it, those are rather important freedoms. As I've said, Lord, our system has many flaws but, on second thought, there is another way of looking at it. Perhaps, if I were forced a little, and given enough time, I could even agree with the view that our democratic political system is indeed the worst—except for all the rest!

PART XI

Church And State

JANUARY 31, 1964

CHRISTIAN NATIONALISM

For some years now it has been evident that an increasing number of evangelical Christians are accepting hatred of certain "enemy" states and glorification of one's own nation as central tenets of their doctrine. A list of contemporary groups and leading individuals who subscribe to this view would be a long one indeed.

One of the leading proponents of this unfortunate fusion of Christianity and nationalism is *Billy James Hargis,* director of Christian Crusade, whose headquarters is in Tulsa, Oklahoma. He has preached his view forcefully and effectively far and wide. Recently he organized an 8-hour radio marathon on the general theme of a return to Christian Americanism. Among his special speakers were such well-known ministers as John R. Rice, Bob Jones Sr., and Bob Jones Jr.

How sad it is that these talented and dedicated servants of God are being drawn in by this cult. One wonders how big a swath it will yet manage to cut. Somehow, in these tension-filled times a gospel of hate seems to have a greater appeal for some than does a Gospel of Love. Let us beware lest we too be drawn into this maelstrom.

I cite the following quotation as an indication of where this fusion of nationalism with Christianity can lead to. I am quoting part of the Profession of Faith formulated by German Christians in April, 1933.

"God has created me a German; Germanism is a gift of God. God wills it that I fight for Germany. War service in no way injures the Christian conscience, but is obedience to God . . . For a German the church is a community of believers, which is under the obligation to fight for a Christian Germany. The object of the Faith Movement of German Christians is one Evangelical German Church for the whole Reich. Adolf Hitler's state calls to the church. The church has heard the call . . ."

AUGUST 14, 1964

CONCERNING THE FLAG

At the time that this is written it seems as if our country will soon have a distinctive national flag. Personally, I favor the idea although I do not consider the issue to be outstandingly important.

A bigger issue, at least as I see it, concerns the reaction of truly Christian churches after we have a flag. Are we going to follow the example of most churches in the United States, including many Mennonite Brethren, and plant the flag next to the pulpit? I believe that to do so would very unwise. As a denomination whose main claim to existence is a strong emphasis on the separated church and the separated life, we would be defeating our own purpose by advertising a supposed, or at least implied, ideological identification of church with state. Let us learn from the experiences of our brethren to the south.

Significantly, more than a few of these American brethren have recently expressed concern over the inroads that the cult of Christian Americanism is making in our own denomination. I share their concern. Yet it seems to me that by placing the flag alongside the Bible, implying thereby that they are somehow equally worthy of adoration and allegiance, some of these brethren are encouraging the very thing which troubles them. The church is neither on a par with the state nor subordinate to it—it is superior to it.

I feel that a major cause of the problem is the failure to understand the concept of "dual allegiance." Many seem to have forgotten that this concept is valid not for the church as such but only for individual Christians. The church has only one allegiance and recognizes only one head. Since the true church represents the claims of Christ it is itself one of the two areas of allegiance for the individual believer.

The symbol of the Kingdom of God is not the swastika, not the American eagle, not the Canadian beaver, not a flag or a country, but the Bible and the cross about which it tells.

UNFLAGGING DEVOTION

Three recent news items pertaining to patriotism and the place of a national flag are worthy of note. Commenting on the current surge of Christian-Americanism the noted historian Arnold Toynbee reported that some French critics of U.S. policies "tore down the American national flag from a Christian cathedral built by Americans in Paris and burned the flag in public." He agrees that such action was extremely rude but asks the pointed question, "What was the symbol of a pagan divinity doing in a Christian church?" The situation is a sad one when the children of light need to be told the truth by the children of darkness.

The second news item contains the report that the U.S. Congress has passed a law making the defacing or burning of Old Glory a major crime. There are, of course, more proper things to do than destroy flags, but the noteworthy point is that flag-defacing is termed "flag desecration." My dictionary tells me that only that which is sacred can be desecrated. The U.S. flag, or any other state flag, is not sacred, and anyone who claims that it is, would therefore seem to be indulging in idol worship, if not outright blasphemy. It is proper to be patriotic and to take pride in one's country and its flag, but to bring in elements of worship is wrong.

The third news story describes a political event which occurred in Sacramento, capital of California. As reported, the State Assembly recently discussed the propriety of passing an Assembly resolution urging every citizen of the state to continue using the phrase "under God" when repeating the pledge of allegiance, even if a court should rule that the phrase is unconstitutional. The resolution, authored by Assemblyman John Quimby, states, in part, "The greatness of our nation is owing in great part to the fact that we have God on our side." Thus it is that sincere, well-meaning people make the God of the universe a mere patron saint and tribal deity.

PENNER VS. BEAVER COUNTY DRAFT BOARD

Jerry Allen Penner, a conscientious objector from Balko, Oklahoma, is finally a free man again. Ever since he registered with his local draft board in 1964 he has faced one problem after the other, largely because the board to which he was assigned refused to grant him CO status. Their stated reasons were specious; their real reasons were probably that they did not want to break their tradition of refusing such requests. Despite the fact that United States law clearly provides for alternative service the Beaver County Board, which is not alone in this stance, refused to grant Penner's request.

After all administrative appeals had been exhausted, the U.S. Department of Justice prosecuted Mr. Penner and on April 8 1968, Judge Fred Daugherty sentenced him to the maximum prison term—five years in the federal penitentiary. This decision by a federal district court was appealed to the next level in that region, the tenth circuit court, where the original decision was upheld.

At this point the MCC Peace Section was consulted for advice and assistance. It was finally decided that despite the uncertainty of the outcome and the high costs involved, the case would be appealed to the Supreme Court of the United States.

The first victory was achieved when the Court agreed to look into the case; the second, more significant victory was announced recently when the U.S. Solicitor General, E.N. Griswold, whose responsibility it is to support the government's decisions in such cases, took the unexpected and virtually unheard of step of supporting Penner. He stated in his recommendations to the Supreme Court that the conviction of Penner was an obvious miscarriage of justice and implied that it was probably related to strong public sentiment against his stand. He recommended that the decision be reversed.

On June 29, 1970 the Supreme Court issued the following order:

> "On the basis of a confession of error by the United States Solicitor General and of an independent review of the record, the petition for writ of certiorari is granted, the judgement of the Court of Appeals is vacated and the case is remanded to the United States District Court for the Western District of Oklahoma with instructions to dismiss the indictment."

The general facts of this case have been widely reported, as they certainly deserve to be. However, several points strike me as being worthy of special emphasis for readers of this periodical.

In the first place, the fact that Penner is a Mennonite Brethren and that he received much assistance from the MCC is somewhat ironic. During my short visits with Mennonite Brethren in Oklahoma and on the basis of general observation I would guess that the MCC, especially the Peace Section, is not a very popular institution in those parts. Nor has it been with Mennonite Brethren generally. Perhaps the Penner case will prompt us all to rethink some of our views.

In the second place it saddens me to hear that some of the strongest opposition to Penner came from fellow Mennonite Brethren. Again we are reminded how easy it is to transform our caesars into gods.

In the third place I wonder what the general Mennonite Brethren reaction would have been if sometime during those six frustrating years Penner would have made his way to Canada. I am convinced that many brethren would have thought of him as an "Un-American" coward, a poor Christian example, and perhaps an anti-freedom "leftist." It took the Supreme Court to spell out justice in this case (quite apart from a Christian ethic) and, unless I am seriously mistaken, to prevent considerable un-Christian condemnation.

Finally, I trust that hereafter the Mennonite Brethren churches will support MCC with greater enthusiasm; not blindly, for our organization invites our suggestions and thoughtful criticisms, but with more zeal.

SEPTEMBER 3, 1976

MISUSING SCRIPTURE

Quite properly, evangelical Christians often cite Scripture to clarify or emphasize some truth. As long as the verses cited are not taken out of context or presented as stating something which they do not in fact state, only those will object who are made uncomfortable by biblical truth. However, in those instances when verses are misused, fellow-Christians presumably have both a right and a duty to try to set things straight; always, of course, being willing to be set straight themselves.

Which brings me to the issue at hand. Throughout the celebration of the Canadian Centennial in 1967, throughout the current American Bicentennial celebration, repeatedly in the statements of spokesmen for Renaissance Canada and other "Christian patriotic" organizations, and often by Mennonite Brethren as well as other evangelical ministers, reference is made to II Chronicles 7:14. The verse reads as follows: "If my people, which are called by my name, shall humble themselves, and pray, and seek my face, and turn from their wicked ways; then will I hear from heaven, and will forgive their sins, and will heal their land."

The standard application of this verse is that if the Canadian population (sometimes the reference is to governments), or the American population as the case may be, will repent of certain evil practices, then God will bless (heal, make prosperous, etc.) the country in question. I suggest that such an application is false and blunts the cutting edge of the true evangelical call to discipleship.

God's promise was made to his people, those who had at some time made a clear commitment to follow him but had fallen into sin, hence, the reference to "my people." Now it seems patently obvious to me that the vast majority of Canadians or Americans have never made that initial commitment and therefore they are not included when God talks about "my people." Nor, of course, are most Americans or Canadians "called by my name," as the inspired writer puts it. In our day, committed Christians are the people who are called by his name. Christians are the New Testament people of Jehovah.

Furthermore, the reference to the "land" does not, I suggest, refer to a modern political state. It refers to actual land all right, the land of

Palestine, but in a situation and at a time when church and state, if we can use the modern equivalent terms, were united in a theocracy with God as functional head. Such a situation does not now prevail in Canada or the United States. Hence the promise does not apply to the recent or present governments of these countries or to the countries themselves.

Of course, God is always ready to forgive all sins of all repentant people, whether general populace or government officials. Should it ever happen that a modern state, together with the government, makes an authentic as contrasted with symbolic, submission to God, then II Chronicles 7:14 would doubtless apply. In the meantime it applies to what God calls "my people," the Christian church—nothing less and nothing more. To preach and teach otherwise probably does great violence to God's Word.

PRAYING FOR GOVERNMENT

Ever since I was a high school student I have had difficulty understanding I Timothy 2:1,2. There we read that "entreaties and prayers, petitions and thanksgivings, be made on behalf of all men, for kings and all who are in authority. . . ".

The comments on these verses which I heard from the pulpit in those years didn't help much. Time and again I heard preachers cite this passage and then, either in the sermon or in a prayer, thank God for "our government," often naming the prime minister (or premier, or president, or king/queen as the case might be) by name.

The whole thing didn't quite make sense; I was perplexed. How could a preacher on Sunday thank God for the prime minister or president by name and then on Monday, for very good and obvious reasons, support a political party that was trying to defeat him in the coming election?

Let me suggest a positive way out of the dilemma. In Paul's day there was virtually no distinction between government offices, or roles, together with the power that flowed from those offices, and the incumbents, that is, those people who exercised that power. The power of the office and of the person were fused. Thus, any reference to a king or to "those in authority" referred to both the people and the offices. Accordingly, while "entreaties, prayers, and petitions" probably referred more to the person and "thanksgiving" more to the office or institutional aspect, Paul made no distinction.

In our day, however, office and incumbent are clearly differentiated. Thus in Canada today when I thank God for our government I thank him specifically for our system of government, for the institutional power centers which regulate society, giving us peace, freedom and order. These offices and institutions are basic and continuous; the elected officials, the politicians, come and go. The governmental power lies in the institutions, not in the people who happen to be entrusted with it for a few short years. In the time of the Pharaohs, the Caesars, and the biblical kings it was different.

For me this means that when I thank God for governmental authority I thank him mainly for that which really constitutes the essence of the matter, the institutions. Only in a secondary sense do I thank him for those individuals who currently happen to occupy those institutions. Frequently, even as I thank God for our free system of government I simultaneously work, in a political and partisan sense, to put different individuals in charge.

I suggest that many preachers, and Christians generally, could avoid the appearance of duplicity if in our prayers we thanked God for our excellent system of political authority instead of focusing on the office-holders. Of course, and I want to stress the point, we should still pray for the office-holders. Whoever they happen to be, they need wisdom, insight, sound judgment, and much more. But that is not the same as making much ado about thankfulness for them. I can in good conscience pray that a prime minister or president be given those gifts, that he govern wisely, and that he be sensitive to divine direction, even as I do my part to have him replaced, should that seem prudent or necessary.

I often thank God for our wonderful system of government and its institutions; I also pray for, make entreaties for, those who hold office. That, in a brief statement, with all too brief an explanation, is how I try to follow the instruction laid down in I Timothy and at the same time to exercise my moral and civic duty as a citizen and voter.

GOD IN THE CONSTITUTION

A big verbal battle took place not long ago in the House of Commons about whether or not Canada's new constitution, assuming it survives the remaining obstacle course, should recognize the supremacy of God. After many words the pro-God forces won. If all goes well Canada will soon officially recognize God—on paper.

Many evangelical Christians who fought hard for this amendment are claiming a great victory. Without in any way wanting to impugn their motives or detract from their zeal, I must say that I remain unimpressed.

There are several reasons why I consider the "victory" to be largely hollow. In the first place, the experience south of the border substantially dilutes any enthusiasm I might have. In the 1950s the U.S. congress passed legislation putting "In God We Trust" on American currency and adding "one nation under God" to the American pledge of alliance. Doubtless many of the legislators had commendable motives but the net result is hardly impressive. One looks in vain for any tangible changes in public policy or governmental behavior resulting from these public assertions. The U.S. acts as other nations act; Americans live as other people live. But there are two major negative results. Having proclaimed these words, more than a few Americans seem to assume that God is on their side—the cult of Christian-Americanism received a great and unfortunate boost. Further, having officially identified the nation with God, some Americans seem to think that somehow that makes them Christians. By themselves of course, these words make no one Christian; words such as these come cheap and mean little. Words such as these produce self-deception.

My second general reason for considering the supposed "evangelical victory" to be mainly meaningless is that it has about it an aura of hypocrisy. If our lawmakers really were serious about giving God some proper place they might begin by allowing the establishment of specifically Christian radio stations across the land. I have written MP's and CRTC officials as well as others, and have concluded that the Ottawa decision-makers, some MP's excluded, are basically opposed to Christian radio. In any of Canada's major cities one is inundated with several (or more) almost identical "rock" and sheer drivel stations. Such proliferation of mindless noise appears to be acceptable even though not even all of the teenagers—and very few others—listen to the stuff. But try to get a licence for a first-rate Christian station, even one which would include much classical and other "good listening" music, and a mountain of resistance develops. If our law-makers began to change their "Act," literally, then I might take them seriously.

In the third place, there is no evidence to suggest that, apart from a score or so of evangelical MP's, our elected lawmakers really consider God's cause to be important. Of the Canadian public at large, some 90% to 95% give so little to charity that they are farther ahead to claim the standard $100 income tax charity deduction; one wonders if our MPs are significantly different. At present our MPs earn a basic $47,100 per year plus major benefits. They are about to vote themselves a substantial increase.

I wonder how much they give to God's cause! It would have been interesting to see how many MPs would have been eligible to vote if only those who tithe had been allowed to speak and to decide the question! Would pious platitudes have yielded to silence, with the exception of the handful of evangelicals? How many lawmakers could have voted? Could it really be that some lawmakers who use the $100 standard charity deduction actually, with a straight and unblushing face, made a great show about the pre-eminence of God?

Since the time of the Old Testament prophets, the God of the heavens has denounced hypocrisy, sham, religious paraphernalia, and empty words. The subsequent millenia have not changed his standard. I hope and pray that in our present case the church of Christ in Canada will not be shamed or embarrassed and the secular masses in this land will not be deceived or misled.

THE MARK OF CAIN

One of the dominant themes in this age of grace is that God's love extends even to those who reject him. People abandon God, but God does not abandon people. That is how it was right from the beginning.

When Cain killed Abel he feared for his life. He knew that he had committed a terrible deed and therefore he said to God, "and it will come about that whoever finds me will kill me."

Then God intervened. We read in Genesis 4:15 that the Lord put a mark on Cain. He was not to be killed by just anyone seeking to practise vengeance, by someone requiring a life for a life. The evil of killing was to be restrained. That is how it happened that civil authority—civil government—was first established. The initial and central purpose of civil authority was to restrain evil.

God's mandate to civil authorities was reaffirmed on several occasions in the New Testament. Romans 13, which must be read in context with the preceding chapter, underscores the point: "Therefore he who resists authority has opposed the ordinance of God; and they who have opposed will receive condemnation upon themselves for rulers are not a cause of fear for good behavior, but for evil." And again, "Do what is good, and you will have praise from the same; for it is a minister of God to you for good. But if you do what is evil, be afraid. . . ."

God thus established and ordained civil authority because he knew that without some sort of over-arching constraint, fallen mankind would run amok—anarchy and chaos would prevail. Besides, in God's great design society should remain sufficiently civil and orderly so that the church could get about its business.

But in our day the structure which was established to restrain evil in sub-Christian society has itself become, at least potentially, the greatest expression of evil. Toying with nuclear weapons capable of total human annihilation, civil authorities are now in a position to magnify incalculably the wanton death and destruction they were established to restrain. The restrainer has become the beast. The major civil authorities have the capability of exterminating God's highest creation on earth. And they are expanding their arsenals, they are shortening "delivery" time (to six minutes in Europe; less in the oceans), and they are raising their rhetoric and threats.

Therefore, the true children of God must insistently remind governments of the "mark of Cain;" governments were established to restrain evil, not to practice it. For while Christians have only one loyalty, we have a dual responsibility. We must affirm the truth which Jesus addressed to the agents of civil authorities, namely, they must not do violence to any one (Luke 3:14 KJV).

We know, of course, that we cannot expect discipleship from non-disciples but we must remind ourselves that from governments we have a right to expect decency, civility, and restraint.

Such a stance means many things, depending on time and place. For us in Canada now it means, among other things, that we strongly affirm Prime Minister Trudeau's attempt to get the nuclear powers to put some brakes on the mindless arms race. His current call may not be consistent with some of his other actions, and perhaps his motives may be mixed, but his call is more than timely.

In secular language our prime minister is reminding governments of the "mark of Cain." As Christians, following our Lord who is still the Prince of Peace, we concur wholeheartedly.

PART XII

War And Peace

OCTOBER 12, 1979

NUCLEAR MADNESS

On August 20, 1945, eleven days after an atomic bomb was dropped on Nagasaki, *Time* magazine stated: "The race had been won, the weapon had been used by those on whom civilization could best hope to depend; but the demonstration of power against living creatures instead of dead matter created a bottomless wound in the living conscience of the human family." If the dropping of those terrible bombs on Nagasaki and Hiroshima instead of on uninhabited areas was folly, then the present nuclear stock-piling can only be described as madness.

The major nuclear powers are set for a hellish overkill. In 1974 the USSR had 2600 nuclear weapons targeted on the US alone, many with multiple warheads which could be independently targeted on separate cities. That same year the US had 7940 nuclear weapons targeted on the Soviet Union. (Source: *The Defence Monitor,* August, 1974.) Since then, the U.S. has produced an average of one new strategic nuclear weapon every 8 hours. Presumably the U.S. now has well over 10,000 strategic nuclear weapons either targeted on the Soviet Union or available for quick delivery.

The reality is so terrifying that the mind cannot comprehend it. Two bombs produced hundreds of thousands of casualties in Japan and brought that powerful country to its knees. Now we are talking about 10,000 bombs in the US alone! The Soviet Union has also increased its nuclear stockpile, adding a bomb every 36 to 48 hours according to informed experts.

The quantum overkill is shocking and sickening. In 1974 the US had about 38 bombs for each one of the 200 or so Soviet cities with a population exceeding 100,000. By 1978 that number had easily exceeded 50! Estimates are that the Soviet Union has at least 15 bombs for each of the 230 or so American cities having 100,000 or more people.

But these staggering, mind-boggling statistics are only part of the story. The destructive power of these thousands of bombs has "mushroomed" drastically. The Hiroshima bomb of August 6, 1945 had an explosive power equal to 13,000 tons of T.N.T. By today's standards that is strictly bush league. The Hiroshima bomb killed more than 68,000 people and injured 76,000 more, many of whom slowly died horrible deaths. Today, the smallest of the 10,000 or so US bombs is about three times as powerful as the Hiroshima bomb and some are 16,000 (repeat, sixteen thousand) times more powerful!

Since 1976, and perhaps earlier, a single US Titan missile, or the Soviet equivalent, can deliver nuclear destructive power five times greater than all of the WW II US bombing raids. A single American B-52 bomber can carry four 24-megaton nuclear bombs, the equivalent of 7,385 Hiroshima bombs!

Ladon Sheats, to whom I am indebted for some of these statistics, has calculated that by 1976 the US had a nuclear striking capability of about 615,385 "Hiroshimas."

I shudder whenever I hear Christians clamor for more nuclear arms. War planners nowadays speak of "mutually assured destruction," MAD for short, and MADness it is. But Christians ought to be found in another camp. Or do we merely celebrate the birth, death, and resurrection of the Prince of Peace without taking his message seriously?

AFFIRMING CHRISTIAN PACIFISM

Were it not for the indescribable horror which stalks our world, one would be inclined to ignore the much-discussed nuclear threat. But how can a person remain silent? The threat is ever-present. The battles involving the Falkland Islands have illustrated once again how perilously close we are at any time to a nuclear holocaust. We cannot keep quiet.

After thirty-seven years of shuddering at the thought of nuclear attacks a certain weariness and fatigue seems to have overcome many of us, and understandably so. Yet the danger at present is greater than ever before. More than 50,000 nuclear weapons, some of them hundreds of times more powerful than the "test" bombs which leveled Hiroshima and Nagasaki, are poised and ready. Even more frightening, the number of countries possessing a nuclear arsenal, now about six or seven, may soon escalate sharply to twenty or more. As long as the nuclear arms race continues, who can tell where the reckless proliferation will end?

What should really pull us up short, however, is the startling fact that we who call ourselves "the historic peace churches" have, to a large degree, let others outpreach and outperform us. At least for many of us Mennonite Brethren that is the case. Consider some key events of the past months.

Billy Graham, who still asserts that he is "not a pacifist," has nevertheless courageously called upon the leaders of the nuclear powers to come to their senses, so to speak. In both Washington and Moscow he has, in the name of God, pled with the top rulers and generals not to destroy God's world. If he, who still presumably supports certain segments of militarism can speak that way, what should we be saying?

In major cities across Europe tens and hundreds of thousands of people are marching for common sense and for peace. That, too, should tell us something.

Even in staid, conservative Canada and across the U.S. many thousands are rallying around the cause. In the tradition of the great Martin Luther King and his kind, they are begging for the right to live. Non-violently they do what they can.

Even more striking is the fact that in several of the Communist countries, significant numbers of people are risking arrest and severe punishment by openly carrying banners against the rushing nuclear madness.

Throughout the world students, scientists, clergymen, physicians, housewives, workingmen, children, senior citizens, academics, middle class suburbanites and even veterans are letting themselves be seen and heard. People far and wide are increasingly realizing that mankind has entered an entirely new age; we are faced with a unique crisis, a threat that we can scarcely comprehend.

To be sure, for the faithful church the proclamation of the Christian gospel remains central, come what may. But that proclamation must now include more far-reaching and more incisive words of prophecy and judgement. When fallen man seeks to play God by toying with the destruction of human life on this planet, then we cannot remain silent. We must speak out or the stones will cry out!

It is a commendable form of Christian pacifism which refuses to become a part of the structures which deal in global death; it is an even higher form of Christian pacifism which, motivated by a caring concern and a limitless love, stands up to challenge those structures themselves.

The faithful church today still preaches the positive message of love, forgiveness, and salvation but it also stands in forthright opposition to that which is blatantly ungodly. Many of us can be easily aroused to condemn pornography, hedonism, exploitation of sex, racism, and a whole range of similar evils. Surely the sin of laying waste what God has made is a greater sin than any of these.

Let us exhort one another to preach and practice the whole gospel of love. If ever the world needed to hear the voice of the historic peace churches, this is the time; this is the historic moment.

PEACE ACTIVISM

In recent months much peace literature has crossed my desk; it constitutes a veritable flood. The mass media conveys a similar emphasis. Tens of thousands of peace marchers are demonstrating in Europe; the "Green Party" is organizing across Canada; the "peace camp" continues its months-long "vigil" on Parliament Hill; scores of limp anti-nuclear crusaders are arrested at various research and bomb-making sites; and on editorial and letters pages, and in pulpits and pews, the debate rages hot and long.

What is our reaction to the whole thing? Many of us, individually and collectively, are already heavily committed and much involved, but many are still questioning what they should do. Here are some propositions which may be useful as we sort out our priorites and shape right responses.

(1) Peace activism is the fruit, not the root of Christian commitment. A life-time of selfless peace activism does not make a person a Christian. Before one becomes a Christian, working for peace among men is a praiseworthy pursuit; after one becomes a Christian, it is a fruit of the Spirit. Only by accepting Christ as Saviour and Lord does a person become a Christian. If, by chance, any of us see peace-witnessing in itself as a means of becoming Christ-like, then we are falling for a new form of "righteousness by works."

(2) Peace activism is a very important pursuit, especially in light of the mind-boggling nuclear stockpile and the rampaging arms race. Today the world has many peace activists; in this climate of militarism the world needs thousands upon thousands of men and women for whom "peace with God" brings with it a powerful concern for "peace among men."

(3) Not all peace activists are Christians. Nor are all firefighters, physicians, nurses, teachers, farmers, fathers, mothers, or volunteers giving selflessly of themselves in "Third World" relief and development service. Of course, it is equally important to remind ourselves that not all peace activists are non-Christians.

(4) In many situations Christians cooperate with non-Christians and work closely with them. Many of us do it every day at work. Many of us do it extensively, even intensively, in our neighborhood, in vocational or professional associations, in business, and in family life.

(5) Not all goals are uniquely Christian. Building houses, combatting ignorance, cleaning up pollution, providing health-care and sponsoring destitute refugees can be undertaken by Christians and by non-Christians. Moreover, if I am part of a bucket brigade trying to save my neighbor's house from destruction by fire, I will not disrupt the emergency proceedings to ascertain if everyone involved in passing the buckets is a Christian. The global nuclear threat is incalculably more important than a house-fire.

(6) In peace activism, as in all Christian activity, the means must never undermine or contradict the ends. We do not practice evil to overcome evil. There are certain kinds of peace activism which are anathema to true Anabaptist peace activists. We do not indulge in activities which bring dishonour to our Lord.

(7) Christian peace activists should not be "unequally yoked together"

with non-Christian peace activists. Close organizational unity may send wrong signals and create serious pitfalls.

(8) Concerning peace activism, Christians are not in agreement, therefore let us be understanding and tolerant. This proposition cuts two ways. Activists must not deride non-activists; non-activists must not denounce activists. Let us be cautious and careful.

(9) Concerning peace activism, its forms, its priority, and especially involvement with non-Christians, the last word has not yet been spoken. Let us be receptive to brotherly counsel and open to additional enlightenment.

PART XIII

Social Issues

JANUARY 7, 1966

ON CAPITAL PUNISHMENT

I do not intend to review all the arguments concerning capital punishment (see Yoder or other writers for that), but I want to point to several vital aspects which many Christians seem to overlook.

(1) The Bible neither orders governments to practice capital punishment nor does it forbid them to do so. True, ancient Hebraic theocracy was to employ it, but neither the New Testament church nor the institutions of modern government can be equated to Hebraic theocracy.

(2) Modern governments have the right to practice capital punishment but this fact does not mean that they should do so; from the government's point of view the decision must be based on arguments and evidence not directly related to Scripture.

(3) There are, I suggest, many Old Testament injunctions and apparent commands which most Christians assume not to be applicable in the age of grace; why should capital punishment not be included in the same category with Exodus 22:18, "Thou shalt not suffer a witch to live"? (Or shall we again undertake the inhuman practice of witch-burning as it was zealously carried out by Christians till 200 years ago?)

(4) I am willing to be corrected if I am wrong, but it seems to me that Christians who urge governments to practice capital punishment have reverted to the logic of sub-Christian society. (Even then they might still be misreading the evidence.) How a Christian filled with Christ's love can urge anyone to kill another human being, even one who has himself killed, puzzles me.

(5) To advocate capital punishment while simultaneously endorsing the principle of Christian non-resistance strikes me as being fundamentally inconsistent.

(6) Evidence relating to the effectiveness of capital punishment as a deterrent to crime is at best inconclusive.

After having studied relevant Scripture and considerable analytical writing on the subject, both pro and con, I am totally opposed to the practice of capital punishment. Our Master instructed us to love all people, even our enemies; I do not want to be associated with any killing, no matter how indirect my connection or responsibility is, for I canot kill in love.

AND THE PEOPLE SAID—NOTHING!

When Castro's communist government executed some 500 Cuban anti-communists, shouts of self-righteous indignation filled the "Free World" skies.

When the Chinese Reds ruthlessly slaughtered thousands in their cruel extermination of "resistance," our mass media, our churches, and our political leaders let their protests be known far and wide.

When the communists in Hanoi recently threatened to execute the approximately 75 American airmen who had bombed North Vietnamese military installations, roads, and bridges, vehement protests and threats filled the air.

But when,as a result of the recent anti-communist military take-over in Indonesia, about 500,000 communists and other leftists were slaughtered without trials, and sometimes without evidence, hardly a whimper of protest was audible. The almost endless cutting of communist throats was simply taken in stride. I read no disapproving editorial and heard no exhortation to caution or justice.

How quickly our standards change. When our own compatriots are threatened, we become loud champions of the sanctity of human life, but when the objects of wrath are colored or Asian masses, and especially when they are Reds, we have nothing to say.

The recent and continuing Indonesian bloodbath is probably the most cruel and vengeful political murder campaign since the Nazis tried to exterminate the Jews (when the "Christian" West was notably silent as well). The colossal butchery is receiving hardly a byline in our North American daily press.

The true church of Christ denounces injustice and inhumanity wherever they occur. Murder never pleases God. Communist and non-communist blood is equally red, and equally precious in his sight.

THE CHAPLAINCY

Few of these columns have triggered as much response to me personally as did the recent one on Billy Graham's visit to Vietnam. Several people have asked me to explain what I meant by the statement, "Chaplains are salve for the conscience; prophets call men to repentance." In brief, here is the explanation.

The type of chaplaincy illustrated by some of Graham's comments relates not to personal "soul care" but to the policy of the country as a whole. This activity involves asking God to bless the nationalistic policies and military undertakings of one's own national government. The temptation to do this has plagued evangelical Christians for centuries, and most appear to have succumbed to the temptation. Many a preacher has urged his congregation to "support our boys in uniform; they are fighting to defend Christianity." Just a few weeks ago a New Westminster, B.C., listener asked the BIOLA Hour panel of experts to speak to the matter of guilt feelings which a soldier had about killing enemy soldiers. The more or less predictable answer was that while it is against God's will for one man to kill another, this divine injunction does not extend to killing while in uniform. "The situation is simply different," is the stock answer; Christian soldiers should have no guilt feelings. If one fights for one's country one should suppress these conscience qualms. It is this type of chaplaincy which I was criticising.

There appears to be no biblical or other justification for Christians to undertake the role of being chaplain to a nation. Who are we to make the God of the universe an ally of "our" army? Was God's will sought in the making of the government's Vietnam policy and the preparation of military plans? Furthermore, how can we assume that it is God's will that our side wins? Is the United States (or the West) a modern Israel? And even if it were, did God always desire ancient Israel to win? True, the Bible exhorts us to pray for our government, but the stated purpose of the prayer is to enable us to live and preach Christianity in a peaceful situation.

I may be in error on this point, but at present it is my conviction that while God may desire the U.S. to be the victor in Vietnam, both sides are guilty in the sight of God. It follows, then, that it is not a disciple's function to declare, unequivocally, that a specific army is fighting for God. Nor, it seems to me, do I have a right to tell people that if they kill while in uniform they should suppress all conscience qualms and guilt feelings.

There is, however, another kind of chaplaincy; that of personal concern. A Christian should witness to people everywhere, and that includes the military. Surely none but the most self-righteous legalist would say that a soldier who seeks spiritual help should not be given spiritual help. At this personal level, many a chaplain, uniformed or not, has helped individuals to become Christians. Some have even ministered to members of the opposing forces (prisoners of war, etc.). This type of witness I support whole-heartedly. The problem is, of course, that many of these chaplain-counsellors also speak out as chaplains to their country and to their government's policy. That aspect of the ministry I cannot support. In the field of battle there is great pressure put on chaplains to combine both roles, and that is why I have serious reservations about the adequacy of American and Canadian chaplaincy programs as presently constituted.

In sum, I support all efforts to help men to become Christians and faithful disciples, but I cannot support the activities of nationalistic "chaplain-Christians" who strive to make the God of the universe a mere tribal deity.

JANUARY 26, 1968

SAVED BY A BLACK HEART

In Sunday School we used to be told that a black heart brought eternal death and a white heart eternal life. Whatever the merits of using such phrases or of talking about "giving your heart to Jesus" (I think it is both distorting and misleading), the world is now witnessing an episode in which a "black" heart brought life.

Dr. Philip Blaiberg lives, at least at present, with a black man's heart beating in his chest. Aside from the fascinating medical and technological aspects of the case, several other facets are significant.

In the first place it is one of those strange twists of history that this most extreme form of racial integration should have occurred in rigidly segregated South Africa. As a part-Negro, Clive Haupt had to go through life with a "C" (for colored) stamped on his identification card. The "C" marked him as a second-class citizen.

While united in death, Haupt and Blaiberg could hardly even have met in life. By law they could not share the same park bench, sit beside each other on a bus, eat at the same restaurant, drink at the same fountain, go to the same restroom, attend the same school, live in the same part of town, or relax at the same beach. In fact, Haupt collapsed with a brain hemorrhage on a segregated beach. A "segregated" ambulance carried him to a segregated hospital. Even in death, and despite his sudden fame, Clive Haupt was buried in a segregated cemetery! Such is the strange nature of South African Apartheid.

Of particular significance to us is the fact that Haupt and Blaiberg could not even attend the same church, and mainly because white Christians clamored for such a law. (One wonders if the white children are taught to sing, "Red and yellow, black and white, All are precious in his sight. . . .") Most Christian observers must surely be filled with amazement and pity as they compare the attitudes and actions of the whites of South Africa with the way in which Jesus treated the socially unacceptable Samaritans.

But let us apply Christian standards not only in South Africa. I suspect that in various areas of our daily living we, too, live by the heresy of Apartheid, rather than by what Jesus lived and taught.

THE DODGERS

It is a sensitive area, as well as a controversial one, and may become even more so before the Vietnam conflict finally comes to an end. Since various church-related agencies are increasingly involving themselves in the problem it is probably time that the matter be raised in this periodical.

What should be our attitude towards American draft-dodgers who, by the thousands, have come, and are coming, to Canada? Views among Christian brethren are sharply divided on the matter; some see these men as irresponsible cowards while others deeply admire them as moral heroes of our day.

It is perhaps necessary that we remind ourselves that the so-called draft-dodgers are breaking no law, at least as far as I know. They are simply removing themselves from a political-legal jurisdication in which they are subject to the draft. They are not in the same legal class as military deserters. (The pros and cons of military desertion for conscience reasons is a major issue in its own right.)

Some observers have argued that Christians in Canada should condemn these evaders because, after all, U.S. laws permit the substitution of various forms of alternate service for military duty. Thus, why should anyone flee from the system?

In response to this argument others contend that unless an applicant is associated with one of the historic peace churches it may be very difficult for an American young man to get a conscientious objector classification. The case of Cassius Clay comes to mind. At the present time scores of young men are in U.S. jails because of their conscientious objection to the draft. Many have tried in vain to get a C.O. classification or reclassification.

Furthermore, many of these young men are conscientiously opposed to the entire draft system. For them the only available options are flight or imprisonment. We and our forefathers have often asked governments and societies to accept our "conscience reasons" even when they seemed weird to the general public. Shall we now do less for a similar dissenting minority?

Let us not forget that many of us are ourselves sons and grandsons of draft-dodgers. It would make a fascinating study to find out how many Canadian Mennonites can trace their origins to people who dodged military and political "obligations." It all began with the first "dodgers," who fled to what is now Canada from the rebelling colonies during the American Revolutionary War, 1775—1783. Thereafter they came mainly from Europe. Some of our most vocal anti-Communist spokesmen who now roundly denounce the present flight from the U.S. were themselves "dodgers" from the Russian draft system. Surely what was right at that time is justifiable now!

If it was right for the von Trapp family to flee from the Nazis (remember "Sound of Music"), if it was right for some of our forebears to flee from the Soviet claims on their lives, and if it is right for Canadian Mennonites at present to press for exemption (for reasons of conscience) from possible future military service, then it surely follows that the young Americans now heading north merit our sympathetic understanding and assistance, and especially if they are motivated by Christian considerations.

Personally, I would suggest that dissenters undertake some alternative service and present as strong a positive witness as possible. That, it seems to me, is the best Christian response to a difficult situation. But I will not condemn those who flee, and I will try to understand and be of help in each case as the opportunities arise.

BREATHTAKING

Most evangelical churches—certainly our own anabaptist-evangelical denomination—have taken some more or less formal stance against the use of tobacco. I agree with that view although I must, in good conscience, add that "Do Not Smoke" should not become the "fifth" spiritual law. It simply seems to me, I dare say "most of us," that smoking is a filthy, costly, offensive and generally degrading habit.

It is also bad for one's health, as we for years reminded ourselves in church rules. Evidence to support that view seems to be mounting steadily. Although I have no experience in this area, I am thoroughly convinced that smoking tobacco is bad and should be shunned by Christians.

Which brings me to the matter of consistency or, more precisely, the lack of it. If one of the main reasons for not smoking is that tobacco-polluted air harms the body, should we not be more concerned about other types of polluted air as well?

A few weeks ago an American Congressman, Mr. Lowell Weicker of Connecticut, stated that "To breathe for half a day in New York City is similar to smoking a pack of cigarettes." Thus, simply living in New York City makes one a "two

pack a day'' smoker year in, year out. Men, women, and children; the healthy and the sickly are all affected.

Admittedly New York is about the most polluted place one can find but numerous other American and some Canadian cities are basically in the same league. Should this not be of some concern to us? Is evil only an individualistic phenomenon?

One can argue, of course, that pollution does not generally involve personal decisions for the average individual and that therefore the matter of ethics is not involved. But that assertion cuts both ways. Is it not immoral to expose infants to a life-destroying environment without pressing for change? Does the combination of at least a latent ability and socio-political opportunity not create responsibility? Does the Biblical imperative to be faithful stewards of our physical bodies not apply in this area?

Traditionally we have talked figuratively and frequently of ''black hearts.'' The point being made remains central. However, there is also the matter of ''black lung'' disease and related ailments. A compelling concern for ''hearts'' need not prevent us from noting trends which may literally become breathtaking, concerning lungs.

Or maybe we should take another look at tobacco. Smoking once or twice a day in rural Alberta is obviously better for the body than living in some large city. On the other hand, we have the option, individually and collectively, of sending our concerns to our political representatives, which is where this column is headed.

KING RICHARD THE POOR

For most people in the Western world the U.S. president is the most important political leader. For Canadians, given our geography and relative size, it is undoubtedly true that our fate is influenced more by the man who lives at 1600 Pennsylvania Avenue than by the resident at 24 Sussex.

That is why we cannot afford to ignore events in Washington nor to dismiss as "foreign" the multi-faceted scandals which have rocked the great republic to the South. In short, the shortcomings, virtues, and values of President Nixon have very great significance for us.

In this connection a recent news story caught my eye. It seems that the President's release of his tax returns showed that the grand total of all his charitable donations in 1972 did not exceed the paltry sum of $290.

Now President Nixon's income is nothing to sneeze at. His annual salary is $200,000 plus large expense accounts. In addition, as a millionaire, he must surely be making much money from his investments, even if they are held in trust accounts. But let's consider only the $200,000 presidential salary. Tithing would have meant a total of $20,000 in charitable donations. Giving 1% (1/10 of the tithe) would have resulted in $2,000 in donations. However 1/10 of 1% would have resulted in about $200 for others in need. Considering that President Nixon counted as a charitable donation a tree which he bought and then planted for some group, that is about what he gave to charity—1/10 of 1% of his salary. He gave nothing from the rest of his income.

I find the revealed information to be disgusting. I had always believed Mr. Nixon when he argued that people should do more to help one another so that governments could do less (and thus lower taxes, etc.) Now it is revealed that he deceived us; by his own actions (more accurately inactions) concerning charity he has shown that he himself neither believes in nor practices what he preaches.

Very little has been made so far in the media about these tax revelations and I think there are several reasons for this. In the first place, most people, including reporters, give almost nothing and thus see nothing unusual in this niggardly stinginess. In the second place, the media people are interested in getting at illegal actions and there is nothing illegal in keeping everything for oneself.

Billy Graham has correctly observed that you can tell a great deal about a person's character by the way he deals with money matters. Despite all the fanfare of church services in the White House, praying to God, associating with big-name religious leaders, etc., President Nixon's fundamental values have been revealed by himself for what they are.

In trying to defend his dismal record on tax matters the president stated that former president Johnson had mentioned to him that he could escape paying taxes by donating his vice-presidential papers to the U.S. and placing a high value on them. President Nixon at once proceeded to do so. However, apparently he never really signed away the papers so that the whole transaction may turn out to have been illegal. In any event, my estimation of Nixon will certainly not be raised upon learning that he took instruction in ethics from Lyndon

Johnson!

For several years many Christians in Canada and the U.S. thanked God for "Christian leaders" such as Agnew and Nixon. How easily we were taken in by empty rhetoric!

DR. MORGENTALER

About eight months ago Dr. Henry Morgentaler of Montreal stood trial on a charge of performing illegal abortions. During that trial he testified freely that during the preceding four years or so he had done between 5,000 and 6,000 abortions. The jury acquitted him. This decision was then appealed by the crown, that is the Government, to an Appeal Court where the lower court decision was reversed. The physician has been sentenced to 18 months in prison. Assuming that he performed 5,500 abortions and assuming that he serves a full 18 months, which is very unlikely, he would be enduring about 2 hours imprisonment for each abortion.

Dr. Morgentaler has appealed this second decision to the Supreme Court of Canada which will this fall make a final ruling. If it should decide in favor of the physician, we can expect to see abortion become an accepted norm in our society. Of course, Parliament can always pass new legislation and one would hope that our good MP's would see their responsibility.

On July 25, when Morgentaler appeared in court for sentencing, he argued that he did not respect Canada's current abortion laws which require that a panel of physicians must agree that an abortion is medically necessary (this covers both physical and mental health) before it can be legally performed. In imposing the sentence Judge Hugessen observed, "The law does not require respect, it demands obedience." If Morgentaler cannot accept the law he, like the rest of us, must be prepared to accept the consequences.

The entire episode has already received wide coverage and the Supreme Court decision will be duly discussed across the nation. A part of one particular news report caught my attention recently. A spokesman for one of the more militant women's liberation groups argued that since Dr. Morgentaler was now prevented from performing all but approved abortions in a hospital, many women were resorting to motel amateurs and back-alley butchers. Many women were dying, she said, and two people had to take the full burden of responsibility for each death, the prosecuting attorney and Judge Hugessen.

Now I agree that two people, aside from the abortionist, must share the responsibility but the two I single out are not the ones to whom she points the accusing finger. Without reviewing my elementary biology too carefully I can assert that both a man and a woman are involved in the initiating of a new human life. An embryo does not get started without a little help. It is with the two initial partners, I suggest, that responsibility must lie. And we had better keep that central truth clear in our minds. Otherwise the advocates of irresponsibility and loose living might yet convince a majority of Canadians, by some perverted form of logic, that pregnancy and kitchen table abortions are somehow caused by law enforcement.

VARIETIES OF VIOLENCE

As I am writing this there is trouble on Parliament Hill. Not only the usual kind of political trouble. The Indians are, so to say, on the warpath. Some red men are scuffling with some red coats, one solitary brave is beating a tom tom, and a few young warriors are trying to put the torch to some green shrubs which refuse to burn.

The sight is not a pleasant one. Hundreds of people are shouting and shoving. Some people are obviously very angry; a few are vicious. One fellow, while being handcuffed, is biting a policeman's hand. It is easy to judge these native Canadians and to condemn them for their violence but their actions are only part of the story. Violence can take many forms.

Is it violence to take the Indians' land at the point of a gun and then thank God for it?

Is it violence to herd Indians on to reservations which almost invariably contain some of the least productive areas to be found anywhere?

Is it violence to break treaties solemnly concluded with their ancestors concerning fishing and hunting rights to be valid "till the rivers cease to flow"?

Is it violence to flood Indian villages around Hudson's Bay, and elsewhere, so that the "civilized" white man can sell electricity to Consolidated Edison of New York and swing a handsome profit?

Is it violence to sell "firewater" to the Indians and then punish them for becoming alcoholics?

Is it violence to destroy the Indian's trapping areas, decimate his herds of buffalo, and pollute his fishing places so that he cannot provide for his family?

Is it violence to dump poisonous industrial mercury into the St. Clair River, into lakes around Kenora, and elsewhere, so that the Indian and his children will die of slow poisoning?

Is it violence to treat the Indian as a second-class citizen when he was a citizen here by birthright at a time when our forebears still believed that the earth was flat?

Is it violence to claim the far North and all the minerals under the land as ours when we have never made a treaty with the natives who live there?

Is it violence when in our school textbooks we depict the Indians as brutal savages when it is the white man who came here and started to fight?

The Speech from the Throne which drones on in the Senate Chamber may sound fine to us but the Canadian Indian knows that the not-so-great White Father who sits on that throne speaks with a forked tongue and seems not to realize it.

MAY 28, 1976

FACING THE FACTS

On May 8th the national newscast carried a most unusual story—you may have seen it. Scores of generally well-known Americans were seated in rows, each holding a small white nameplate. The group included such diverse celebrities as astronaut Edwin Aldrin, actor Dick Van Dyck. politician Wilbur Mills, TV personality Gary Moore, Indian Chief Sylvester Tinker, the Rev. Joseph Kerine, and the great baseball pitcher Don Newcombe.

As they were introduced, many began their little speeches by simply stating, "I'm an alcoholic." That's what they all had in common. Apparently a major purpose of this strange publicity stunt organized by the National Council on Alcoholism was to remove the "stigma of alcoholism." Also, the organizers hoped that more alcoholics would be encouraged to seek treatment for their problem.

Since there are about 10 million alcoholics in the U.S. out of a total population of about 210 million (almost one out of 20!), the sponsoring Council faces a mammoth task and deserves much praise for tackling a frightening social crisis.

Likewise, the prominent citizens who exposed themselves to the world as alcoholics deserve credit for their honesty and their willingness to deal with their problems. Some tried to joke about the whole situation but most, it seemed to me, felt embarrassed or at least very uncomfortable. Understandably so.

Unfortunately, despite all the candor and confessing, both the organizers and the participants were not ready to face all the facts. They kept on insisting that alcoholism was a disease, presumably like other diseases. Of course, no one ever got around to explaining which germ, virus, etc. causes the disease.

All insisted that in the future they did not want to be known as "reformed alcoholics" but as "recovered alcoholics." Dr. Luther Cloud, the Council's vice-chairman explained that "reformed" was objectionable because it "implies erroneously that alcoholism is a moral straying rather than an illness." He added, "Being sick is not being bad." As he spoke, the entire group applauded.

Well, well! There's an interesting twist. Alcoholism, we are told, cripples or kills millions of people each year. Incalculable financial and emotional costs result. Millions of careers and homes are destroyed. And all of this comes about because people who had total freedom to leave the alcohol alone or to stick with purely minimal consumption chose of their own free will not to do so.

Now we are supposed to be so utterly naive and simple-minded as to believe that they are not responsible for what they brought upon themselves and society! If alcoholism is not a moral straying then I don't know what is. Who knows, maybe we who denounce alcoholism and criticize those who lure people to it as well as those who drink themselves into it will soon be labelled as the immoral ones!

The mind boggles at the "logic" of the children of darkness. I suppose ere long we will hear of the illness of laziness, the malady of mugging, the disease of bank-robbing, the sickness of committing murder and who knows what else. No longer will there be evil, only illness; no longer responsibility, only excuses.

THE AMERICAN BICENTENNIAL

The current celebration of the American bicentennial has evoked considerable controversy in the U.S. but also elsewhere. Expressions of patriotism and thanksgiving are matched by equally emotional demonstrations of criticism and denunciation.

Since I have lived in the U.S. for about eight years and simply because I am a Canadian, I take great interest in the activities associated with this 200th anniversary. Together with the dissenting minority I, too, can "point the finger." One can certainly argue that the Indochina intervention and certain other foreign policies were misguided, that domestic race relations leave something to be desired, and that the disproportionate consumption of the earth's resources is unconscionable. And many other issues come to mind.

But that is only part of the picture. My reaction to the U.S., which I have studied for many years, is much more positive than negative, and when I think of individual Americans my feelings are even more positive. In no other country, except perhaps my native land, have I found people, large numbers of people, as hospitable, friendly, generous, and warm. (Time and again their acceptance of us was so overwhelming that I quickly forgave them for their ignorance about Canada and even overlooked the not infrequent propensity for equating national economic achievements with Christian virtue or military might with moral pre-eminence!)

It is precisely because I have basically warm feelings towards my "second homeland" that I have, on occasion, expressed certain criticisms. Presumably a friend should be expected to be both concerned and candid.

I suppose what triggered my recent thinking in this area was the shrill criticism of the current U.S. celebrations expressed by some Canadian Christians, including some Mennonites.

The following, I think, needs to be said to some of my fellow Mennonites.

* The main reason we have no black-white racial problems in Canada is that cotton does not grow here. (Native Indians are mistreated the same in both countries as also were Japanese citizens during World War II).
* The disproportionate consumption of global resources is as great in Canada as in the U.S. except to the extent that slight income differences might dictate lower consumption here.
* In the main, Canadian public opinion closely parallels American opinion on foreign affairs. Our attitudes are hardly more—or less—virtuous.

Even more to the point, I find it strange that people who make so much about loving one's enemies, a praiseworthy stance, seem to find it so hard to love their friendly neighbors even if there are value or policy differences. It seems to me that without setting aside our critical faculties, Canadian Mennonites should follow the Biblical directive of rejoicing with those who are glad. If we can't even get along with our friends, we should stop talking about loving our enemies.

To my American friends I want to say, "Don't listen only to the foreign cynics. None of them, as far as I know, is planning to move to Poland or Czechoslovakia so that they can live closer to the U.S.S.R. than to the U.S. Remember, also, that when Canadians decide to go on holidays or to migrate, almost all head south. And as far as MB's are concerned, we Canadians want to stress that we are one brotherhood. Therefore we share your joys and sorrows and try to understand your problems. Therefore, also, we need to speak openly and honestly to each other.

"Right now you are especially grateful and happy as you thank God for your freedoms and other benefits. And because you are happy we also are happy."

LOTTERIES

With the Montreal Olympics upon us, we watch with great interest as the athletes expend every possible ounce of energy to run a little faster, jump a little higher, or throw the discus a little farther. It's all very exciting, especially when the Canadians win.

But there is one aspect of the whole games phenomenon which is somewhat less exciting and that is the growing tendency of governments to rely on lotteries to pay their expenses, in this case the ridiculously high Olympic deficit.

Now I am not saying that I will never buy a raffle ticket when my neighbor's daughter comes to our door promoting a worthy cause, or that I will not purchase some other ticket. But when I do so, I act on the assumption that I am donating money to a cause which I support or that I want to maintian a good relationship and am willing to donate a small amount of money in order to do so. Maybe my judgment needs correction but that's how I operate at present. When I buy a ticket, I consider it a donation; that money is gone.

Nonetheless, what really upsets me is the sudden enthusiasm of our governments to generate revenue by cultivating crass selfishness and greed. Throughout society, from management to employees, rich elites to poor people, and young people to the elderly, we already have more than enough of the notion of getting something for nothing.

Personally, I resent the fact that my tax money is being used (misused?) by governments to con the public. The particularly unfortunate part of this whole venture is that the slick advertising is most effective on those who can least afford to gamble their money away. The smooth-talking promotion about a tax-free million and the subtle implication that buyers may well win—which is only technically true given the massive negative odds—is positively repulsive to me.

I am not suggesting that governments should,or realistically can, outlaw all lotteries but I am strongly suggesting that governments, whether Conservative in Ontario, Liberal in Ottawa, or whatever, should not try to entice as many millions of Canadians as possible to get hooked on this vice. It does little good to have morality squads cracking down on bookie joints while Ottawa itself operates the biggest bookie joint of all!

The argument is often advanced that bookie joints must be suppressed because their illegal betting operations operate without the taxman getting his ''legitimate'' share, but even that secular argument does not hold for most of the government-run lotteries because the winnings are also tax free.

It is all rather sad. A lot of poor people, in a desperate attempt to get rich quick, are losing a lot of money which they can't afford to lose.

Perhaps, if you really must gamble, you should go back to the Irish Sweepstakes. There, at least, the profits, such as they are, go to hospitals. Better still, don't gamble.

DECEMBER 10, 1976

LOVING QUEBEC

The words sound odd, even peculiar, perhaps because so many people in our society now seem bent on cultivating animosity instead.

Of course, many Canadians, including some Christians, don't stop to think what they are doing. Their perverted logic goes something like this:

"Since we don't know individual French-Canadians, how can we be expected to like them, let alone love them? Besides, they are different; so much so that its just as well that we don't have much to do with them.

"And many speak with an accent and don't want to be assimilated into the Canadian mainstream. Also, they're always asking for special privileges involving schools and languages, etc. and in both world wars most of them opposed the Canadian government's conscription laws. Some of their leaders also clamor for special immigration regulations which favor their group. How can we ever build a great country with such people?"

As I glance over the lines I've just written a powerful feeling of sameness comes to mind. I think of the closed, ethnic community in which I grew up; assimilation was frowned upon, if not officially denounced.

My thoughts flash back to my highly revered grandparents, pillars in the community. They were civic-minded and real Christian saints but they could never have understood all the present public controversy over Quebec because during their fifty years in Canada they never learned English. They chose not to.

And then I remember the Mennonite Educational Institute, that separated high school which I attended 25 years ago. It functioned then, and still operates today, because governments allowed Christian groups to operate private schools. Glancing at the old yearbook pictures I see my former teachers who were allowed by Ottawa to do alternate service during World War II. Then my eyes fall on former classmates—Gerhard, Anna, and the rest—who came to Canada when the government waived the regular immigration regulations for certain categories of refugees.

Over there, that's a picture of one of my favorite teachers, F.C. Thiessen. He used to tell us all about the "Privilegium" in Russia which allowed pacifists to avoid military conscription. And he talked about self-governing Mennonite communities with unpronounceable names.

Just a minute, a CBC commentator is now talking about the special privileges for which certain Canadians are clamoring. I missed his opening lines and until I heard him mention "Quebecois" I thought he was talking about traditional Mennonites. After all, as far as "demands," pressures, and privileges are concerned, is there really much differences? You be the judge.

CAN WE TAKE FREEDOM?

Increasingly, and very, reluctantly, I am coming around to the view that people in Canada today probably have more freedom than they can profitably use. Doubtless that is a very controversial suggestion—let me explain.

At the outset we should be clear on one basic point, namely, that total freedom without any restraint creates anarchy which is hardly a viable option in any situation. Hence, the question is not whether a line should be drawn limiting freedom but, rather, where that line should be drawn. My suggestion is that today it is not drawn at the right place or places.

Let me illustrate. Observing the moral situation in our high schools and universities I am forced to conclude that many, if not most, of the students have more freedom than they can handle. Looking at much of organized labor, certain segments of the business world, large sectors of the media, the bulk of the "popular" movie industry, and even society in general I perceive similar situations. Almost everywhere I look I find people clamoring for more and more freedom (often associated with power even though they already have difficulty acting responsibly in the present climate of broad freedoms).

The real problem, as I see it, involves a fundamental misconception. People seem to assume that the more freedom they have, be it in group pressure, sexual activity, education, language, "cultural" consumption, or social behavior generally, the happier they will be. The fact of the matter, of course, is that freedom in itself is an invaluable means to achieve meaningfulness but it does not tell us what is good! We may have all the freedoms we want but if we are not committed to any specific values, then those freedoms will not give us any real satisfaction or purpose in living.

The answer does not lie in harsh censorship, rigid regulations or some kind of authoritarianism. Freedom, if it is to be anything, must include, within limits, the right to do wrong; at least the right to do some things and believe some things which the majority thinks are wrong. But there must be limits. And I suggest that at present in our society the areas of freedom may be too broad.

You see, I happen to believe that children should not be allowed to smoke or drink; that alcoholics should be banned from the highways; that smokers should not be allowed to smoke in enclosed public places; that Playboy should not be available in grade school libraries; that the legal drinking age should probably be raised to 20 years; that strikers should have no special rights; that resource developers should not be allowed to poison the environment; that banks should not be allowed to charge exorbitant rates; that high school students should not be allowed to choose just any courses they happen to fancy and thus avoid the core areas; and that criminals must be removed from society (and helped) until they change their ways.

Maybe such a stance makes me a reactionary; but that doesn't particularly bother me since I suppose there are some trends against which Christians should always react. Of course, we must be careful not always to be reactionary or to expect discipleship from non-disciples.

Maybe Christian integrity requires us to speak up concerning both excessive freedom and abuse of freedom. After all, a civilized environment is profitable for Christians and non-Christians alike and we should do what we can to develop and restrain it.

WOMEN'S LIB

From time to time I read something in the daily press which strikes me as being so outlandish and far-fetched that I am utterly puzzled as to why the whole thing is taken seriously.

Such was my reaction the other day to a newspaper account of a Winnipeg speech by women's lib advocate, Germaine Greer. Perhaps I should add that I am not objective when it comes to Greer's pontifications; her perception puzzles me, her "logic" escapes me, and her conclusions turn me off.

Of course, when she or any other women's lib spokesman advocates equal justice, equal pay, etc., the points are valid. Historical injustices and exploitation must be terminated.

But "Ms." Greer's observations are of another kind. According to the Canadian Press account she said that "Women will not be liberated while they are under capitalism, and while they're still getting married." Wrong, utterly wrong, on both counts—though today space limitations allow me to deal only with item one.

Has Ms. Greer ever travelled to the Communist countries? If she has, did she notice all the liberated women sweeping the streets, working on construction projects and often doing other demanding physical tasks while their children were off in some state-run nursery or preschool already memorizing the "party line"? She calls that liberation?

True, there is official legal equality for men and women in the Communist countries but, at least as far as I can tell, that has not really helped the women very much. Constitutional equality has put many women into menial, low-status jobs alongside men but it has not brought them parity in political life, in the media, in the business world, or in the professions, with the possible exception of medicine and certain sports.

If emancipated women fare so well in the non-capitalist world, why does Ms. Greer not bring some of them with her on her lecture tours so that reporters and listeners generally could get the whole story first hand? Doubtless the "oppressed" women in middle class suburbia in North America would be delighted to discover how they could be emancipated straight into street-sweeping, construction, and truck-driving.

Let these fuzzy thinking "liberationists" have their full freedom. Most women in our society, even in low income groups, are much too sensible and sophisticated to believe that remedies for existing injustices can be found in Ms. Greer's prescriptions. Some women may be taken in by her distorted notions but their numbers will be few.

It's a pity that frustrated crusaders as Ms. Greer do not accept true liberation, that which Jesus epitomized when he talked to the woman at the well. For ultimately, real liberation is to be found not in capitalism, and certainly not in communism, but in the community of liberated, disciplined, and sharing believers.

JULY 7, 1978

BILLY GRAHAM IN TORONTO

The local and regional media people have, in the main, done a less than adequate job reporting Billy Graham's recent one-week crusade in Toronto. Apparently perplexed by the whole thing, some tried to ignore it. For example, on Sunday June 11, the CBC-TV Toronto station totally ignored the event. *It may be* understandable that "The National" 11:00 p.m. news would have no report but surely the metro-Toronto news which follows "The National" should at least have noted the fact that 18,000 people packed out Maple Leaf Gardens and another 8,000 of us didn't make it inside! (I did manage to be part of Thursday's 31,000 crowd at the CNE stadium.) But nothing was said! During the entire week the secular TV and radio people were virtually silent.

The daily press had more to say, but was generally not objective. Those of you who read the June 10 *Weekend Magazine,* distributed in newspapers across Canada, know what I mean. The cover showed Graham tightly clutching a bag of money, with a total of 8 such bags forming a cross on the entire picture.

Most reporters (I followed the *Toronto Star, Globe and Mail,* and the *Kitchener-Waterloo Record)* seemed to be baffled and confused. Most focused on style rather than substance. Apparently they could not get themselves to believe that Graham was "in it" for anything else than the money, even when their own facts contradicted their conclusions.

The general trend was to depict Graham as a master at the art of evangelism, as someone who had made "original contributions to the theory and practise of evangelism;" as if Christian evangelism is just another type of entertianment or form of "show."

Not one reporter came to grips with what Billy Graham actually said! The *Record's* Roswitha Guggi, who at least reported the main points, was easily the most responsible of the lot. She, at least, stuck to reporting (interviews, description of facts and events, impressions) rather than attributing pecuniary motives to the preacher.

Most reporters repeatedly harped on the crusade budget. Did they really expect that such a venture requires no budget? I got the impression that they would have been critical of the fundraising, which was very low-key, no matter what the size of the budget might have been.

I was disappointed to see that the supposedly informed and sophisticated big-city reporters and columnists failed entirely to distinguish between the different types of evangelists, e.g., the ubiquitous late A.A. Allen and Billy Graham. I suppose they simply could not bring themselves to make Graham look good.

The basic problem, it seems, is that most of the media people don't understand Graham's motives. One

referred to "his life's work of being saved," thus reflecting utter ignorance of what salvation means as well as a misreading of his motivation.

I suppose we should not be surprised when non-Christians present Christian evangelism as just another business. (Guggi, whatever her personal beliefs, may be, was fair.) After all, to non-Christians the Gospel is foolishness.

In his *Weekend Magazine* article Ken Lefolii probably revealed more than he intended when he wrote that during his interaction with Graham there came a point when "it seemed to the reporter that he had now reached the shoreline of the dark gulf that separates the saved from the unsaved." Lefolii's figure of speech is also, as once again revealed by most media reports of the crusade, a literal statement of fact.

OCTOBER 13, 1978

PROFIT NOT A BAD WORD

Profit is not a dirty word, despite what a few of my socialist friends say. Without the profit, and the profit motive, a free economy stagnates. It would be nice if people would hurry to work, gladly work overtime, put in extra hours in the evening, and press themselves to be more productive on the job—all for the public good and only for the public good. But, unfortunately, human nature, especially in its fallen state, does not operate that way. By and large, people only exert themselves on the job if there's something in it for themselves, some desirable rewards be they financial or non-financial.

I have been thinking about this topic for a long time, as many of you doubtless have. A news item on the CBC this morning triggered additional thoughts. As I am writing this it appears that some 12,000 unionized employees of INCO in Ontario will shortly be on strike. Why? Have not thousands of INCO employees already been laid off because of high production costs and massive unsold stockpiles of nickel in Canada? Yes! Does INCO not have massive stockpiles? Yes! Then why the strike, one which might well last many months and financially cripple thousands of households?

The answer, according to a union spokesman, was that "last year INCO made a $90,000,000 profit" and, to paraphrase him, "we can't let them get away with that."

The union leaders strike me as being very naive. Granted, the 90 million dollar profit looks great but, as I understand it, even with that profit the large number of shareholders would have been farther ahead financially if they had simply invested their funds in government bonds. Do the union leaders really believe that somehow people should invest in private companies when there are no financial rewards for doing so?

Are the union leaders so upset by the fact that the entrepreneurs, who have risked their capital, are making a profit that they are willing to have more jobs go overseas and lose millions in employee income just to whittle down that profit? Apparently. How sad. Let me remind you, the union leader did not say that employee wages were too low, his point of concern was the profit!

How should Christians react to the notion of profit? What with increasing numbers of our fellow church members becoming enterpreneurs and major investors, the question appears to be timely.

Jesus, you will recall, told a story of what three men had done with sums entrusted to them. He was very critical of that man who had done nothing, who had not even put his money to earn interest.

The point to remember, I think is that we must all be diligent, always, of course, practicing integrity. If we have money, we should not neglect opportunity. For a person in business the earning of a profit is as proper and natural as is harvest time for a farmer. Let us not begrudge people their due. A field plowed and money invested can both serve fellowman. They can both represent honest work and public, even Christian, service. A reasonable return is proper in both cases.

After harvest time, or receipt of dividends, let us all practise good stewardship—that is a major test of our spiritual commitment. What we do with what we earn is a basic moral question; whether we earn our income as wages or as reasonable profit is not.

MAY 25, 1979

CHAIN LETTERS

The other day I got one—another one. This one began with, "Trust in the Lord with all good faith and he will acknowledge and he will light the way." The letter stated that "it," (the reference could be to either the prayer or the letter), had "been around the world 9 times." I wonder who keeps track of how many times it has circled the globe and then changes the number in all the existing copies! Maybe, by some miraculous way, the letter began with a nine-fold circumnavigation under its belt at the outset!

The letter stated that if in four days I sent copies "to people you think need good luck," I would receive "good luck." The only good luck I had was to forget about the letter for a week or more. But, then, I didn't send out any copies either.

Come to think of it, why should the letter constantly speak about good luck? Does it not say at the outset that we are to trust in the Lord and he will direct our paths? Maybe the original letter writer had a lapse of memory.

Supposedly the letter has triggered both pleasant and dire results. "An RAF officer received $70,000. Joe Elliot received $450,000 and lost it because he broke the chain." Joe Elliot? Do you know Joe Elliot? "While in the Philippines, General Welch lost his wife six days after he received the letter. He failed to circulate the prayer. However, before his death he received $775,000." Not bad for the General! And he didn't even send a letter. But poor Mrs. Welch. And all because of a letter!

The letter claims to emanate from "Saul Anthony de Caoif, a missionary from South America," at least at some earlier time. Has anybody heard of de Caoif? The letter continues, "I myself forward it to you." I wish I knew the identity of that compassionate soul who concluded that I needed good luck.

I am asked to make 20 copies. That costs $3.40 just to mail the stuff! My Depression mentality resists. But the letter, continues, "Constantine Dias received the chain in 1953." That means it had circulated the globe 9 times by 1953! "He asked his secretary to make 20 copies and send them out. A few days later he won a lottery for $2,000,000." Sounds impressive.

Poor Belon Fairchild. He "received the chain and, not believing in it, threw it away. Nine days later, he died."

There is still more. *"Do not send money,* for fate has no price." I'll let others go by fate, I'll stick with faith And, besides, it's illegal to send a chain letter through the mail. Also illogical, silly, and, in this case, sacreligious as well.

DEALING WITH THE DIVORCED

Although our denomination has adopted a statement which seeks to help people who have experienced the tragedy of a divorce, much questioning persists. I would like to comment on some of the issues which are being raised.

Some brothers and sisters are saying, "Isn't it high time that we make clear to our children where we stand—for their good and ours?" Or we may hear the following, "In light of the very high divorce rates, we need to stand firm." Still others have said, "Divorces are now happening more and more right in our churches, what shall we do?" All are making valid points; the problem is reaching serious proportions. But let us be careful how we react.

First, have we any biblical basis for putting divorce and adultery in a special category as some seem to do? I suggest that we do not. Time and again in the Bible this type of transgression is listed with the others. Nowhere is it described as an unpardonable sin though its consequences are exceptionally deplorable. Second, how did Jesus react? In situations that can be seen as analagous Jesus demonstrated love and forgiveness. To the promiscuous woman at the well he offered healing. To the woman caught in the act of adultery he showed compassion. In both instances the law would have required severe punishment. But Jesus, it seems, concluded that such punishment would serve no redemptive purpose. In the latter instance, the ones who wanted to initiate punishment certainly had the law on their side. Yet Jesus stayed their hands and, with his challenge about their own guilt in other areas, he apparently also stayed their mouths. He would have been justified in letting the requirement of God's law, as given through Moses, be enforced but he chose not to go that route. In his mercy he still extends forgiveness today, be the offender a total pagan or a stumbling believer like Peter was.

What about the matter of teaching the young people? What will impress them most, the rejection and setting apart of those who have thus sinned, or a readiness to forgive a repentant person and to help? Will our young people be more impressed by rigidity and rejection than by forgiveness and compassion? Further, can we not have a very high view of marriage as well as forgiveness for those who sin in this area? I think that we can. We do not have to choose between the two. Jesus did not use "the fallen" to make an example—should we?

But some still say, "Can the divorced claim a full place in the church?" In a sense, of course, none of us can claim any place. However, we should note what Paul says in I Corinthians chapter 6. Having catalogued, in the first 10 verses, a range of gross immoral behavior (divorce is not specifically mentioned but can be inferred) the apostle adds, "And such were some of you; but you were washed, but you were sanctified, but you were justified in the name of the Lord Jesus Christ. . . ." I find no suggestion that these redeemed violators of God's sexual and marriage norms were in any way second class.

I am convinced that in the final analysis Jesus will not criticize the church, so to speak, for being too forgiving, too compassionate. It is more likely that our inadequacy will involve our having been too rigid.

Billy Graham has written, ''Christ came to forgive us, and if God forgives someone for their sinful past, so should we.'' He continues: ''If a divorced person has repented of sin and been converted to Christ, I can see no reason why that person should not be allowed to make a contribution to the life of the church.'' We do well to heed his words.

$38,000 MORE!

This column may strain a few personal friendships but I am sufficiently perturbed by the specific as well as the general issue at hand that I must speak up.

Our fellow citizens in the medical profession generally deserve much gratitude and praise. By and large they serve selflessly and often sacrificially. But on occasion some baser tendencies appear. One such instance presently involves British Columbia's 3,700 practising physicians.

I suppose it can be argued that the past year's average salary, after expenses, of about $64,000 a year was too low. For many taxpayers who paid the bulk of the medical training expenses such a salary must surely look good but in comparison to average American medical salaries, exorbitant as they are in many states, the B.C. figure could be termed reasonable.

However, the recent settlement has diluted my trust in the commitment of the B.C. physicians. Pressuring the government first with a strike threat and then with massive illegal extra billing, the doctors finally extracted a huge increase in their income. Over the next two years their average salaries will go up by $38,000 which is almost 60%! Of course, the patients and the public will ante up this major cost, $170 million to begin with.

Given the power and professional clout of the physicians pressure group, there probably was little else that the B.C. government could do. No one can force physicians to practise good medicine. If they ever really want to hurt the public, or the public's government, they certainly are in a position to do so. We are at their mercy. Fortunately they rarely abuse their power or deny us their vital services. When they do, there is little that the rest of us can do but acquiesce.

Of course, the extorting physicians are not alone. In Canada today certain labor groups and certain businesses seem bent on gouging the public as much as they can. In various instances what remained of a traditional sense of public responsibility has gone out the window. Students and patients, air passengers and residents in nursing homes, as well as mail-users and those who require fire protection have on numerous occasions been summarily abandoned.

Where will it all end? Has human carnality degenerated to the point where special interest groups with powerful clout are ready virtually to shatter our society in order to satisfy their selfish, short-term goals? The signs are ominous. When fishermen, policemen, and physicians hold the public at ransom, what can be done?

More than a century ago Karl Marx argued that rising moral consciousness on the part of the working class would destroy an ecomomic system given to exploitation. He may yet be proven partly right. Maybe an economic system given to self-exploitation will be destroyed not by rising moral consciousness but by pervasive personal greed.

Of course, committed Christians will not be found giving leadership to the various ventures of greed. Those Christians who find themselves in irresponsible and exploiting groups as members will need to interact much more closely and intensively with fellow members of the household of faith. Wise counsel, moral support, prayer intercession, and economic assistance from the church community will be needed if we want to be faithful to our cause. Difficult times may lie ahead. We may be pressed hard to compromise on essentials but with God's promised help and assistance from fellow saints we can prevail. The world will increasingly seek to shape us into its mold but it must not succeed.

A LIFE IS A LIFE

In recent weeks, because of a variety of personal experiences and observations, I have become convinced that many of us, myself certainly included, need to develop a more consistent view about the sanctity of human life. On a piecemeal basis our denomination has over the years addressed several of the key questions but I am not aware of any systematic and thorough attempt to spell out an inclusive, integrated, and biblically-based statement.

This column is not the place to set forth such a statement but I shall suggest what should probably be included.

My underlying assumption is that as disciples of Christ who believe that every person is made in the image of God, and who have experienced his mercy and love, we are fully committed to the goal of saving life. Consequently our areas of concern must include at least the following.

1. *Death at the hands of the military.* For centuries our Anabaptist peace/love witness has been well known. At present we need to re-emphasize it and address ourselves to at least two vital issues. First, we must ensure that this biblical tenet is clearly proclaimed in our pulpits, taught in our schools, and reinforced in our homes. If we fail in this endeavor, our children may someday hold us accountable for our dereliction. Second, we need to speak with increased boldness to governments (ours, Allied, Communist, and others) about the incredible and frightening arms build-up. As Christians we fail our Master if we remain quiet while militarists around the globe develop and stockpile ghastly means of biological, chemical, "conventional," laser, and nuclear weapons.

Though we cannot expect Christian ethics from non-Christians or sub-Christian structures, we proclaim ourselves unashamedly as opposed to killing—we are "merchants" of life!

2. *Death at the hands of the executioner.* Though governments, in both the defense function and police function, possess the right to use force, and in their sub-Christian mileu may even claim a legal right to take life, we as Christians, and particularly as peace-making Christians, stand strongly opposed to capital punishment. Justice may demand death; Christian love may not. We do not clamor for blood.

3. *Death of the unborn.* Sometime back physician Robert MacMillan, the outgoing president of the 14,500-member Ontario Medical Association said that in 90 percent of abortions approved for reasons of health, there is no unusual health factor involved. Stating that he is not a "Catholic or a Right-to-Lifer," this knowledgeable physician asserted that he was simply concerned that no one seems willing to deal with the reality of the abortion situation. Christians, by definition, are pro-life. Of course there are libertarian and other arguments which can be marshalled in support of widespread abortion, but we stand for life! The unborn cannot speak for themselves.

4. *Death on the road.* Much more than half of Canada's approximately 5,000 annual traffic deaths are caused by drinking drivers. Such senseless slaughter must be stopped. Let us vigorously support the various agencies combating drunkenness and strongly endorse the increasing

attempts by certain governments to crack down on those who put their weaving bodies and dulled minds behind the wheel. As Christians we oppose death by piercing glass or grinding steel.

5. *Death by civilian gun use.* Increasing numbers of Canadians, not to mention Americans and others, are slaughtered because millions of hand guns are readily available for use across the continent. As Christians we support all responsible efforts to cope with this plague. We don't need hand guns, we don't use hand guns; rather, we support responsible gun control efforts.

Additional kinds of death could be mentioned but let these five major categories suffice for now.

My challenge is that individually and collectively we proclaim our Christian stance. As we state our case consistently—something which we have not always done—our witness for life will take on added credibility.

Let the merchants of death, whatever their stripe, work for death; we are called to work for life. A life is a life; we defend it. Even as we save lives by our charitable deeds of mercy, our crusade to oppose killing, by whatever means, must assume new urgency. Let us be equal to, and consistent in, this awesome task.

MISAPPROPRIATING GOD'S PROMISE

Our Daily Bread, a daily devotional guide published in Grand Rapids, Michigan by the Radio Bible Class, remains one of the finest guides available. We have used it for years and recommend it highly. In combination with our denominational *Rejoice* it provides excellent family-oriented material.

On rare occasions, however, *Our Daily Bread* serves a useful purpose by illustrating, unintentionally, how not to apply God's promise. Such an instance is found in the reading for last August 27.

The title for that day, based on Psalm 27:5, was "a God-sent cloud." The writer's central theme is that the Lord often protects Christians "in marvelous and unexpected ways." The illustrating story described a World War II incident in the Pacific war zone.

One day, "one of America's mighty bombers" took off from Guam, "headed for Kokura, Japan, with a deadly cargo." Because of cloud cover "the sleek B-29" circled the target area until its fuel supply ran low. "Frustrated because they were right over the primary target area yet not able to fulfill their mission," the crew finally headed off to an alternate target and dumped their deadly payload, the world's second atomic bomb used in battle, on the city of Nagasaki. On that bright morning, August 9, 1945, about 70,000 Japanese were blasted into eternity.

The writer asks, "Was that foggy cover, which rolled in from an otherwise sunlit sea, a mere happenstance? Hardly!" You see, about a week previously the Japanese authorities had transferred large numbers of captured Americans to Kokura. The American military commanders were unaware of that fact. When, shortly after the devastation of the nuclear blast, that fact became known one of the American officers exclaimed, "Thank God for that protecting cloud! If the city hadn't been hidden from the bomber, it would have been destroyed and thousands of American boys would have died."

The writer closes with the words, "No wonder Psalm 27:5 became one of the favorite texts of our God-protected Christian servicemen!"

Small wonder that the reading of this account at our supper table evoked gasps of incredulity and dismay. Can Christians really be so blinded by nationalistic fervor? Where in God's Word do Christians find any assurance that they ought to take up arms to kill fellowmen for whom Christ also died?

Where do we read that "a God-sent cloud" will, or probably will, protect Christians when they put the state's mandate ahead of the Biblical injunction?

Why should we conclude that the lives of American boys are more precious in God's sight than the lives of Japanese boys? (In the second World War American rhetoric about the unique significance of American casualties prompted allies and enemies to coin and repeat this couplet, "American boys are like no others, Only American boys have mothers.")

Does the death of tens of thousands of Japanese mean nothing to the (at least partially Christian) American service men?

How can Christian writers of devotionals today accept the blatant hypocrisy of thanking God that "thousands of American boys" did not die in the nuclear inferno and of also thanking God, at least by implication, that thousands of Japanese, including vast numbers of innocent civilians, did?

What kind of biblical exegesis allows one to take promises given to God's people, living world-wide, and apply them to the American (or for that matter any other) military establishment?

How do we know that there were no Christian Japanese under that cloud covering Kokura? Does God place a higher value on American Christians than on Japanese Christians? Maybe the cloud was put there to protect Japanese Christians?

The remaining questions that come to mind could fill much more space but let me close with one more. Could that billowy cloud over Kokura not have been placed there by God as an obstruction and a clear message to the Americans not to drop that deadly payload at all? The August 6 nuclear devastation of Hiroshima, in which 68,000 people died immediately and another 76,000 were badly injured, was already forcing the Japanese imperial government to seek surrender terms. Maybe God was warning Americans not to shed more blood!

Let all who have ears to hear, hear.

DANGER ON THE RIGHT

For more than 20 years I have been intrigued by what is commonly called "the Far Right," a peculiar movement in which Christian fundamentalism, patriotism, anti-communism, defense of free enterprise, and some other elements are supported vigorously.

I have read scores of books and articles on this almost exclusively North American (mainly American) phenomenon. I have interviewed numerous Far Right leaders, visited Far Right organization headquarters, publicly debated with Far Rightists and have written a book entitled, *The American Far Right,* Eerdmans, 1968.

This particular para-church movement has really mushroomed following the beginning of the U.S.—USSR cold war in 1946. It consists of more than 20 separate organizations, some more religious than others, spanning most of the U.S. and reaching far into Canada, including many supposedly Anabaptist communities. That's one reason why it intrigues me. Additionally its activities arouse my interest because of the blend of truth and distortion, perhaps even falsity, which it disseminates.

Then, too, I am perplexed why significant numbers of Mennonite Brethren accept and support it. Also, I must add in all fairness that I am disturbed and dismayed that the mass media generally treat Far Rightists very unfairly, It is one thing to disagree basically with the Far Right application of Scripture, as I do; it is something quite different and certainly deplorable to make them look silly by innuendo, bias, and lies. I find that simply letting Far Right spokesmen speak for themselves makes my point quite adequately for me.

In the May-June, 1981 issue of *Christian Crusade,* which calls itself "America's Number One Christian Conservative Publication," the Rev. Billy James Hargis has an article entitled, "Fundamentalism, The Case For 'Christian Americanism'." In quoting from it, and commenting briefly, I shall illustrate what lies at the centre of the Far Right and why I think we should avoid it. Secondarily, the excerpts also illustrate why we should not call ourselves fundamentalists; Anabaptist, evangelical, or evangelical-Anabaptist are better labels. Let me add one caveat at this point. I am not saying that Far Rightists are not Christian. Many of them do preach the gospel; God will do the final evaluating.

Here are some quotations. I think that Rev. Hargis, whom I have known personally for more than 16 years, would not accuse me of taking them out of context.

"The fundamentalist Christian American is a person who believes the Bible is literally inspired from cover to cover. Furthermore, we believe that the United States of America is God's greatest nation under the Living Son." Where, I say, is there any biblical or other justification for the second assertion? And what does it do to the notions of the universality of the Church and the primacy of church over state for every disciple of our Saviour and Lord?

"Our enthusiasm for America, our constitutional concepts, our democratic ideals, our free enterprise economy, and our Judaic-Christian traditions are not unlike the religious nationalism that you find among the returning Jews in Israel." Surely, Billy James, you don't seriously mean to imply that the U.S., rather than the Christian Church, is God's "new Israel?"

"We, the fundamentalist Christians of America, feel that no other nation, save Israel, has ever been blessed as God Almighty has blessed the United States." My dear Billy James, in this age is God working mainly through the church or through a country?

"We see in the founding of this nation a people guided by God to set up a near perfect Christian democracy that would be an example to peoples everywhere." The native Indians, among others, see it differently. Their forefathers saw the settlers fall on their knees and then on the aborigines.

"We look upon communism as the greatest enemy that the church of Jesus Christ faces." I, too, see communism as a great evil but surely the church's greatest enemy is Satan, not communism!

"Christian fundamentalists can never be at *peace with this world.* We are constantly working to bring it to an acceptance of Jesus Christ as Saviour and King, and the *American way* as God's way in government." Isn't that rather presumptuous, Billy James? What makes the American way God's way?

"Our prayer is for America and the continuation of her freedom. It is best expressed in II Chronicles 7:14: 'If my people, which are called by my name, shall humble themselves, and pray, and seek my face, and turn from their wicked ways; then will I hear from heaven, and will forgive their sin, and will heal their land'." Be careful not to misuse Scripture, Billy James! Since when are Americans called after God's name? They are called after America! This verse originally applied to Israel; today it applies to God's people wherever they may be, in the U.S., Canada, the Soviet Union, or elsewhere. Political citizenship is not a basis on which God divides people.

And thus it is. Let us opt for a better way.

DANGER ON THE LEFT

Several months ago I wrote a column entitled, "Danger on the Right." Since that time I have received numerous requests/suggestions that there should also be a critical appraisal of the "leftist" danger.

The respondents are, of course, correct; reaction should be balanced. Over the years this column has repeatedly discussed the inadequacies of communist regimes, of militant nationalism, and super patriotism. An attempt to tie Christianity to any one of these is heretical and needs to be exposed and opposed.

If it seems that I have been particularly sensitive about right-wing extremism, there is an explanation. During the last several decades there has been a fairly widespread tendency in Canada and the U.S. to identify evangelical Christianity with right-wing politics. Even in certain Mennonite churches the impact has been considerable. We seem to come to terms quite easily with the political-religious evangelists on the Right!

However, with reference to the Left, the situation is quite different. During the past 20 years or so I have visited about 100 to 150 Mennonite Brethren churches in Canada and the U.S.; I have had the privilege of speaking in about half of those. Not once did I encounter any situation where the pastor or leading group was trying to tie the Gospel to leftist politics. Marxism seems not to have penetrated the Mennonite Brethren clergy; "Liberation Theology" has cut no swath. I have seen numerous flags in church but never one that was red!

Of course, the above does not mean that there is no danger from the left; there is! Let me be more specific.

1. Some of our church members, even some leaders, seem to invoke a double standard. If a fundamentalist or a right-wing preacher "adds to the Gospel," they jump all over him but if a left-wing or liberal minded theologian demythologizes and humanizes the Gospel, his error is conveniently ignored.

Similarly, if a right-wing government, e.g. South Africa's, practices despicable racism it is quite properly criticized, but if a Communist government, e.g. Vietnam's or the Soviet Union's, practices similar racial oppression, assorted varieties of historical and sociological explanations are sometimes trotted out.

2. Certain ethical stances associated (not only) with the Left are gaining support among segments of our brotherhood. Thus violence and revolution by Marxist guerrilla movements have sometimes been justified. A few times I have even heard certain Anabaptists justify, or at least rationalize, communist oppression of entrepreneurs and those who own property. Then, too, there have been some indications—though I have found none among Mennonite Brethren clergy—of support for Latin American Liberation Theology. This "end justifies the means" theology should have no place in our midst.

3. On more than a few occasions I have heard certain Anabaptist spokesmen suggest that we need to cooperate more closely with the Marxists. Of course, in many respects we can cooperate with all kinds of people and we should be willing to dialogue with anyone. But surely, on fundamental questions, Anabaptists stand diametrically opposed to the Marxists. A Bible-believing Anabaptist

cannot accept the following Marxist essentials:

- there is no God; God is a figment of man's imagination.
- man has no soul; man is simply the highest of the animals.
- all ethics are relative; there are no final, fixed standards of right and wrong.
- the end justifies the means; anything that promotes the cause of Marxist "Liberation" is right.
- all government is only an expression of class struggle.
- mankind is not inherently evil; it is the environment that makes man evil.
- religion is the opiate of the people; there is no "other world" and "other-worldliness" must be suppressed.
- the ownership of property and the earning of a reasonable profit are both evil.
- the family is an inferior social structure and its interests must always be subordinated to those of party and class.
- children belong to the state; parental responsibility and control are always secondary.

The list could be much longer. It is abundantly clear that on fundamental ethical and religious issues we cannot accept the standard Marxist/Communist views. The fact that certain leftists camouflage themselves with rhetoric about peace does not change the situation. We stand by our convictions, yielding ground neither on the right nor on the left.

PRISON REFORM

Perennially, Christians make much of prison reform, which is hardly surprising since Jesus himself mentioned concern for prisoners as a hallmark of saintly people (Matthew 25). With the ever-swelling prison population and the consequent overcrowding, not to mention abusive treatment, this is not the time to terminate sensitivity and compassion.

Yet one current question puzzles me. Here is the issue. Several of my Christian acquaintances, including at least one expert on the topic, are firmly convinced that the ultimate Christian response to the prison dilemma is to abolish prisons. ''Prisons train criminals,'' they argue, so the best available option is to unlock the gates and let the prisoners go. Rehabilitation, they insist, is more likely to occur in society than in the cell blocks.

To reinforce their sometimes compelling arguments, these acquaintances point to the alarming rates of recidivism. Most law-breakers who are sent to prison are again into criminal pursuits soon after their release, and thus the presumably pointless treadmill routine continues.

Unfortunately the data is indeed depressing; one wishes that incarceration would be more therapeutic and rehabilitative than it actually is. But even so, it seems to me, my zealous acquaintances are partially missing the point.

Society, I insist, deserves to be protected from burglars, rapists, drunken drivers, muggers, thieves, vandals, murderers, extortionists, and the like. When arrested, tried, convicted, and imprisoned, they are put behind bars not only because they need to be helped, and some people would add ''punished,'' but also because society needs to be protected. Just because the goal of rehabilitation cannot be achieved does not mean that the goal of protection should be abandoned. A failure to distinguish between these two goals represents fuzzy thinking. And that's the nub of the problem.

What, then, should a responsible Christian stance be? I think that we should abandon the unrealistic notion of prison abolition and urge, even press, authorities to take prison reform much more seriously than they do. Often prisoners are ignored and mistreated to an incredibly shocking degree. A civilized society with a Christian conscience should not permit such inhumane mistreatment. Convicts may not have electoral clout or community status but they are still human beings. To crowd them into filthy cells, to destroy any semblance of self-respect, and to brutalize them cannot be tolerated.

I am not necessarily in favor of sentencing people to prison but if they cannot live by the basic laws of the land and refuse to be rehabilitated, then there seems to be no other option.

Through the Mennonite Central Committee and other agencies let us continue programs of prison visitation and prisoner rehabilitation. Let us also be leaders in convincing governments that adequate facilities, counselling, treatment, and training must be made available.

More than one wise observer has noted that you can gauge the moral quality of a society by visiting its prisons. The point is well taken. Let us take note and act accordingly. But I cannot go along with the further idea that if we wish to be truly mature in our Christian response, we should press for the abolition of prisons. The rights of citizens, Christian and non-Christian alike, cannot so easily be dismissed!

ACTIONS LOUDER THAN WORDS

As a child I was indoctrinated with the notion that it was not good enough to give token amounts to "missions" and other worthy causes; a person should give of his "substance," proportionately and joyfully. I can also recall hearing the admonition that a person could not discharge his obligation to "the needy" simply by making donations—personal involvement of some sort was required.

The idea of private citizens helping other private citizens, of groups helping families and other groups, has had much appeal in these "conservative" times. Should that not be the natural state of affairs? Should those who "have" not be helping those who "need"?

Certain political sectors in Canada and the U.S. have, of course, been advocating such a stance for generations. "Cut back on government hand-outs and let the private sector pick up the slack" constitutes the gist of that argument.

This attitude has won widespread support among large segments of evangelical, conservative Christianity. It incorporates many of the values which Jesus taught and practiced. In recent decades Christian identification with this "limited government" stance has increased markedly as more and more people in our ranks have become affluent. Many of us have loudly echoed slogans about "less goverment welfare and more private aid."

These thoughts rushed through my mind the other night as I watched my favorite news program. Sandwiched between two major stories was a brief statement about President Reagan's 1982 income tax form which he had just completed for the U.S. Internal Revenue Department and given to the eager journalists.

I was shocked. Here is a man who for decades has espoused the virtues of private sector charity and what is he doing by way of example? Out of a reported 1982 income of about $750,000, ($200,000 or which he earns for being U.S. president) his total charitable donations reached the paltry sum of about $15,000 or 2 percent of his income. What a disillusionment! Naively, I suppose, I had honestly thought that this convincing spokesman for the "private charity" crowd actually practiced what he preached. Further, given the nature of the itemized contributions which the newsman read, it is unlikely that substantial other charitable donations were made but not listed.

Doubtless, some readers will wish to point out that $15,000 is a significant sum; my response is that relatively, and especially in light of the man's eloquent words, it is a niggardly pittance. The $750,000, after all, does not represent the man's total financial worth but only his income for 1982. Considering his total assets President Reagan is an extremely wealthy man. And 2 percent remains 2 percent.

President Reagan's deeds have spoken louder than his words. In charity he is almost as poor as the masses. Or have you forgotten the news item which informed us that in a certain recent tax year the average Canadian tax-payer who claimed the standard $100 deduction (for which no receipts are required) actually donated the total princely sum of $13?

Fortunately, the faithful church does not operate in such a miserly manner; unfortunately most of society, from top to bottom, apparently does!

AUGUST 19, 1983

TECHNOLOGY—THE FOURFOLD REVOLUTION

The twentieth century has brought numerous major "advances" to the human race; supersonic air travel, the penetration of space, cures for various diseases and the almost global impact of the pill, come to mind.

However, four phenomena, I suggest, have played an especially important role in weakening social bonds and individual well-being. Of course, in each case the strong arguments are not all on one side but the enormous disintegrating effect can hardly be denied.

These four awesome technological achievements have become both bane and blessing.

(1) *Television.* Focussing first on the level of the individual, the tube must be given pre-eminent place. In privacy and without much financial cost, countless individuals now spend much of each day, and much of a lifetime, observing without participating and perceiving without thinking (or at least without reflecting). In large part, entertainment has degenerated into mere diversion or even false reality. Most important of all, aside from the sheer waste of time for many addicts, is the widespread replacement of human relationships with vicarious identification.

The result of this massive assault on an individual's time, mind and human interaction can be a veritable personality disintegration. Numbed, indeed transfixed, by the endless audio-visual barrage, a person eventually becomes little more than a Nielsen statistic.

(2) *The automobile.* What television has done to millions of individuals, the automobile has done to millions of families. Mobility has wreaked havoc with family schedules and undermined their traditional and natural interdependence. Family tensions need no longer be faced, let alone resolved; the means of escape is parked in the driveway. The possibility of increased togetherness has yielded to the probability of greater dispersion. The automobile is a major culprit concerning family disintegration.

(3) *The nuclear bomb.* As the automobile is a major cause of weaker family ties, so the nuclear bomb has fundamentally changed the family of nations. As Churchill phrased it, "Security has become the twin of terror." A return to normalcy seems impossible. Mutual annihilation is an ever-present threat. The cost in money is staggering, the cost in human disillusionment and dread is incalculable. Who can predict the ultimate consequences?

(4) *The microchip.* The particular significance of this little hero, or villain, is that the cumulative impact of the three technological achievements cited above, and many more besides, have become less costly, more refined and more widespread. Beyond that, according to some futurologists, in the long run subsequent generations of the chip will not only "robotize" whole new areas of human endeavor but bring a perilous dehumanization of man himself. Many people will become superfluous.

Despite the major negative effect of these four expressions of technology, the main message for us is not gloom and doom but rather the need for awareness. The forces of disintegration are with us and must be recognized and consciously as well as conscientiously combatted. They will not overwhelm the church nor will they thwart God's dealings with mankind but they must be taken seriously.

PART XIV

The International Scene

MAY 20, 1966

CHINA

Engulfed by an emotional wave of opposition to Red China and hatred of everything Peking stands for, the Western world conveniently forgets some important events of the past. We tend to have very short memories when it is to our advantage. Indeed, we even manage to overlook some unpleasant aspects of the present situation.

I'm not trying to suggest that Red Chinese motives are praiseworthy or that Communism is less than evil, but rather I'm suggesting that there is a good bit of justification for Red Chinese hatred of the whole, "enlightened," "civilized," "Christian," white West.

Item: For several centuries most Europeans, and later on Americans as well, looked upon the Orient as something between an arena for prestige-laden power plays and a handy backyard which should be worked over for whatever profits could be squeezed out of it. Brandishing guns and cannon, the leaders of the "advanced" nations forced China to submit to the humiliation of becoming mere "spheres of influence." The patient Chinese, long on both pride and memory, have not forgotten how they were trampled underfoot.

Item: Despite all its protestations about racial equality and its heart-warming orations about human dignity, the West has consistently treated Orientals as an inferior race. Immigration barriers, property laws, and employment practices have all added to the hurt. The Oriental felt insulted because he was insulted.

Item: The West alienated the Oriental not only by its formal practices but also by its informal folkways, habits of thought, and derisive designations. References to "the yellow peril" used to be commonplace, and "coolies" were ranked even lower than servants. The Chinese in particular were made to look silly. Their long civilization and proud traditions were ground into the dust.

Now, at last, the tables are turned. It seems proper to say that injustice is bearing fruit, and it is bearing fruit after its own kind. The fruit is bitter. It is no pleasant thing to have the evil of many past generations being visited upon us.

I am now and intend to remain anti-Communist, but I need to remind myself that when the West denounces Red China for being aggressive, for preaching divisiveness, for practicing prejudice, hatred, and racism, it should remember that we were the self-appointed tutors of a people who learned only too well the vices we practiced.

GRAHAM IN VIETNAM

In past centuries the Christian Church in various countries has frequently been tempted to become chaplain rather than alternative, to the political-military power structures of the day. After reading Billy Graham's statements made during and after his recent Vietnam trip I get the impression that he has caused millions of people throughout the world to conclude that at least as he sees it, the cause of Christ and the cause of the United States in Vietnam are one and the same thing.

Graham would perhaps disagree with this description of his perspective and his influence, yet I cannot see how one can reach any other conclusion if one looks at the evidence! Speaking to an assembly of battle-ready servicemen at an American military base he said,

"I can assure you that you are in the prayers and thoughts of millions of Americans from coast to coast who are proud of the job you are doing out here."

Technically the statement may be true, but the implication that Graham shares this view and the further implication that true and responsible followers of Christ identify with this verdict disturb me.

Furthermore, I suggest that Graham distorts the biblical depiction of the Christian battle against evil when, again by subtle implication, he links it with the American intervention in Vietnam.

"There is not only a war in Vietnam, but there is a world war, a spiritual war between good and evil. Is there any hope for peace? There's only one way we can find it: that is in Jesus Christ."

Simply capping a questionable suggestion with a reference to Christ as the solution to our problems is inadequate.

No doubt President Johnson knew what he was doing when he invited Graham to be the government's guest on a trip to the bloodstained war zone. Graham has not disappointed, let alone embarrassed, his host. The American government has reaped valuable propaganda. The President has made it appear as if Western evangelicals support his Vietnam policy unequivocally.

Graham would have done better, it seems to me, if he would have declined the official invitation and paid his own way. Having seen the terrible distruction at first hand he ought to have reminded Christians everywhere that Christ is not only personal Saviour but Lord of life and Prince of Peace. Clearly, such an exhortation would not have endeared him to the White House, the State Department, or the Joint Chiefs of Staff. Five-Star Generals might not like to be told that the destruction of Vietnam is not simply a case of right against wrong.

The preaching of the full gospel does not make the prophet popular. It never has. Jesus Christ himself was run out of town and crucified. Anybody who calls people to a life of true discipleship can expect to be rejected by the powers of this world. Chaplains are salve for the conscience; prophets call men to repentence.

3 VIET CONG

The amount of money which the United States spends on the ''dirty little war'' in Vietnam staggers the mind. The present rate is approximately $2 billion per month. With this massive expenditure the U.S. is able to lay waste large areas in both South and North Vietnam, to destroy buildings, bridges and roads, and to kill hordes of Viet Cong.

Assuming, as military leaders likely do, that the aim is to destroy the enemy, how much does it actually cost the United States to kill one V.C.? An eminent Washington news analyst has come up with an interesting answer to this question. Dividing the monthly U.S. war costs by the number of the ''enemy'' killed during that time period he produces the astonishing fact that it costs the U.S. $332,000 to kill one of the Viet Cong.

Actually, the cost per ''kill'' is even higher, because the cost figure cited above does not include the expenditures of the Australians, New Zealanders, Koreans, or the South Vietnamese themselves. On the other side of the balance sheet one should, of course, enter the additional ''achievements'' or ''assets'' accruing from the tremendous outlay of funds. These include the thousands of ''enemy'' persons maimed or wounded, the hundreds of thousands of civilians killed or crippled by bullets, bombs, and napalm, and the incalculable destruction of property.

As I contemplate the figure of $332,000 I cannot help but compare it to certain other statistics. The entire annual foreign missions contributions of our United States and Canadian churches is about enough to kill 3 Viet Cong — and there might be sufficient left over to burn out a village or two.

We sometimes think that we are doing quite well in our missions program, that by our ''generous'' giving we are an example to other less zealous denominations. The fact of the matter is, at least in the United States, that as taxpayers we are giving much more to deliver the message of death, than as church members we are donating to deliver Words of Life.

TWO SIDES

Generally speaking, public opinion in North America tends to side with Israel in the perennial Arab-Israel crisis. When the state of Israel was established in 1947-48 most people in the United States and Canada applauded the event, and most have rejoiced at every Israeli victory since that time.

There are various reasons for this widespread pro-Israeli orientation. Sympathy for a people brutally slaughtered by Hitler, admiration for a democratic and progressive state surrounded by traditionalist regimes, identification with a valiant underdog, reassurance at seeing "prophecy fulfilled," and satisfaction at seeing the forces of Islam defeated are some of the more significant factors. For some, no doubt, the fact of a successful Israel eases the conscience pangs which come from life-long anti-Semitic prejudices.

But there is another side to the picture, one which emerges from the Arab perspective. By what right did the British in their 1917 Balfour Declaration promise international Jewry a homeland in Palestine in exchange for financial support in the war against Germany? By what right did the British give away Arab real estate? Furthermore, if the Western world is so deeply concerned about fair treatment for the Jews why did these governments not complain when Hitler started his gassings in the 1930s, and why did they not accept the thousands of Jews Hitler tried to barter away at that time? Why should the Arabs have to give up their homelands so that the rest of the civilized world can perpetuate its subtle racial hatreds? When no one else would take them in, the Jews found refuge with the Arabs. Why should the Arabs now quietly submit and accept as a just result the fact that the guests, once they were sufficiently numerous and strong, have driven out their hosts? This is how the Arabs view the situation and they are largely right.

Nobody who has seen the hundreds of thousands of undernourished Palestinian refugees languishing in miserable desert camps, as I saw them, can possibly rejoice to hear that their numbers have been increased by the recent war.

If I were an Arab I would likely be seething with righteous indignation. Before the June hostilities began, U.S. Ambassador Arthur Goldberg repeatedly asserted that his government was honor-bound to uphold the territorial integrity of all Middle East countries. No doubt some sort of intervention would have taken place if Israel had lost the war, but with Israel victorious over her neighbors, the pledge seems to have been forgotten. At least so it appears at the time of writing. Granted, the Israeli bombing was triggered by an Arab blockade but from the Arab perspective the Aqaba blockade was merely a delayed reaction to the 1947 Israeli assertion of independence.

The Arab record is also sullied, but the point is, the evidence and the logic are not all on one side.

DECEMBER 14, 1973

BREAD AND OIL

For centuries the so-called Christian West has had control of the bulk of the world's wealth. The peoples of the underdeveloped countries, including the Arab lands of the Middle East, had to be satisfied with what little assistance the West gave them to help improve their generally sorry lot.

And it didn't bother our consciences much either. When mass famine struck out there we thanked God for our bountiful or at least adequate harvests. When floods swept through river valleys we felt sorry. When disease decimated populations we were grateful for our inoculations and got booster shots when we planned to travel abroad.

Oh yes, we prayed that pestilence and plague, flood and famine, and disease and drought would come to an end. We sent parcels and persons. But we never accepted the idea that we should share our bread and clothing and savings and shelter with them till they had just as much (or little) as we had. Somehow most of us thought it quite fair and Christian not to share, except a little. Furthermore, one must avoid the pitfalls of the "social Gospel."

But now things have changed. The Arabs, many of whose countries are still relatively very poor, have no right to keep their oil! We need it! Who are they to think that they can have the last word about their black gold?

How hypocritical the "Christian" West is. Till recently we destroyed foodstuffs in vast quantities to keep prices high. Never mind that half the world goes to bed hungry every night. They are not our neighbors, we said. We elected governments that looked after us.

The Middle East oil regions are finally acting mildly like we have for centuries and we don't like it. Can we learn anything? Or maybe we have all become little Khrushchevs playing the salami game. I take my share, you take your share, and then I take as much of your share as I want.

You need our wheat and equipment, etc.? That's too bad. We'll sell it to the highest bidder elsewhere. But we need your oil and you better give us some—or else!

THE BOAT PEOPLE

In recent weeks the world has once again witnessed a heart-rending tragedy. The privileged protect themselves and their status while the downtrodden suffer and have nowhere to go. Man's inhumanity to man persists.

The suffering, starving, desperate and sometimes drowning boat people fleeing the Red terror in Vietnam and Laos are the Warsaw Jews forty years later. Nobody wants them and nobody, it seems, cares. Human blood, if it's Vietnamese, comes cheap!

Some months before World War II broke out in 1939 a shipload of Jews managed, after months of begging, to get out of Germany. They sailed for the New World. Doubtless they knew that Canada had taken in millions of destitute immigrants. Surely they also knew that inscribed on the Statue of Liberty in New York harbor was (and is) a message to the destitute, the helpless, and the homeless in the world to come to freedom in the U.S.A. But for that shipload of desperate Jews those words had a hollow ring—they were only words. The ship was not allowed to dock. The desperate boatload sailed to Canada. Again it was forced away. Nobody would take in these marked people. Eventually supplies ran out and sadly they returned to Nazi Germany where Hitler, taunting the liberty-mouthing democracies, gassed the helpless boatload.

Now the crisis is upon us again. Anywhere from 8,000 to 20,000 people a month are leaving everything to get out of Red Indochina. Probably half—some estimates go as high as 80 percent—are either killed, captured, or drowned at sea. The 50 percent or so who escape hardly fare better. Nobody wants them; they are human rejects.

The terribleness of the whole thing boggles my mind. How can the governments of Malaysia and Thailand tow these ships with their starving, teeming masses back out to sea knowing full well that likely a watery grave awaits them?

But we must not be too critical. What is Canada doing? Precious little. Oh, we'll take some hundreds but that's about it. The thousands are shunted aside. Now I know that it would make no sense to open the doors of immigration without restriction, Canada couldn't absorb 100 million people, but this is a special case. These people are starving at sea!

In 1968 when refugees from Communist Czechoslovakia poured into Germany and Austria our government chartered special planes to fly the freedom-seekers to Canada. But they were white and European. We had done the same thing when refugees fled Hungary in 1956.

But the Vietnamese are not white. Nor were the 376 Sikhs who, following the letter of the 1908 Canadian Law that East Indians could come to Canada only by "continuous passage," actually rented a ship and did so. The Canadian government backed by public opinion in B.C., refused to let the ship into port. For three months the ship sat in Vancouver harbor and then it was finally driven away, back to India.

Now, after persistent pressure from the beleaguered government of Malaysia, Canada has finally agreed to take 500 or so carefully selected refugees from the slum ship Hai Hong. The U.S. has also agreed to take a token number.

Our songs of liberty begin to ring hollow. Perhaps the North American governments, and their smug, indifferent peoples, should hang their collective heads in shame. We spend tens of millions of dollars on dog food but have nothing for the starving boat people. Of course, we could always recite the U.N. Declaration of Human Rights, which Canada signed, or those beautiful lines from the Statue of Liberty:

"Give me your tired, your poor,
Your huddled masses yearning to breathe free,
The wretched refuse of your teeming shore,
Send these, the homeless, tempest-tost to me!"

CHRISTIANS IN THE USSR

Several decades ago, as a student, I was intrigued by certain specific guarantees found in the Soviet constitution of 1936. The fact that the "impressive" document was proclaimed in 1936, at the height of Stalin's bloody purges, made it all the more fascinating for me.

The Stalin constitution, for example, states in Article 124 that "In order to ensure to citizens freedom of conscience, the church in the U.S.S.R. is separated from the state, and the school from the church. Freedom of religious worship and freedom of anti-religious propaganda is recognized for all citizens." Article 125 adds the following, "guaranteed by law; freedom of speech; freedom of the press; freedom of assembly, including the holding of mass meetings; freedom of street processions and demonstrations."

Particularly incongruous, given the ruthless and arbitrary dictatorship under Stalin, is the added assurance in Article 125 that "These civil rights are ensured by placing at the disposal of the working people and their organization printing presses, stocks of paper, public buildings, the streets, communications facilities and other material requisites for the exercise of these rights."

I wonder if the thousands who faced firing squads and the slightly more fortunate thousands who were exiled to Siberia ever knew about, or thought of, these flowery phrases!

A few weeks ago my student-age reflections on these matters came back to me as I perused a copy of the current constitution, issued in 1977, as Leonid Brezhnev phrased it, "on the eve of the 60th anniversary of the Great October Socialist Revolution." I wanted to check whether the substance of Articles 124 and 125 had been changed. It had not.

Chapter 7, Article 50 guarantees "freedom of speech, of the press, and of assembly, meetings, street meetings, processions and demonstrations." Article 52 states: "Citizens of the U.S.S.R. are guaranteed freedom of conscience, that is, the right to profess or not to profess any religion, and to conduct religious worship or atheistic propaganda." There are some minor changes in the quoted and the other relevant sections but the substance is the same.

Nothing has changed. Freedom is promised but rigid controls and suppression is practiced. Even so, the Soviet government has not won its battle against the Faith!

Consider these statistics, issued about two months ago by the Munich-based "Licht Im Osten" organization of concerned Christians. According to the best sources religious groups in the U.S.S.R. number approximately as follows: Moslems, 30,000,000; Jews, 4,000,000; Russians Orthodox Church, 50,000,000; Roman Catholics, 3,000,000; Protestants (registered churches): 800,000 Lutherans; 100,000 Reformed; 3,000,000 others including Baptists, Mennonites, Adventists, Pentecostals, Church of the Brethren, etc.; and probably about 4,000,000 in unregistered groups. In total, approximately 95,000,000 of about 245,000,000 people in the U.S.S.R. belong to some religious group.

Lenin and Stalin would be dumbfounded. They did not expect organized religion to survive. The constitutional phrases were doubtless intended as useful propaganda for foreign consumption.

But the churches persist, and faith thrives. The powers of darkness will not win.

DO THE REFUGEES FLEE COMMUNISM?

Ever since the great "boat people" tragedy hit the headlines I have been struck by the fact that many western government spokesmen and leaders of various relief agencies in North America have been reluctant to call a spade a spade.

Time and again I hear it said, even by Christians, that the reasons for the boat people fleeing are "very complex" or they have "a long historical basis." Sometimes there is a strong implication that the fleeing thousands are opportunists, seeking to advance their material status. Writing in various dailies a Toronto freelance journalist, Edward Carrigan, actually asserted that "more than 80 per cent of the people fleeing Vietnam are of Chinese origin, and therefore do not meet the test of refugee status. . . ." What utter hogwash!

Since when is common race or ethnicity a test of refugee status? Were the fleeing Armenians not refugees in 1921 when certain Turks tried to exterminate them? Were the Jewish "boat people" who tried to flee Nazi Germany in the 1930s not refugees?

The fact of the matter is that often refugees are refugees precisely because they are a persecuted minority. Certainly that was true of a score of brutally persecuted minorities under Stalin!

As for the notion that a money motive drives these people to risk their lives, well, the argument is equally silly. By what logic would residents in Vietnam undertake a frightful ocean voyage which they know will claim the lives of more than half who undertake it, and hope to make it to some shabby and crowded refugee camp, if their only motive were to improve what we are to conclude is a reasonably decent life in Vietnam? It would make no sense!

Let's say it like it is. These pathetic boatloads, be they Vietnamese, Chinese, Cambodians, or whatever, are risking all for a chance to escape a brutal communist dictatorship. For months I have read scores of articles on the matter, I have interviewed numerous refugees, and have analyzed the situation for myself. I find the evidence compelling and the reality not at all complex. Life under the Vietnamese Communists is so bad for most people that they will do almost anything for even a chance to escape.

Without working my way through even half of my file, I could cite case after case of Communist inhumanity and terror. But let me summarize the report of Otmar Kauck as carried in the *Mennonitische Rundschau* in the June 6 issue. Significantly, Gwynne Dyer, writing from London on July 14, corroborated all the important details.

Shortly after the Communist takeover in 1975, the middle class businessmen and proprietors and others were systematically stripped of their possessions. Of course, all semblance of political and religious freedom also disappeared.

Often the entire family, but almost always at least the family head, were put on a starvation diet and sent to "New Economic" regions. All day long these dispossessed people had to clear bamboo forests with their bare hands! They tore their hands till the blood flowed but the heartless officials merely laughed, "Good for the revolution!" To add to the terrible plight, the vindictive guards would not even allow the workers to build themselves makeshift shelters.

Anybody who got sick suffered or died. No medicines or medical help were provided. It is hardly surprising that many committed suicide. And it is hardly surprising that hundreds of thousands tried to flee.

Read the accounts for yourself. And don't be brainwashed by people who did not hesitate to denounce the ill-conceived American intervention by name but somehow can't get themselves to name the Communist oppressors.

The Indochina holocaust is no more complex that the Nazi holocaust—and hardly less gruesome.

GRAHAM IN MOSCOW

For the past several weeks there has been a lot of flak in the media, especially in certain segments of the religious press, concerning Billy Graham's mid-May trip to the Soviet Union. Readers will recall that the famous evangelist went to the heartland of Communism to participate in a Soviet-sponsored peace conference attended by about 450 clergymen from more than 80 countries.

Some of the more fundamentalist Western critics have come down hard on the good "Reverend" for supposedly being duped by the hooded leaders of the Russian Orthodox church into abetting the Kremlin's propaganda. In part these critics may be right. For the most part the speakers vigorously condemned American policies while simultaneously remaining silent about, or even defending, Soviet aggression in Afghanistan, its brutal suppression of "satellite" peoples, and its headlong rush into the nuclear arms race. During much of the anti-Western haranguing the world-renowned American evangelist, named an honorary member of the conference presidium, sat silently amidst the Russian patriarchs.

Despite the exploitation of the visit, Graham deserves to be highly commended for his venture. At a time when many evangelists seem totally oblivious to the mindboggling nuclear threat, Graham has at last committed his great prestige to doing something about it. More "peace power" to him. Years ago he seemed almost to be a perennial chaplain to the U.S. military establishment; now he has moved beyond that role; he is stressing the full dimensions of the Gospel of Peace. Those of us who belong to the peace churches should be encouraging and supporting him.

Unfortunately much of the Western secular press distorted Graham's statements on religious freedom. When pressed for comments the preacher stated that "it would be wrong to say there is no freedom to worship in this communist state" and "I have experienced total liberty of what I wanted to say." Technically he was right. More than 900 people were allowed to hear him preach the gospel in Moscow's only Baptist church. But, of course, there is no full freedom of religion. The Soviet Tass news agency, for example, refused to transmit certain pictures of the crowded church. But surely the Western Associated Press, or at least some headline writers, did Graham a great disservice by boldly proclaiming that "Graham finds no religious coercion." That is clearly not what Graham said. He asserted that there was some freedom, which is true, and that among the more than 50 countries in which he has preached there are "various kinds of restrictions," which is also true.

I, for one, greatly admire Graham's readiness to risk alienating part of his traditional support base in his determination to help prevent a nuclear holocaust. He was willing to take that risk for a greater cause.

One other aspect deserves a comment. During his Moscow visit, according to reports, Billy Graham in no uncertain terms told his listening Soviet citizens to "obey the authorities." For emphasizing that biblical statement he is now being criticized. But much of the criticism, I suggest, missed the point. Given his general church-state views, what else could Graham say? Until he is willing to put that biblical statement in perspective and fully separate the Christian gospel from the American flag and to make civil obedience conditional even in the U.S., he can hardly make civil obedience conditional in the USSR. That is his biggest dilemma. Having for decades urged American Christians to live by a citizenship of almost blind obedience to a cultic Christian-Americanism, he now finds himself in a bind and, in the name of consistency, has little other citizenship advice to give his Russian hearers except to repeat what he has told his American audiences.

Graham has come a long way. He will surely move even farther. Are Western Christians prepared to have him describe all governments as secular, all Christian citizenship as conditional, and all militarism as anti-Christian?

"COMRADES" IN ARMS

During the 16 or more centuries since the Roman Emperor, Constantine, militarized the Christian church in 313 A.D., there have been countless instances when individual believers and groups of Christians, from small to large, have tried to advance the cause of Christ by the use of sword, cannon, and bombs.

Time and again followers of the Prince of Peace have overlooked the indisputable ethic which he taught and practiced and have, instead, sought somehow to fuse our Lord's ethic of love with the ethic of killing.

Perhaps the most depressing and lamentable instances of such a contrived ethic of "Christian death" have involved situations in which political leaders have enjoyed widespread "evangelical" support because their opponents were also self-declared opponents of evangelical Christianity.

One is reminded, for example, of the considerable endorsement the racist and militarist Adolf Hitler enjoyed during the 1930s, and even, in some places, into the 1940s, because he was opposing the anti-Christian communists.

In our day, the patterns persist. Two especially depressing situations involving Latin America come to mind.

Let us first consider the battered little republic known as El Salvador. Many North American Christians, including Anabaptists, heartily endorse President Reagan's policies of supporting the present government's ruthless policies and practices. After all, so the reasoning goes,is not the El Salvadoran leader, Robert D'Aubuisson, trying to defeat "communist" guerrillas? Whether or not the reform-oriented guerrillas are democratic socialists or not is still debatable but what is certainly not debatable is the oppression, exploitation and cruelty of the El Salvadoran government.

According to its own strongest backers in Washington, D.C., last year that government murdered, for political reasons, "only 2,630 of its citizens," supposedly a praiseworthy improvement from the 5,439 the year before.

Recently a delegation of three Canadian MPs, two of them ordained clergymen, visited that war-torn state and corroborated our worst fears. The government has become the enemy of the people. As my MP, Rev. Walter McLean, put it: "We learned that repression and violation of human rights is a daily reality. Some 4,272 civilian assassinations—victims of the security and para-military forces—were reported during a recent 10-month period."

The fact-finding mission met with all major sectors of El Salvadoran society, groups representing the government, the opposition forces, the churches and human rights organizations. The three MP's concluded, "The Salvadoran government and military forces have been methodically eliminating even the most minimal forms of opposition."

How can we, as North American Christians, give our support to such anti-Christians regimes? The world today has many terrorist governments which, like Hitler's, claim to be fighting godless communism, but should that make us their allies?

A second particularly sad situation involves Guatemala, another war-weary Central American state. Its president is Efrain Rios Montt, who categorically asserts that he is a born-again Christian. The utterly shocking and complicating fact is, however, that Montt and his comrades in arms have systematically slaughtered people. The well documented cases are numerous. In one especially ironic situation, given Montt's widespread support among fundamentalist and evangelical Christians in the U.S. and Canada, Montt's troops rounded up 350 villagers, locked them in a church and burned it.

Let us not get caught up in simplistic and misleading slogans about "God versus Communism" or "good versus evil." The situation is not that simple. Montt and many other dictators are oppressive and God-dishonoring leaders—just like Hitler and Stalin both were. Let us not be conned into supporting anyone who claims to be Christian and anti-communist. We need to practice careful discernment and restraint. We have not been called to urge governments to arm or to fight, let alone to exploit and to torture. Ours is a higher calling.

Some evangelical leaders are loudly urging us to be comrades in arms. Let us be very wary!

MORAL DILEMMA IN INTERNATIONAL AFFAIRS

The early months of 1984 have indicated once again the moral morass of international affairs. Lebanon, El Salvador, Afghanistan, Honduras and a score of other grim theatres haunt us. Many concerned Christian citizens are asking, "How should we respond to these tragedies?" Four general options come to mind.

(1)**Non-involvement.** A more correct label would be "attempted non-involvement." A minority has chosen this option. These people try to ignore reality by focussing on Kingdom-building, narrowly defined. But this option is not credible. We can try to minimize involvement, which may be good, and even knowledge, which is unfortunate, but in a society where civilian and military resources and personnel blur into one, irrelevance is not possible. A commitment to ignorance is not commendable, and to total non-involvement is not possible.

(2) **Nationalistic support.** A blind endorsement of one's country's policies may make sense for non-Christians who are short on social conscience, but it makes no sense for Christians. Our church is universal and God is neither a tribal deity nor commander-in-chief for any country.

(3) **Support for anti-Communists.** This option is probably dominant among evangelical Christians in North America. The basic assumption, generally valid, is that non-communist governments are, by and large, better than communist governments.

However, the widespread further assumption that governments which oppose Communist governments are therefore Christian is, of course, unwarranted. Such a view is false because it defines something as good on the basis of what it is not. Such an assumption would make Mussolini and Hitler virtuous!

Today many Christians support President Reagan's foreign policies. True, his credentials as an eloquent and consistent anti-communist are impeccable, but in striving to support the lesser evil, for example in El Salvador, he ends up supporting a brutal and exploitative dictatorship.

This option is understandable and popular but, in my view, not praiseworthy. An unqualified political anti-communism is hardly better than an unqualified nationalism.

(4) **Christian realism.** This option emcompasses several propositions. (a) Total irrelevance is impossible, therefore Christians opt for limited, selective imvolvement. (b) In our age all national governments, although differing markedly in their commitment to freedom and humanitarianism, are sub-Christian. (c) All national governments commit grievous errors; all are capable of proposing some sensible policies. We therefore focus more on specific policies than on governments or countries per se. (d) No political system is worthy of unconditional support, although some deserve more support than others.

Individuals and organizations accepting this fourth option do what they can to ease suffering, reduce exploitation, enhance human dignity, provide assistance, and promote peace. But we are under no illusion. We do what we can mainly because of who we are and whom we serve, not because we believe that large-scale success awaits us down the road or because we believe that a little more criticism will make our country Christian. Rather, we know that our country, be it Canada, the US, or the USSR, is part of a fallen order. Our task is to acknowledge reality and to do what we can in this fallen world. We address specific issues and policies. Our agenda is lengthy and our exhortations unabashed. We act with diligence but not with unwarranted optimism.

If we live in societies where voices are suppressed, we still seek to be faithful. If we live in societies where freedom prevails, we seek to be faithful, diligent and thankful.

PART XV

Puzzle Pieces

NOVEMBER 1, 1968

A LETTER FROM ASIA

Dear Christian:

I write to you because I have a big question to ask and because you told me in your last letter to ask you whatever I wanted to. Yesterday I read in our neighbor's *Kowloon Daily News* that the Canadian government, "Ottawa" you once called it in a letter, has decided to spend millions of dollars to help about two thousand refugees from Czechoslovakia to come to Canada. According to the report which I read, many of these people are highly educated individuals who just happen to be on a vacation outside their country at the time of the Soviet intervention. No doubt they will get very good jobs and "make money" as our local G.I.'s say. Many will soon have their own bicycles or even motorcycles. I envy them and wish them well. I am glad that your country is trying to help these people who chose freedom instead of communism.

And now, because I know you so well, although I have never met you, let me ask you the question which has been on my mind. And please do not get angry with me for asking it; please try to understand my situation. Why is it that Canadians are suddenly so much concerned about helping these few thousand people who were rich enough to go on a vacation and why does there seem to be so little concern about the tens of thousands who live with me here in the refugee camps?

I have tried to tell myself that Canadians were shocked when they first heard the news about the freedom-crushing tanks rumbling onward from the East in the darkness of the night. But then, our condition is shocking too! It has been more than six years since I fled the Red oppression on the mainland and still there is no place to go. There have been no emergency Hercules airlifts or government-chartered planes to our area although many children here are dying because they do not get enough proteins.

As I have told you in an earlier letter,many of us have no homes here. My two younger brothers and I sleep in a tiny shack which is very cold in the winter and sometimes we hardly get enough to eat. Often we eat only once a day. Once in a while I get a job for a few days but mostly we just beg and wait for the distribution at the local MCC center. I do not know what we would do without the food and clothing which your churches send us. Please thank them again.

We have tried to migrate to Canada but the local Canadian consul says that we "do not qualify." Why not? We too are refugees from communism and as orphans we perhaps need help more than those Czechs which your government is flying across from Europe. Is it because we are Chinese? Is an oriental person of less value?

Well, I guess I should not complain. Many of my former friends are worse off. Some have been trucked back to the People's Republic because there is no room for them here and because no country will accept them. Others have died. Tell me, Christian, is your country not big and rich?

Sometimes when I am very depressed I tell myself that there are millions of people in Africa and the Middle East who have been refugees much longer than I have been. When I think of them I can go to sleep sooner.

Sincerely,
Soo Long,
Refugee Camp C, Hong Kong.

INDIAN JOE

If you believe that the Christian emphasis on real charity, sometimes referred to as the spirit of Christmas, is an inappropriate topic for this time of year, read no further. If your touching words (uttered last December) about reflecting God's love have been tucked safely away with the floodlights and the fake Christmas tree go back to the letters to the editor or reread the editorial. I'll write what follows because the account doesn't want to leave me.

A bit unevenly but with full harmony the singers' voices penetrated the old frame shack. Indian Joe heard them and his face gradually tensed. A year ago, almost to the day, they had sung for him, and left him a hamper and some Christmas tracts. It had lasted him some days and then he was back to his meagre fare. They had spent about five minutes at his place; having done their charity for him they left him with more things but less dignity and had rushed back to their upper middle class homes.

Now he heard them again. He could surely use some more groceries but the thought that he was again being used so that some consciences could be a little less sullied—at least for a short time—made him angry. Who did they think he was? A person without feelings? A person who needed food only two weeks a year? A person who could keep his dignity while being used.

The singing stopped. He waited. Someone knocked. Ready to respond with something besides a fake season greeting Joe opened the door. "Donations for the poor please!" a youthful voice appealed. Swallowing his words Joe relaxed, went into his bedroom and brought out a dollar—that left him with two. He actually managed a faint smile. The well-dressed young fellow thanked him and as the twenty-odd well-dressed folk piled into their nice cars, Joe forgot at least some of his long pent-up resentment. He closed the squeaking door firmly. With less money but more dignity he soon turned in for the night.

The main moral of the story could be one of several things, but the one that lingers in my mind is that . . . .

OPEN MIND; CLOSED CLUB

The other day I met a fine group of people. What struck me about them was their friendliness, frankness to each other, obvious acceptance of one another, sense of unity and purpose, enthusiasm, loyalty to the group and to its ideals, general dedication and, I might add, their thrift. They seemed to have a cause for which to live and since this is relatively rare these days I decided to investigate the matter further.

I soon discovered that the friendly people belonged to The St. Andrews and Caledonian Society—or something like it. Some of them soon schooled me about their group, its purposes, and, most significantly, its great traditions. They seemed to relish traditions. I heard about the clans, the Highlands, the tartans, the kilts, the haggis ("take a small helping first"), their "games," the kirk, and much else. It was amazing to see what they all had in common and what it meant to them.

Something which is that improtant to somebody is worth looking into. I did. The thing was and is for real. These people stand for something of which they are not ashamed and they talk about it. Their enthusiasm was contagious so I asked whether I could join. That's when the trouble started.

It seems that one has to have the right name, or background, or at least be married to someone who does. Since I'm already married to someone who cannot trace her ancestry back to the Highlands, the Lowlands, or anywhere else in Scotland, or even to some acceptable parts of Northern Ireland, and who cooks great "Porzeltche" but probably doesn't know whether haggis should be boiled, beaten, or dried, that option was clearly out. (Just as well; I wouldn't want it any other way.)

I then worked the name angle. Several possibilities arose. First I tried what seemed to me most obvious: J.H. McRedekop. It was not accepted; apparently there is no McRedekop clan. I then tried MacRedekop. No better. There was no record of such a clan or even a tartan. My next attempt involved hyphenation. I tried Redekop-Edinborough, Strachan-Redekop, Douglas-Redekop, etc. but they just shook their heads. I stopped working this approach when one of their leaders told me that hyphenation came only by marriage. At this point their earlier openness seemed less open, at least as far as I was concerned. I then tried the last option. O'Redekop; perhaps they would let me sneak in that way and besides, I was already designing a new tartan based on the motif of leafless poplar trees set against a dust-bowl background. I struck out again. They were having great fun—even fellowship!

At about that time several of them got out a huge book of names and family trees and they eagerly tried to fill in some blanks. (Apparently this is done each year in an attempt to trace down those who have somehow drifted away.) Some blanks were filled.

Sadly I left the group. Evidently there was no place in it for me. Obviously this account is not true, but maybe the moral is.

A PARABLE OF HARVESTERS

(1) Now it happened in the fourth month of the fourteenth year of King Erreip 1, eleven months after the time of the Great Proclamation, that Jesus was sojourning in Britalsamanont, that great empire west of the mighty rushing river. (2)And there came to him vast multitudes of leaders, church builders, zealous media specialists—also known as sons of thunder—and other sincere believers including sons of Luther, Calvin, and Menno. And they crowded round about him.

(3) And finding a hillock in a park near a town centre in Clearcoalverherbwink, nigh unto Calvanregwinnonto, he commanded that the masses be seated. Then he lifted up his voice and spoke this parable unto them.

(4) A certain graingrower, seeing his fields almost ripe unto harvest, set his heart to prepare for the season of reaping. In preparation for his task he travelled many miles unto Alms Springs. There, for a fortnight, he sat at the feet of experts, men full of knowledge and of great repute. (5) These authorities told him to treat his crops carefully, to fertilize and to spray them, to irrigate and to weed them. That graingrower grew a great crop but he was so taken up with treating it right that he never got around to harvesting the grain.

(6) And, lo, a second graingrower also beheld his fields and he, too, saw that they would soon be ready for harvest. And he became anxious and said, "If I do not harvest my fields then the ravens might come, or the hail might strike, or the grasshoppers infest the field!" (7) So this harvester cut and threshed his crops that same day, but much of the grain was not yet ripe and after the harvest season many kernels shrivelled and had to be thrown away.

(8) Then a third graingrower looked at his large field and said unto himself, "There are yet many days until the frosts come and the snow flies." (9) Then he travelled into a far country and while he was gone a great blizzard struck that region and flattened his fields. Some grain could be harvested in spring but most of it was lost.

(10) A fourth graingrower, who also noticed some heads ripening, said unto himself, "I will wait until all is ripe, then I will harvest it and store it in my enlarged barn." (11) And he did as he had said. When all the grain was ripe he drove his mighty scythe machine throughout his fields. (12) This thoughtful farmer worked hard, but not carefully, and much of his crop was ground into the soil and lost.

(13) Then the last of the five graingrowers beheld his rolling field; it was turning golden. Each day he inspected his crop and tended it. (14) Finally, on the right day, and in the right way, he carefully harvested a bountiful crop of good grain. (15) He who has ears to hear, let him hear.

(16) Now the sons of Luther, and Calvin, and Menno asked one another; What meaneth this parable?

(17) Then Jesus, beholding their perplexity, said unto them: O ye of much learning and little understanding. This is the interpretation. The fields are the world and the grain thereon are the people who have heard the Word but some have not yet come to the knowledge of the truth. The graingrowers are ye!

(18) The first graingrower observed correctly and he nurtured his crops

faithfully. He did many alms and good deeds but he harvested no crop and he gathered no souls.

(19) The second graingrower lacked patience and would not let the grain develop. He rushed matters thoughtlessly and destroyed the faith of many. His harvest of souls was small.

(20) The third graingrower was distracted by the enticements of other things. He neglected his people and they were overcome by the storms of life.

(21) The fourth graingrower lacked sensitivity and tact. His tactless and heavy-handed manner caused many to stumble, to fall, and to fail.

(22) Now the fifth graingrower did that which was right. He neglected not the harvest, he waited patiently for the right season, he was not distracted by the other matters, and he harvested his crop with much care. (23) Because of him many people were brought into the Kingdom. (24) On the final day of reckoning my heavenly Father will say unto him, ''Well done thou good and faithful harvester, enter into the gates of the owner of the fields—you have harvested well!''

(25) Now go ye and learn from this wise harvester.

INDEX

About the Author

Dr. John H. Redekop was born and raised in Western Canada. He studied at Columbia Bible Institute, Clearbrook, BC, the University of British Columbia, Vancouver, Heidelberg University in Germany, the University of California, Berkley, and the University of Washington, Seattle. He has held teaching positions at several universities. Since 1968 he has been Professor of Political Science at Wilfred Laurier University, Waterloo, Ontario. Dr. Redekop is currently the Moderator of the Canadian Conference of the Mennonite Brethren Churches. The John and Doris Redekop, who live in Waterloo, have four children: Wendy, Gary, Heather, and Bonnie.

About the Illustrator

Lorlie Barkman was born and raised in Saskatchewan. He graduated from Bethany Bible Institute, Hepburn, Saskatchewan, and then studied commercial art for two years. From 1964 until 1975 he served as pastor of the Regal Heights Mennonite Brethren Church in Moose Jaw, Saskatchewan. Since 1975 Lorlie has produced television programming and Served as English Media Director at Mennonite Brethren Communications, Winnipeg. Lorlie and Deanna Barkman and their children, Barry, Bonnah and Christy, make their home in Winnipeg, Manitoba.